Impossible Data Warehouse Situations

Addison-Wesley Information Technology Series
Capers Jones and David S. Linthicum, Consulting Editors

The information technology (IT) industry is in the public eye now more than ever before because of a number of major issues in which software technology and national policies are closely related. As the use of software expands, there is a continuing need for business and software professionals to stay current with the state of the art in software methodologies and technologies. The goal of the Addison-Wesley Information Technology Series is to cover any and all topics that affect the IT community. These books illustrate and explore how information technology can be aligned with business practices to achieve business goals and support business imperatives. Addison-Wesley has created this innovative series to empower you with the benefits of the industry experts' experience.

For more information point your browser to http://www.awprofessional.com/itseries

Sid Adelman, Larissa Terpeluk Moss, *Data Warehouse Project Management*. ISBN: 0-201-61635-1

Sid Adelman, Joyce Bischoff, Jill Dyché, Douglas Hackney, Sean Ivoghli, Chuck Kelley, David Marco, Larissa Moss, and Clay Rehm, *Impossible Data Warehouse Situations: Solutions from the Experts*. ISBN: 0-201-76033-9

Wayne Applehans, Alden Globe, and Greg Laugero, *Managing Knowledge: A Practical Web-Based Approach*. ISBN: 0-201-43315-X

Michael H. Brackett, *Data Resource Quality: Turning Bad Habits into Good Practices*. ISBN: 0-201-71306-3

David Leon Clark, *Enterprise Security: The Manager's Defense Guide*. ISBN: 0-201-71972-X

Frank P. Coyle, *Wireless Web: A Manager's Guide*. ISBN: 0-201-72217-8

Frank P. Coyle, *XML, Web Services, and the Data Revolution*. ISBN: 0-201-77641-3

James Craig and Dawn Jutla, *e-Business Readiness: A Customer-Focused Framework*. ISBN: 0-201-71006-4

Kevin Dick, *XML, Second Edition: A Manager's Guide*. ISBN: 0-201-77006-7

Jill Dyché, *e-Data: Turning Data into Information with Data Warehousing*. ISBN: 0-201-65780-5

Jill Dyché, *The CRM Handbook: A Business Guide to Customer Relationship Management*. ISBN: 0-201-73062-6

Patricia L. Ferdinandi, *A Requirements Pattern: Succeeding in the Internet Economy*. ISBN: 0-201-73826-0

Nick V. Flor, *Web Business Engineering: Using Offline Activites to Drive Internet Strategies*. ISBN: 0-201-60468-X

David Garmus and David Herron, *Function Point Analysis: Measurement Practices for Successful Software Projects*. ISBN: 0-201-69944-3

John Harney, *Application Service Providers (ASPs): A Manager's Guide*. ISBN: 0-201-72659-9

International Function Point Users Group, *IT Measurement: Practical Advice from the Experts*. ISBN: 0-201-74158-X

Capers Jones, *Software Assessments, Benchmarks, and Best Practices*. ISBN: 0-201-48542-7

Ravi Kalakota and Marcia Robinson, *e-Business 2.0: Roadmap for Success*. ISBN: 0-201-72165-1

Greg Laugero and Alden Globe, *Enterprise Content Services: Connecting Information and Profitability*. ISBN: 0-201-73016-2

David S. Linthicum, *B2B Application Integration: e-Business-Enable Your Enterprise*. ISBN: 0-201-70936-8

Sergio Lozinsky, *Enterprise-Wide Software Solutions: Integration Strategies and Practices*. ISBN: 0-201-30971-8

Joanne Neidorf and Robin Neidorf, *e-Merchant: Retail Strategies for e-Commerce*. ISBN: 0-201-72169-4

Bud Porter-Roth, *Request for Proposal: A Guide to Effective RFP Development*. ISBN: 0-201-77575-1

Mai-lan Tomsen, *Killer Content: Strategies for Web Content and E-Commerce*. ISBN: 0-201-65786-4

Karl E. Wiegers, *Peer Reviews in Software: A Practical Guide*. ISBN: 0-201-73485-0

Ralph R. Young, *Effective Requirements Practices*. ISBN: 0-201-70912-0

Bill Zoellick, *CyberRegs: A Business Guide to Web Property, Privacy, and Patents*. ISBN: 0-201-72230-5

Impossible Data Warehouse Situations

Solutions from the Experts

Sid Adelman

With contributions from:

Joyce Bischoff

Jill Dyché

Douglas Hackney

Sean Ivoghli

Chuck Kelley

David Marco

Larissa Moss

Clay Rehm

✦ Addison-Wesley

Boston • San Francisco • New York • Toronto • Montreal
London • Munich • Paris • Madrid
Capetown • Sydney • Tokyo • Singapore • Mexico City

The publisher offers discounts on this book when ordered in quantity for bulk purchases and special sales. For more information, please contact:

U.S. Corporate and Government Sales
(800) 382-3419
corpsales@pearsontechgroup.com

For sales outside of the U.S., please contact:

International Sales
(317) 581-3793
international@pearsontechgroup.com

Visit Addison-Wesley on the Web: www.awprofessional.com

Library of Congress Cataloging-in-Publication Data

Adelman, Sid.
    Impossible data warehouse situations : solutions from the experts / Sid Adelman, with contributions from Joyce Bischoff ... [et al.].
       p. cm. —(Addison-Wesley information technology series)
    Includes bibliographical references and index.
    ISBN 0-201-76033-9 (alk. paper)
    1. Data warehousing. I. Bischoff, Joyce, 1938- II. Title. III. Series.

QA76.9.D37 A35 2003
658.4'038'028574—dc21

2002074381

ISBN 0-201-76033-9
Text printed on recycled paper
1 2 3 4 5 6 7 8 9 10—MA—0605040302
First printing, October 2002

Contents

Chapter Eleven   Data Quality   249

Chapter Twelve   Integration   275

Chapter Thirteen   Data Warehouse Architecture   303

Chapter Fourteen   Performance   333

Preface

In the seminars, presentations, and classes we teach on data warehousing, we are often subjected to what appear to be "impossible situations." Likewise, in the *DM Review* "Ask the Experts" forum (*http://www.dmreview.com*) we are confronted with questions that, at first glance, appear to have no answers or solutions. However, they *do* have solutions, and that's what this book is all about.

We took the 91 impossible situations discussed in this book from our classes, from the *DM Review* "Ask the Experts" forum, from data warehouse consultants, and from colleagues in the field who have experienced these situations. These are all real situations, but we have disguised them to protect the authors as well as to protect the organizations experiencing the situations from the attendant shame and humiliation. As a side note, reviewers of specific situations in our manuscript were quick to say, "I know what company this describes," and they were almost always wrong.

THE PURPOSE OF THIS BOOK

There is no reason that each organization, as it begins and continues to develop data warehouse projects, must wrestle with many of the very difficult situations that have confounded other organizations. The same impossible situations continue to raise their ugly heads, often with surprisingly little relation to the industry, the size of the organization, or the organizational structure. In this book we let you know you are not alone and your problems are not unique. We also offer hope to the perplexed who see no obvious solutions to their problems.

Some of the situations should resonate with those of you planning to enhance your data warehouse by adding new data, additional users, or new applications. It may be that the impossible situation has not yet emerged, but you definitely see it just around the bend. After reading this book, you should be able to avoid the situation rather than needing to fix it after it has developed.

WHO SHOULD READ THIS BOOK

Every stakeholder, data warehouse architect, data warehouse project manager, and user liaison responsible for any portion of a data warehouse faces the challenges identified in these pages. These people are looking for solutions to situations that, at first, appear to have no possible answer.

This book does not present an introduction to data warehousing. To benefit most from this book, you should have some level of familiarity with data warehousing through practical experience, conferences, or previous reading of data warehouse texts. This book is also not geared to any primary topic such as meta data or data quality; instead, it covers a broad range of areas. The reference section lists both introductory and more advanced suggested reading material.

User liaisons and managers may wish to read only Part I (Impossible Management Situations). All others will want to read both Part I and Part II (Impossible Technical Situations).

HOW THIS BOOK IS ORGANIZED

As mentioned, the first part of the book deals with managerial situations and the second part with technical situations. The order within these sections is very roughly the order in which projects are developed and situations are encountered, but each chapter stands alone without depending on those that precede it. You can read the book from front to back, but more likely you will be drawn to the chapters describing the problems that cause you the most pain. For example, if you struggle with data quality issues, Chapter 11, Data Quality, is the place to start. Each subsection of a chapter presents a different impossible situation related to the chapter's topic, followed by the experts' suggested solutions (presented in the alphabetical order of the experts' last names).

The Data Warehouse Glossary at the back of the book clarifies some terms and helps keep you from going down the wrong path. Misunderstanding the terminology used in this fast-changing field has caused significant misinterpretation that has resulted in wasted time and money, dissension, and hurt feelings. The Data Warehouse Glossary contains acronyms as well as data warehouse and information technology terms. A few of these have more than one definition. Please refer to the definitions to avoid any misunderstandings as you read through the situations and solutions. If your native language is not English, you will find the Colloquialism Glossary useful since the experts used many colloquial expressions in their contributions to this book.

You will notice strong biases in the experts' responses. The experts came to these dearly held opinions honestly through extensive experience in real-world situations. A few of the answers are embarrassingly similar, while some sharply disagree, appearing to contradict each other. Recognizing that there is usually more than one answer to every problem, very much depending on the organization and the situation, we made no attempt to reconcile the differences. We trust you will astutely choose the solution that will work best in your organization.

THE EXPERTS WHO WROTE THIS BOOK

The following people contributed their expertise to address the situations we present in this book:

- Sid Adelman
- Joyce Bischoff
- Jill Dyché
- Douglas Hackney
- Sean Ivoghli
- Chuck Kelley
- David Marco
- Larissa Moss
- Clay Rehm

True experts, these men and women have worked in the data warehouse arena for a cumulative 142 years. If anyone can address these impossible situations, they can.

The experts suggested best practices based on their experiences with both successful and unsuccessful implementations. The experts correctly identified many of the situations as reflecting the symptoms of a dysfunctional organization, knowing that without understanding the real causes, no effective solution could be honestly recommended. When presented with insufficient information, the experts resorted to making assumptions about the situations.

The experts' bios appear in the back of the book.

How to Contribute New Impossible Situations

A number of impossible situations came to our attention after the experts received the original batch of 91 situations, and we all feel sure more will appear. If you want to contribute a new situation for consideration, please send it to *impossibles@sidadelman.com*. We may include your situation in a second edition of this book.

ACKNOWLEDGMENTS

The situations in this book were gleaned from a variety of sources. A major source was my Data Warehouse Project Management Seminar, in which students would present seemingly impossible situations. I'd like to thank all the students in this seminar who were brave enough to expose their extremely difficult if not impossible situations.

My clients, my colleagues, and the experts represented in this book contributed many of the other situations. There are no attributions for the impossible situations themselves. This was intentional to protect the reputations and careers of those who submitted them.

A number of situations were pulled from submissions to *DM Review*'s "Ask the Experts" forum, mentioned earlier. My thanks to the publishers of *DM Review* who allowed us to use those submissions and to Mary Jo Nott, the Web Editor at *DM Review* who manages the forum.

This book is a compilation of hard-won wisdom from the experts—my colleagues I've been privileged to know and work with. As you will see in their solutions, there would not have been a book without their insightful contributions. Thanks especially to Larissa Moss and Joyce Bischoff for their excellent ideas and suggestions that went well beyond their expert solutions.

Thanks also go to the original reviewers who made excellent suggestions about ways to improve the book and make it more readable and informative. Thanks to Jean Schauer, Editor in Chief of *DM Review*; Majid Abai, President of Seena Technologies; and Dennis Fitzpatrick. I also thank Lou Russell and Cort Pahl for their ideas and insights.

Anyone who has written a book knows the work and expertise of the various editors. I salute the editing savvy of the folks at Addison-Wesley, including Mary O'Brien, Alicia Carey, and Simone Payment. Steven King in *On Writing* wrote that your editor is always right. This was especially true for this book. Special thanks to my copyeditor, Chrysta Meadowbrooke.

If you are actually reading this book, it's due to the marketing skills of Curt Johnson and Chanda Leary-Coutu.

Any finally thanks to Sisyphus who graces the book's cover for being the model for all those who believe their role in this difficult data warehousing environment is an uphill struggle with no solution in sight.

—*Sid Adelman*
Mammoth Lakes, California
July 2002

Credits

Epigraphs

Albrecht, Karl, and Ron Zemke. 1990. *Service America!: Doing Business in the New Economy.* New York: Warner Books.

Drucker, Peter D. 1979. *Adventures of a Bystander.* New York: Harper and Row.

————. 1974. *Management: Tasks, Responsibilities, Practices.* New York: HarperCollins.

Harrington, H. James. 1987. *The Improvement Process: How America's Leading Companies Improve Quality.* New York: McGraw-Hill.

Juran, J. M. 1995. *Managerial Breakthrough,* 30th anniversary ed. New York: McGraw-Hill.

Likert, Rensis. 1967. *The Human Organization: Its Management and Value.* New York: McGraw-Hill.

Mayle, Peter. 1995. *A Dog's Life.* New York: Knopf.

Pirsig, Robert. 1974. *Zen and the Art of Motorcycle Maintenance: An Inquiry into Values.* New York: Morrow.

Repository Data Model Strategy Paper. 1986. GUIDE GRP-153, September.

Walton, Mary. 1991. *Deming Management at Work.* New York: Perigee Books.

Zachman, John. 1987. "A Framework for Information Systems Architecture." *IBM Systems Journal* 26(3).

PART I

Impossible Management Situations

CHAPTER ONE

Management Issues

*Whenever anything is being accomplished, it is being done, I
have learned, by a monomaniac with a mission.*

—Peter F. Drucker

OVERVIEW

A sound management structure is one of the critical
success factors for a data warehouse. A strong, positive
attitude by managers in both the business and information technology (IT) departments is critical to success; projects have come to a halt when the project's
sponsor left. Some sponsoring managers don't stay
long enough in their positions to see projects through
to completion, not due to incompetence but because of
the dynamic nature of the organization. Thus the loss
of a sponsor before a project completes is a likely event.
A strong, dedicated sponsor present throughout the
process is a critical success factor for a data warehouse.

Management often does not know what is going on
with the data warehouse and does not understand its
value. Without this understanding, there won't be
funds to support existing data warehouse systems, nor
will there be funds for future systems. Some organizations have a terrible track record, collecting multiple
data warehouse failures. These failures are usually the
result of management not understanding, not caring,
and not devoting the necessary resources to make the

data warehouse successful. Success requires a change in the way management views data warehouse projects.

Data Sharing

Information is power, and division heads are loath to give up any power they see leaking from their empires as a result of a data warehouse. Following a norm to not share data has implications for the entire organization and affects the ability to maintain a single version of the truth.

Often users don't share data for a number of reasons. The users may genuinely believe they are the only ones smart enough to receive, validate, and interpret the results of a query or report. Some managers may believe that sharing their departmental data would give their bitter rivals ammunition to be critical. Sharing data may give supervisors the ability to micromanage (a management activity that is definitely not appreciated by their staff). Since data is power, managers may correctly believe they lose some of their power by sharing data. And finally, managers may not want to share their data because, before it is released, they may want to adjust the results, sometimes putting their own spin on the numbers. These managers may want enough time to be able to justify poor results or to actually change the numbers before the rest of the organization's members see the results.

We have seen situations where people in management, for reasons of power and politics or sometimes fear, have fought against the project from the beginning and continue to do so as the project is developed. They may continue to sabotage the project or sabotage its reputation even after the project has been implemented.

Criteria for Success

Some data warehouse implementations fail. It's possible that many of those "failures" would be considered by some to be successes (or at least to be positioned someplace between failure and success). The criteria for success are often determined after the fact. This is a dangerous practice since those involved with the project don't really know their targets and will make poor decisions about where to put their energies and resources.

Users are instrumental in setting these criteria, but managers must set realistic goals for performance and address what data will be provided in each phase. The list below presents a suggested set of criteria for evaluating the success of a data warehouse project.

- The data warehouse is used and useful.
- The company makes an acceptable return on investment (ROI).
- The project meets business- and performance-based benchmarks, for example, improvement of customer satisfaction ratings.
- The users generate new requirements, for example, more users want more data warehouse capabilities, increased access, and new data sources.
- The users are satisfied with the response time and the overall performance of the data warehouse. This is not only a question of the system giving quick response but also a function of what the users expect. The data warehouse team should set users' performance expectations early and often (with compliments to the late Mayor Richard Daley of Chicago).
- Satisfied users are willing to sing your praises. Be sure to ask.
- The goals and objectives for the data warehouse (assuming they have been identified and accepted) have been met.
- The data warehouse helped solve a business problem. For example, a manufacturing company could experience a problem due to inadequate quality information, which a data warehouse could resolve.
- The company realized a business opportunity. For example, a data warehouse that provides customers with critical information unavailable from your competitors could help your company secure large clients.
- The data warehouse has become an agent of change. For example, a data warehouse that fundamentally changes the way an organization approaches decision making could result in more timely decisions based on higher quality information.

In the remainder of this chapter, we'll explore seven situations that arise in the realm of management issues and present suggested solutions for each one.

THE DATA WAREHOUSE HAS A RECORD OF FAILURE

This is the third attempt at a data warehouse. The first two failed, and the general feeling is that this one will also fail. What can the project manager do to dispel the negative conventional wisdom about the data warehouse?

Sid Adelman

Talking up the data warehouse and telling everyone how good it's going to be is a wasted effort. The only thing that will convince this organization is a successful implementation. The project manager should deliver something of value and deliver it quickly. He or she should ask the project's business sponsor to tout the success of the project and to point out specifics on how the data warehouse made a difference to the department.

Joyce Bischoff

First, the project manager must understand why the first two projects failed and address those issues in the project plan. He or she must ensure that project members are well trained and that the organizational issues are addressed. It would probably be helpful to bring in a high-level data warehouse expert from a consulting firm to act in an advisory capacity to ensure that the project addresses critical issues.

Douglas Hackney

The first step is to perform the due diligence necessary to fully understand the failure drivers for the prior efforts and to mitigate those drivers in the current initiative. During the very important second step, the project manager must create a new brand name for the project that does not use the term *data warehouse*. Finally, for the third step the project manager must focus specifically and exclusively on delivering incremental relief of life-threatening business pain.

Chuck Kelley

Well, you know the old saying, "Third time is a charm!" It would be nice to know why the first two attempts failed. There are many reasons for failure, and most of them are not technical but political and/or personal.

The project manager's critical role in this third attempt involves completing the following tasks.

- Define a clear business case, and develop the consensus understanding of what the data warehouse will and will not do.
- Create the appropriate committees of the right people (representing the business side and the technology side) to aid in the development of the data warehouse.

- Keep a constant presence with business users, letting them know what is happening and what will happen next.
- Continue to capture feedback on what is going well and not so well.

The project manager needs to find a senior management champion, someone who understands the need for the data warehouse and can articulate it to the other members of the senior management team. The data warehouse champion will support the building of the data warehouse and act as the arbitrator of any issues that arise between the groups.

David Marco

It is important to understand why the previous initiatives failed and to have a plan that will mitigate these issues for this third attempt. The project manager must be honest about why the previous attempts failed. He or she shouldn't gloss over the problems; the team making the new attempt will likely face the same problems.

Larissa Moss

Hopefully the project team conducted postimplementation reviews on the two prior data warehouse projects to learn from the mistakes. The project manager can use the review results and other sources of information about data warehouse development to show the users and management that the third attempt will be different. He or she should set up a meeting with all stakeholders and briefly cover the reasons for the prior failures, followed by a review of the different approach planned for the next project, showing how the team will avoid the prior pitfalls. The project manager should also set up a weekly communication channel (through meetings, e-mails, or an intranet Web site) to convey ongoing progress as well as roadblocks and resolutions on the project. He or she should also engage the users and the sponsor to promote the data warehouse efforts and their progress.

A bad reputation is not easy to overcome. But given good communication and enough time, a well-organized and well-managed project should produce positive results—and positive results are the best way to recover from a bad reputation.

Clay Rehm

Instead of spending time talking, the project manager should just do it. How? Every single project team member must work hard to produce deliverables each week, to communicate every day, to hold a positive attitude even when other people are negative, and most importantly, to keep up the effort. One rule for project success: "Always have a smile on your face and tell yourself and everyone you meet that the team will succeed!"

So how can the project manager motivate the team? It is up to him or her to keep everyone excited about the data warehouse project. The disposition of the project manager will rub off on the team, good or bad. The body language, tone of voice, and expressions on the face of the project manager can do a lot for the morale of the team.

The project manager should staff the project with team members who have positive attitudes, who have experience with difficult projects, and who are willing and able to do what it takes to get the job done on time. This means assigning to the project people who are willing, if asked, to work 15-hour days or 7-day weeks.

Even if a team member does not have experience with a given tool or technology that the data warehouse will use, the project manager should determine whether the team member is willing to learn and is quick to learn a new tool under the most trying of circumstances.

Since there is a history of failure, the project manager should consider retaining a consultant who has experience with data warehousing and have that consultant provide best practices, standards, and templates.

The following best practices can keep a project from failing.

- Get close to the users and become their friend.
- Get to know what the users need, and support those needs.
- Take a personal interest in the project.
- Communicate through the use of diagrams; everyone loves visuals.
- Document the current state of the project and the desired future state, and show the steps planned to get to the goal over time.
- Always have a positive attitude and be easy to get along with.
- Tell yourself that failure is not an option.
- Sit close to your users.

The moral of the story: A team filled with pride and positive attitudes can go a long way.

IT Is Unresponsive

The data warehouse is fairly new in the organization. The data warehouse manager reports two levels below the chief information officer (CIO). The IT people on the operational/transaction side are not cooperating with those on the data warehouse side. The IT people on the operational side were unresponsive to requests for resources and information about the operational systems, and now they're not responding to requests for source data that will go into the extract/transform/load process. What should the project manager (who reports to the data warehouse manager) do?

Joyce Bischoff

Does the data warehouse manager report to the CIO through other managers? If so, it is in the CIO's interest to ensure IT's cooperation. If not, the highest levels of executive management need to be involved in supporting the project. Forming a data warehouse advisory committee with responsibility and authority may solve the problem.

Douglas Hackney

The project manager must immediately escalate the issue to the highest level possible. He or she must discover exactly how much support can be expected from the key stakeholders. If the project manager cannot gain support, then he or she will need to adjust the goals and methods accordingly.

Chuck Kelley

The project manager needs to keep a strict log of requests and delivery times, keeping the data warehouse manager up-to-date about specific problems. The data warehouse manager needs to get to the operational side and see what can be done. If that doesn't resolve the problem, then the data warehouse manager needs to get the ear of the CIO. During this time, the members of the data warehouse team need to continue to build relationships with the operations staff to see if they can alleviate the situation.

Larissa Moss

Clearly data warehousing is not a strategic business initiative in this organization. This is evidenced by the placement of the data warehouse team—two levels below the CIO—and by the mere fact that another IT group can snub the data warehouse team and get away with it. The only hope for the project manager is to have a strong and influential business sponsor supporting the data warehouse initiative.

The project manager should meet with the data warehouse manager and the business sponsor to discuss the situation and to prepare a strategy to force the operational team to cooperate. As part of the strategy, the business sponsor should take this issue to the business executives whose departments originate the source data needed for the data warehouse. The data warehouse manager and the sponsor should also meet with the CIO to discuss the issue. If those efforts fail, it will be evident that the business sponsor is not at a high enough position in the organization and does not have enough influence to remove this roadblock.

Bottom line: If the data warehouse project was initiated by this sponsor, she or he has an uphill political battle to fight. If it was originated by an executive higher in the organization, possibly even the chief executive officer (CEO), then this issue must be taken to him or her. If the data warehouse project is an IT initiative, this would be a good time to give it up.

Clay Rehm

This sounds like some research needs to be done to find out why the online transaction processing (OLTP) IT people are jealous of the data warehouse staff. There could be many reasons why the OLTP IT staff members are not cooperating.

- They are too busy.
- They are bitter that the data warehouse team has stolen their talent.
- The data warehouse team gets to play with new technologies.
- The data warehouse team may have new offices, cubicles, or work surroundings.
- The data warehouse team may have gotten bonuses or awards for building the data warehouse.
- Members of the OLTP team may have wanted to be on the data warehouse team but were not selected.

The project manager must spend the appropriate time researching and identifying the reasons the OLTP team is not cooperating. After identifying the true reasons for noncooperation, the project manager must determine a course of action to resolve the problem quickly and without much fanfare. Since the data warehouse team relies so heavily on source systems, everyone must consider themselves as one big team.

Here are some possible suggestions for how the project manager can bridge the gap between the teams.

- Find a way to let the OLTP IT people temporarily "intern" on the data warehouse team for a specific project or task.
- Offer the resources of the data warehouse team to intern on the OLTP team for a specific task.
- Offer training on new technologies to the OLTP IT staff.
- Ask the OLTP IT management to give visible praise, bonuses, and so on to the OLTP IT staff members when they accomplish some tasks that are related to the data warehouse project.
- When openings appear on the data warehouse team, consider filling them from the OLTP IT team.
- When the data warehouse team does any marketing efforts or presentations on the data warehouse, give recognition to the OLTP IT staff members, indicating that the data warehouse could not have been implemented without their involvement.

Bottom line: Instead of simple finger-pointing, this effort requires tact, sensitivity, and professionalism.

MANAGEMENT CONSTANTLY CHANGES

A very dynamic organization is constantly changing management. It is unlikely that the corporate sponsor will remain for the duration of the project. What should the project manager do?

Sid Adelman

The project manager should get a backup sponsor or, better yet, solicit a few high-ranking sponsors who will be able to support the project even if the initial sponsor leaves. The project manager should choose sponsors who are politically powerful, have a substantial interest in the project's success, accept problems (since a project will always have problems), and have both a long-term and short-term perspective of what needs to be accomplished.

Joyce Bischoff

The project manager must try to obtain broad support from the business community, making sure that more than one person has a strong interest in the success of the project. The project manager should consider forming an advisory committee of high-level managers to provide stable support for the project and keep them well informed through regular meetings and communication.

Douglas Hackney

First, the project manager should focus on group-level pain rather than individual-level pain. Second, he or she should have a fully detailed scope statement in place with the data warehouse steering committee. This ensures that the directions and deliverables of the project will outlast any single individual. Third, the project manager should deliver incremental solutions based on a very tight scope, keeping the project time lines in the range of 60–120 days. This affords maximum flexibility as the business changes directions in response to the changing personalities.

Chuck Kelley

In this case, at all times it will be important to have more than one data warehouse champion within the management group. As the organization dynamically changes, it is the job of the project manager and the remaining data warehouse champions to make sure they find new champions. Spending a large amount of time with the new members of the management team, whether they become new champions or not, helps continue the project's growth and expansion.

David Marco

It is important to make sure that the data warehouse will provide value to the front-line workers of the organization, as opposed to executive reporting. Since the sponsor will be leaving, the project manager must make sure that funding is set for the duration of the project.

Larissa Moss

The most solid justification for a data warehouse project is not a corporate sponsor but a business problem that needs a data warehouse solution. Having a strong sponsor to champion the data warehouse initiative is certainly crucial to its success, but without a strong business justification the risk of having a data warehouse project cancelled is even higher. The project manager should perform a business case assessment and prepare a data warehouse justification and cost/benefit document that will outlast the current sponsor. The project manager needs to solicit buy-in from the CEO and other business executives to ensure that a new sponsor will not be able to cancel the data warehouse project.

Clay Rehm

The project manager must prepare for the worst: that the sponsor will leave. This advice holds true for any project manager, even in the instance of a seemingly static and stable sponsor—the sponsor could leave unexpectedly.

If the project manager doesn't have a well-documented data warehouse, he or she must start the documentation immediately. It is preferable to document the business problem(s), scope, and requirements in writing before the sponsor leaves. Additionally, before the sponsor leaves, the project manager should get written approval on all the documentation and store the documentation in a safe place.

The point of having solid documentation is that the project manager can present the purpose, goals, challenges, and benefits of the data warehouse project to anyone at anytime. Managing a data warehouse is difficult enough, and documenting the decisions, architecture, and processes is a quick win/win strategy.

Documentation should be written in a style that nontechnical folks can read easily. This means the documentation and presentations must have an "executive summary" and also provide necessary details. The nontechnical people won't read the technical details, but plenty of other folks will.

In summary: The data warehouse project definition, scope, and requirements should by very well documented.

IT Is the Assassin

The business brought in a competent data warehouse consulting organization to deliver a specific data warehouse application. The cooperation of the IT staff is necessary to build and support the data warehouse infrastructure and to supply the source data. The CIO saw the data warehouse initiative as a challenge to her position and authority and is taking every opportunity to undermine the consultant and the project. What should the consultant do?

Sid Adelman

The consultant must have an important meeting with the business sponsor. Important meetings differ from casual or regular meetings; the consultant should let the sponsor know this meeting is crucial. In the meeting, the consultant should explain the situation to the business sponsor—that without the cooperation of IT, the project will fail. The consultant should also get input from the business sponsor. The business sponsor knows the organization, knows the CIO, and should also be able to help in getting cooperation from the CIO.

Joyce Bischoff

The consultant should go to the business sponsor and ask her or him to work with the CIO on behalf of the project. If possible, the CIO should be a cosponsor of the project. It is unlikely that the CIO will cooperate unless there is a possibility that she will get credit for the implementation.

Douglas Hackney

The consultant should escalate the issue immediately to the highest-level business stakeholders, ideally the CEO and the board of directors. If the cooperation of the CIO and the IT organization cannot be gained, then the consultant should resign the account.

Sean Ivoghli

The consultant should make sure the business sponsor knows what is happening. Saving relevant correspondence and proof of sabotage in a situation like this can protect the consultant from blame. The consultant must not make a frontal assault on the IT team members—they have more power than may be obvious. After all, the consultant is only a visitor in that company and thus should do his or her best to adopt the standards of the IT staffers and to make them feel comfortable that the system will be maintainable. The consultant should allow IT to participate enough to feel involved but not enough to hurt the consultant. He or she should even give the IT staffers some credit for some of his or her accomplishments but not enough to undermine the consultant. If he or she can win the friendship or approval of the IT staffers, great. If not, the consultant should take comfort that he or she is not alone in this situation. No matter what, the consultant should do his or her best to deliver and should not be discouraged. That's the best way to win the IT staffers' trust.

Chuck Kelley

The consulting organization needs to keep a strict record of what was requested, the date promised, who promised it, and the actual delivery. Documentation is critical for the success of this project and the consulting organization's reputation. The consulting organization's management needs to work with the CIO to make sure she understands that the organization is not working on the project to threaten her position but to help strengthen it. This occurs by providing expertise in an area where her team may not be as strong as the consulting organization and by encouraging the desire of the consulting team to work with her IT group as partners.

David Marco

It is critical to document each and every problem that occurs in the project. The consultant needs to take this problem log to the business sponsor to show him or her what is occurring on the project. Hopefully the business sponsor can meet with the CIO and convince her that if they work together, the end project will be a victory for both of them.

Clay Rehm

The consultant should immediately do two things about this situation.

1. Tell the business sponsor what's happening.
2. Work proactively with the CIO to win her over as an ally.

The consultant needs to tell the business sponsor (verbally and in writing) about the situation as soon as he or she identifies this threat. Why? After a few weeks or months on the project, the consultant may get blamed for something he or she did not do or something that may harm the consultant's image. It is also important for the consultant to tell the sponsor that he or she will work immediately to resolve the problem.

The consultant also needs to get the CIO to become an ally. This is a challenge, perhaps an impossible one. If she is smart, she will know what the consultant is doing. The consultant must communicate honestly and face-to-face, not only through e-mails. If his or her personality makes it easy to talk honestly with people, he or she will be much further ahead!

The consultant should try to make friends with the CIO while minimizing her feelings of suspicion. The consultant could initiate a discussion with the CIO immediately and be open and honest with her: "I understand and can appreciate your feelings about a possible threat to your career, but I wish you no harm. I only want to advance your career as well as the careers of others involved with this project."

The consultant must find a way to include the CIO in the project. She could lead or participate in a new data warehouse advisory group or technical advisory group. The consultant must involve the CIO quickly, getting her to see the benefits and challenges of her involvement as soon as possible. Throughout the course of the project, the consultant should make sure to ask the CIO's advice on different topics. If it is sound advice, the consultant should use it and make reference to her as the source.

A data warehouse project is difficult enough without the presence of powerful internal resources trying to undermine it. Resolution of this situation requires swift action, great communication skills, tact, professionalism, and honesty.

THE PILOT MUST BE PERFECT

Management thinks the data warehouse implementation must be perfect; as a result, the scheduled implementation date has already passed. The managers expect the quality assurance (QA) on the pilot to be at the same level as that of a production system. What can the project management team do to convince management that a pilot system and a production system should have different levels of QA?

Sid Adelman

A pilot is the first version of the data warehouse application that uses real data that has been understood, documented, properly selected, cleansed, transformed, and summarized. It takes more time to create a pilot than a prototype, but when the pilot is complete, the organization has something meaningful and useful. If done properly, the pilot is not a throwaway project; it can be expanded and enhanced. For example, the number and types of users can be expanded. The pilot data warehouse can incorporate additional data entities, attributes, subject areas, and historical data for trend analysis and can begin to incorporate external data.

However, since some of the benefits of a pilot are that it takes less time to implement and provides a learning experience for the organization, some mistakes will occur. The deliverable will not have the same robustness as a production system. The organization, including the QA team, should understand the purpose of a pilot and not hold the pilot system to the same standards as a production system.

Joyce Bischoff

Although the testing of a pilot system should have a high level of QA, the emphasis while testing a data warehouse implementation is on data quality and availability. In an operational environment, data quality and availability are still important, but there is more emphasis on front-end programs and their accuracy. Education about these differences and their implications for QA is the key to success.

Douglas Hackney

In this situation, working with someone who has IT experience as a manager (or, at a minimum, as an IT project liaison) is invaluable. The project management team should seek out someone who has this type of experience in the business organization and request to have this person appointed as the primary liaison between the data warehouse project and the business stakeholders. This person is more likely to understand the differences between the pilot level implementation and a production release. Failing this, the project management team should make a presentation to the data warehouse steering committee specifically addressing the differences between a pilot and a production release system. The team must be very specific in requests for deliverables, capabilities, and time lines.

Chuck Kelley

The project leader needs to spend time with management to show that the goal is perfection, but the reality is that a pilot rarely allows enough time for a common understanding of the data requirements now or in the future. The smart approach is to get data in front of the business users in order to get quality feedback during this pilot phase. Letting the business leaders see the data allows them to think in ways they may not have thought before. Until this occurs, the requirements will not be genuine. During the pilot, there will be feedback that discusses why certain measurements are calculated a certain way, which is going to help improve the quality of the whole data warehouse that eventually gets delivered.

Larissa Moss

The data warehouse manager should explain to management and the QA team the software release concept and how it applies to data warehouses. Operational systems and traditional decision support systems used to be built as silos with definitive start and end dates. Once these systems were implemented in production, the only changes applied to them by the maintenance staff were program fixes and a few minor enhancements. A data warehouse is different. It is not a system in and of itself but an environment of many integrated and reconciled databases and applications. This environment cannot be built like a big-bang delivery with definitive start and end dates but must evolve over time. That means that not only will fixes and minor enhancements be applied to this environment but also major new functionality and data will be added over time.

This concept can also apply to individual data warehouse applications, that is, they too can be developed and rolled out iteratively (the first iteration being the pilot). Therefore, the data warehouse team will have ample opportunities to correct any quality problems that slipped through the cracks. The motto of "just enough" may not be appropriate for an operational production system, which is not meant to be reworked, but it is quite appropriate for a data warehouse, especially when it is only a pilot. This does not mean that the team should ignore quality completely, but the team must balance quality with the other constraints of scope, time, resources, and money.

Bottom line: As long as the users and the data warehouse team understand that the data warehouse databases and applications will be revisited and revised as a matter of policy and approach, quality does not have to be 100 percent from the start.

Clay Rehm

The data warehouse team should always strive for perfection, even if the scheduled implementation date slips a little. However, testing a pilot does not require the depth, documentation, and complexity that testing a production system does.

Pilot is another term for *proof-of-concept* or *prototype*. All three terms presume an incomplete system. *Webster's Ninth New Collegiate Dictionary* gives the relevant definition of *pilot* as "serving as an experimental or trial undertaking prior to full-scale operation or use." With that in mind, the pilot is an experiment meant to prove a point or to determine whether the project is worth pursuing.

It is wise to recommend to management that since minimal effort was given to the analysis, design, and development of the pilot, it would indeed be a waste of time, money, and effort to thoroughly test the pilot.

The moral of the story: A pilot is a quick, easy, and inexpensive way to prove a point.

USER DEPARTMENTS DON'T WANT TO SHARE DATA

The feeling seems to be—no one actually says this aloud—"By giving another department access to our data, we will be giving them the ability to criticize us or even take over our jobs." Department heads sometimes give lip service to the idea of sharing data, but in the case of the data in their department, they maintain that no other group has the expertise to accurately analyze their data. They want to be in control of who sees what data and when. How can the data warehouse team get department heads to share access to their data?

Sid Adelman

The data warehouse team may not be able to get department managers to share data. They often do not want anyone to see their data for fear that the department may be exposed to criticism or be micromanaged. The departments heads often want to explain their results or put their own spin on the measurements before others review the data. Few organizations have real data sharing. It happens only in the rare circumstances when the CEO makes clear that everyone must share data and cannot hold anything back. Some organizations do not have the internal politics that impede sharing; however, I have seen only one such organization during my career.

Joyce Bischoff

This situation requires a change in the corporate culture, which may not be easy to effect. The emphasis on teamwork and data sharing must come from the executive ranks. If executives are serious about data sharing, they should address this issue during personnel evaluations.

Jill Dyché

Ahhh. A corporate culture that doesn't encourage business accountability. I hear the question, "Who should own the data?" all too frequently. The fact is, while the business should define the successful use of data, it's the company that owns the data, not one individual organization. People tend to forget for whom they work.

Unfortunately, since this situation is reflective not only of data management but also of cultural issues that represent a barrier to progress, it mandates executive involvement. The CIO should answer the question, "Is data a corporate asset at this company?"

Now, almost every CIO I've ever met answers this question in the affirmative. "Of course data is a corporate asset!" he or she replies while making a mental note to begin describing data as a corporate asset. However, the follow-up question is a bit tougher: "Are you willing to treat data like you do your other corporate assets?" Yes, it's a loaded question that implies everything from solid business processes to structured governance to organizational change. CIOs usually don't answer this question as directly.

The CIO needs to be willing to institute a corporate data management group in charge of managing key enterprise information. (This group could be the existing data administration group.) This group ensures that corporate data is inventoried, that the systems of record are established, that key business rules are understood and socialized, and that departments, in exchange for relinquishing control over their data, get the information and support they need, when they need it.

If the CIO isn't willing to make this decision, then the departments should be left to fight it out until the business pain resulting from different versions of the same data, varied business definitions, nonstandardized decision making, and even incomplete customer profiles becomes great enough to trigger action. Unfortunately, this might culminate in lost customers, reduced market share, and lower satisfaction scores. These are the prices the CIO will have to pay for not managing data as the corporate asset it should be.

Douglas Hackney

In order to gain buy-in for the sharing of information, the department heads and their constituencies must understand the value the organization as a whole will gain from the interchange, exchange, and open access to each department's data. It's very difficult to gain buy-in from powerful functional leaders in decentralized organizations without a clear mandate from the board of directors and the CEO. In these scenarios, the top-down approach is the most effective one for gaining cooperation from powerful constituencies since it requires a clear mandate from the top levels of the organization.

Chuck Kelley

Without a strong data warehouse champion or the backing of upper management, this is a difficult situation to solve. There must be a sense of ownership throughout the whole organization for the success of the data warehouse. Having members of each of the sources as members of the data warehouse team as a place to get the "right" expertise can help reduce, though not alleviate, the unwillingness to share data.

Larissa Moss

Building a data warehouse is a cross-organizational business initiative, and it is not up to the department heads to decide whether and how they will participate. In the scenario given here, either the business executives do not understand or support this concept or the message has not trickled down yet to the department heads. In either case the project manager is in no position to tell the department heads what they should or should not do. He or she can attempt to educate and persuade them, but that will probably have little effect on their attitudes.

A more effective approach is to make the business sponsor of the data warehouse project aware of the department heads' reluctance as soon as their resistance impacts the project. Caution: Unless the project manager knows that the business sponsor also suspects there will be a problem with data sharing, the project manager should not act based solely on a "general feeling" or hearsay but should wait until he or she has hard evidence that the department heads refuse to cooperate. The sponsor must then take up this issue with the department heads or their superiors.

If the sponsor is either unwilling or unable (due to low rank within the organization) to resolve this business issue, the project manager could bring this problem to the CIO's attention. However, it is doubtful that the CIO would have any influence over the department heads unless the CIO takes this issue to other chief officers (CEO, CFO, COO), who then enforce cooperation. This scenario will work only if the business executives understand and support the data warehouse as a cross-organizational business initiative. If they don't, the project manager would be better off switching to another project because this situation will not get resolved in the near future.

Clay Rehm

It's easy to think that anytime you provide your data to additional people, you increase your chances of criticism. However, the data warehouse team should encourage the department heads to use a different perspective: to believe that when outsiders view the data, they will be able to see problems as well as opportunities that the department heads may not see.

The department heads need to have a good reason to share data with outsiders. The benefits for the whole organization may be difficult to see from the perspective of a small department.

If the department heads don't share the data, they will limit the company's opportunities for growth and the possibilities of identifying any data anomalies. Department heads must become "thick skinned" to handle the criticisms, knowing that good can come from it. Sometimes you have to take the good with the bad.

SENIOR MANAGEMENT DOESN'T KNOW WHAT THE DATA WAREHOUSE TEAM DOES

A newly built data warehouse meets almost all the measures of success. The response from upper management has been lukewarm. It seems management does not recognize the success of the project. What should the data warehouse team do?

Joyce Bischoff

What were the measures of success? Does the business sponsor consider it a success? In fact, was there a business sponsor or was it an IT project? If it was an IT project, it may be difficult if not impossible to prove that it was successful.

The data warehouse team should conduct surveys of managers and users to identify the business benefits of the data warehouse. Team members should interview key people. Although managers may not actually use the warehouse directly, their employees probably provide them information from the data warehouse, and the team can determine the effectiveness of the warehouse from that point of view. Team members should ask managers such questions as those listed below.

- Do you use or receive information from the data warehouse?
- Have you personally benefited from the warehouse in terms of improved decision making, better productivity, identification of potential business opportunities, and so on?

The team should also consider sending a questionnaire to all users regarding their opinions of the warehouse. It is rare to receive more than a 30 percent response rate on questionnaires, so it is important to conduct interviews to be sure to obtain a more complete perspective. Team members should ask users such questions as those listed below.

- How often do you use the warehouse?
- Do you consider yourself to be a novice user, a moderately experienced user, or a very experienced user?
- Which end-user tools do you use?
- On a scale of 1–5, where 5 is high, how satisfied are you with the following aspects of the data warehouse?
  - Overall performance
  - Ease of understanding the data design
  - Ease of understanding the data
  - Usability of the data
  - Accuracy of the data

- Availability of the data
- Effectiveness of the end-user tools
- Standard reports and queries
- Query and reporting tools
- Help desk support
- Availability of user training
- Quality of user training
- Process for communicating changes to the upcoming production schedule
- Responses to requests for additions or changes to the warehouse

The team members should always ask for free-form comments, which provide valuable information that might not have been adequately covered in the general questions. After assessing the results of the interviews and questionnaires, the team can more easily document the success and/or possible points in need of improvement.

Jill Dyché

Senior management doesn't care about whether a data warehouse has met its success metrics. Senior management cares about whether the data warehouse saved or earned the company more money than it cost. In other words, it's all about the bottom line.

The question here is not "Why doesn't senior management care?" as much as "Is it really important for senior management to care?" If the end-users are using the data warehouse for critical business functions, if they are helping to fund it, and if those sponsoring the data warehouse agree that it has done its job, then perhaps the data warehouse has proven all it needs to prove.

However, if senior management has begun to ask questions—the proverbial "How has this data warehouse benefited us?" belongs in the Data Warehouse Hall of Fame—then it's time to pull out the pre-facto ROI estimates made during the construction of the data warehouse business case and back them up with hard numbers.

No ROI estimates? No hard numbers? Then it's back to the end-users to help the team corroborate both the tangible and intangible benefits of consolidated, clean, and meaningful business data. Perhaps the data warehouse has meant more inventory turns per year. Perhaps it has reduced staff data-gathering time by 95 percent. Perhaps it replaced a dozen departmental servers, saving the company $1.2 million in licensing fees.

If the data warehouse has done its job, the users should be able to sing its praises. And if it hasn't, senior management is the least of the data warehouse team's worries. The business users aren't happy. The team should be afraid.

Douglas Hackney

In this common example, the measures of success for the data warehouse were tied to technological goals or IT goals rather than the goals and values of the business. It is critical that success measures be defined between the business and the team prior to implementation of the system. In a case such as this where the measures of success are unimportant to the business, the system will continue to be viewed as marginal until capabilities are added that are meaningful to and measurable by the business.

Chuck Kelley

The data warehouse team needs to spend time with senior management doing "dog and pony" shows (including bits on the corporate Web site and in any newsletters) to show how the data warehouse has been successful. It would not be a surprise to me, however, if senior management would not feel excited about the system unless they could see the real benefit (ROI in real dollars) of the data warehouse. Anything that shows the ROI would increase the recognition of the project's success.

David Marco

Marketing a data warehouse project can be as important as the physical implementation. Remember, perception becomes reality. If management perceives that the data warehouse has not been valuable, it could spell trouble for the future of the team.

The data warehouse team needs to document the measures of success and get the business users, especially the sponsor, to support these findings. The data warehouse team then needs to take this information, preferably with the business sponsor, to management to present the success of the data warehousing initiative.

Larissa Moss

Management does not seem to perceive any business problems that needed a data warehouse solution, and the success factors by which the data warehouse team measured its success must not have been business factors. It is possible that the IT department and/or a lone-ranger business sponsor of low rank saw a business need and built a data warehouse in the hope that the users would come around. Most likely, the team performed no business case assessment, prepared no cost justification, and obtained no management buy-in. The IT team members must now prepare and present their business case to management, showing the business pain in dollars and cents and demonstrating how the data warehouse is solving that pain. It may be too little too late, but without buy-in from management this data warehouse has no future.

Clay Rehm

Assuming the data warehouse is meeting the needs of the people who really need it, assuming they are using it, and assuming it is providing ease of use and accessibility to data that was not accomplished before, the data warehouse team has no choice but to enlist the marketing expertise of the business users. It is critical that the users market and present the benefits and success of the data warehouse.

Instead of doing something dry and boring, the business users can put on an "expo" that spotlights all the benefits of the data warehouse, including enhanced technology, beneficial changes to business processes and organizational change management, and improved availability of data. This can be accomplished through demonstrations of the data delivery interface.

If the users don't like that idea, why not take the presentation on the road? A road show is a great way to expose a product to many people in the organization.

If there is a company intranet site, the team can put a blurb on the home page about the new data warehouse and the road show and/or education schedule.

These methods should specifically target upper management, even taking into account what format best holds their interest. Do they like expos, demos, road shows, intranet education, paper handouts?

CHAPTER TWO

Changing Requirements and Objectives

If one does not know to which port one is sailing, no wind is favorable.

—Seneca

OVERVIEW

Change Control

The nature of a data warehouse is such that new requests will constantly be added to the original requirements. These requests may ask for new data from current source files, new canned reports, a different delivery vehicle such as the Web, the integration of new source files, or access by more users.

Most project managers include a small amount of fat in their estimates so they can accommodate unforeseen contingencies and small scope changes. Sometimes, the small changes begin to creep up to the point that the existing schedule can no longer handle the additional requirements. This is *scope creep*. When the requests are for large changes, such as new and complex source data or some new technology implementation, it is referred to as *scope gallop*.

If the schedule derived from the project plan was realistic, a major change cannot be accommodated within an existing schedule. The list below presents the project variables.

- *Function:* The project will deliver this capability.
- *Resources:* This includes budget, skilled personnel, and management commitment.
- *Quality:* An unrealistic schedule may push the team to take shortcuts such as minimal testing, incomplete documentation, and inadequate training.
- *Team health:* Some managers believe they can drive their teams 12 hours each day and seven days each week. This can work only for a short time. After that, the team members may be present, but their productivity and work quality will suffer.

It's difficult to hit a moving target, and the scope of a data warehouse project is no exception. Somehow there is the notion that with a data warehouse we can abandon all we know about change management, believing that a data warehouse gives us the license to make changes without having to incur additional costs and time delays.

Some data warehouse projects are developed in parallel with major changes to existing operational systems or with the introduction of new operational systems that provide the source data. Ideally, we would like to freeze new requirements and changes to existing requirements, but the reality is that there is no way to stop these requests.

Goals and Objectives

It would seem that everyone involved with a data warehouse would know why it is being built, but that often is not the case. Sometimes the objectives are expressed in lofty terms that have little concrete definition, nor can these terms provide much direction to the people executing the projects. Without clear objectives, a data warehouse project will go astray. In these cases, we see effort being spent on tasks that make no real contribution (for example, cleaning up data that will never be accessed), tasks that duplicate effort (for example, multiple efforts evaluating the same set of tools), or tasks that conflict with each other (for example, the implementation of incompatible keys resulting in integration problems).

Once the project is complete, some organizations have great difficulty determining whether their objectives were met and whether the project was successful. Most often, organizations don't even take the time to compare their results with their original objectives. Project leaders are often at a loss to demonstrate the value of their project. Many projects have been successful but management has not recognized that success. In fact, management may not even recognize the value of the data warehouse system.

The reasons for developing prototypes are often misunderstood, resulting in a push to turn the prototype into a production system. Often, users have demanded the prototype becomes a production system. This inevitably leads to disappointment since prototypes rarely are robust enough to provide meaningful capability to the business users.

In the remainder of this chapter, we discuss solutions for six situations that often occur due to changes in requirements and objectives.

THE OPERATIONAL SYSTEM IS CHANGING

The data warehouse project has been in development for six months. Right in the middle of the project the team discovers that the operational source systems are being rewritten, with the new systems expected to be live in eight months. What should the data warehouse team do?

Sid Adelman

The obvious answer is to put the development of the data warehouse on hold until the operational source is reasonably stable. However, the danger is that the team will be scattered to the wind, and trying to reconstitute the team when the time is right will be close to impossible.

There is a way to keep the team together, interested, and motivated. The team can work on project activities that will still provide value to the organization. There should be a certain amount of commonality between the new and the old operational systems. User requirements may be somewhat different, but most of those requirements can still be salvaged. The logical modeling will require some changes, but most of the logical modeling effort can still be used for the new system as well as for the old. Many of the reports and queries will be the same. There should be no need to change out the access and analysis software, nor should there be any reason to change the extract/transform/load (ETL) software. Be aware that even though the new system is expected to be live in eight months, the actual delivery time may be much longer, so retaining the team may be even more of a challenge.

Joyce Bischoff

If the data warehouse design is based on known requirements, the target data structures in the warehouse may not require major changes. By modifying the sources in the source-target mappings, the team should be able to proceed with the project.

Douglas Hackney

First, the data warehouse team should determine whether any new critical metrics and measures will be present in the new operational system that were absent in the old. If so, the team should modify the target model to include these measures. Second, the team should review and reconfirm the target model with the business stakeholders in the context of the new operational system. Third, at least one data warehouse team member should be assigned to the new OLTP system team. That person's mission is to bring back an accurate and stable OLTP logical model as early in the process as possible. Fourth, the project manager should revisit the project timeline and deliverables with the data warehouse steering committee, making adjustments as necessary.

Sean Ivoghli

This issue needs to be dealt with primarily at a political level between project managers and project sponsors. As a defensive measure to reduce the chance of surprises, the data warehouse team can develop a script that reads the relational database management system (RDBMS) catalog and compares the current data definition language (DDL) of the source system(s) to the DDL of the source system(s) at the time of the previous extract. The team might want to consider saving all the different versions of the source DDLs as evidence in order to fuel the political effort. Once in production, the team members should consider running this script before every extract to prevent surprises. Then they can determine how to handle the ETL process in the event of errors.

Chuck Kelley

We always need to remember what Heraclitus the Obscure (who was born at Ephesus about 530 B.C.) said: "There is nothing permanent except change." Even that long ago, they understood the development process!

The data warehouse team should continue with development using the current system. Unless it is a very small system, the chance that the new system will be live in eight months is pretty slim. Even if it is, the functionality will not change a great deal. Therefore, the major changes will be reflected in the input to the transformation process. While continuing the development on the current system, it would be wise to place into the schedule regular meetings with the people working on the new system to find out what is happening.

David Marco

Since the data model for the data warehouse is subject oriented, this change in source systems should not impact that area of the development effort. If I believed that the new system would go live in eight months and that the existing source system would go away at that time too, I would wait on the construction of the ETL process. The data warehouse team should stay together and make sure to construct good data marts, a metadata repository, and error-handling mechanisms.

Larissa Moss

Hopefully the data warehouse team members developed a logical (business) data model (not the same as a logical database design) reflecting the operational data objects and data elements, and hopefully they analyzed and modeled the domain (content) of the operational data elements according to the business rules. If they did, the team can now use this model for impact analysis and the source-to-target mapping document as a guide for the necessary changes.

If the data to be delivered is still the same before and after the new operational system, the logical data model would not need to change, and neither would the target data warehouse databases and the data warehouse data delivery application. Only the ETL process would be affected. The source data would have to be remapped from the new system to the target databases, and the extract and transformation modules would have to be rewritten or revised.

If the data to be delivered is different, that is, if there are new data elements or if some old data elements are removed for some business reason, the logical data model would have to be modified to reflect the changes. Since the data content of a logical data model is reflective of the data content in the data warehouse databases (regardless of the database design schema), the designs of the target databases and the data access and analysis applications would have to be modified. In addition, the ETL process would have to be rewritten or revised.

In either case, to avoid a lot of rework, the development work on the data warehouse project should not continue until the data impact is analyzed. This can be done only after the new source system is stable (not necessarily implemented) and the final operational data content of the new system is understood and modeled.

Clay Rehm

I would continue on the path to deliver the first release of the data warehouse as planned. Even though the new operational source systems are expected to go live in eight months, there is a very good chance it will take longer.

This is a great opportunity to demonstrate the value of the data warehouse, to test the current system, and to test the new system when it gets in. The users can see value now and not have to wait until the new source systems are in place.

The management team must make it clear to all participants that more time and money will be required to make the changes when the new systems come in.

So the current data warehouse design can accommodate the future changes, the data warehouse team must collect the following right now:

- Source systems data models
- Business rules
- Worked examples
- Use cases

The moral of the story: Learn and document as much as possible about potential new source systems so the data warehouse design is flexible and scalable.

THE SOURCE SYSTEM CONSTANTLY CHANGES

The source system is being built at the same time as the data warehouse. Although the design of the source system is supposed to be "frozen," it is constantly changing. The source system development team does not communicate the changes—the data warehouse team discovers changes during testing when the system fails. The lack of communication may be intentional. What should the data warehouse team do?

Sid Adelman

How does the data warehouse team get the source system development team to communicate what it is doing? There are three approaches.

1. Escalate the problem to management and get management to force the development team to communicate. This may work for a time, but it is far from optimal. The development team members will always have some excuse for being late or incomplete with their communications, and they will surely resent you for going over their heads.
2. Develop a rapport between the teams and a rapport between the teams' managers. Outings and athletic or other types of competition can help develop the relationship. The success of this approach very much depends on a previous history of friendships and working together. If reasonably good relationships do not already exist or, more importantly, if there is much animosity, this approach will not work.
3. Create some common incentives for the teams. If the source system development team participates in the success of the data warehouse project (that is, both teams are eligible for bonuses), communications will start to flow as never before.

Douglas Hackney

The data warehouse team manager should immediately meet with the OLTP team manager to discuss the issues and attempt to reach a resolution. If this effort fails, the issue should be escalated to the data warehouse steering committee. A prerequisite for success is the cooperation of the source system data owners and stewards. If this cooperation is not present, chances for data warehousing success are slim.

Sean Ivoghli

This issue needs to be dealt with at a political level. To reduce the chance of surprises, the data warehouse team can develop a script that reads the relational database management system (RDBMS) catalog and compares the current data definition language (DDL) of the source system(s) to the DDL of the source system(s) at the time of the previous extract. The team might want to consider saving all the different versions of the source DDLs to fuel the political effort. Once in production, the team members should consider running this script before every extract to prevent surprises. Then they can determine how to handle the ETL process in the event of errors.

Chuck Kelley

First, it should be understood that this will always happen, not just when building the source system and data warehouse at the same time. There will be many times that the source system will change and the data warehouse team will not be notified, causing all the ETL processes to fail.

The data warehouse team should try to get someone on the source system team as a listener to report back to the data warehouse team any design changes that are occurring. Of course, this will not catch all the changes. It is important to put into place a reconciliation process. Some items to check are listed below.

- How many new customers were added to the source system and then to the data warehouse?
- How much money was reported on the operational reports versus the data warehouse? How much money was reported in the source file versus the data warehouse load?
- How many new items were posted into the source system versus the data warehouse? (Remember that these may not be equal, depending on grouping or aggregation!)

Once this reconciliation process is in place, there must be a defined way to reverse items that could not be reconciled (based on the terms of the service-level agreements). One way to do this is to place a job run number in every table. Keeping track of what "run" originally inserted each piece of the data into the database will help in reversing them. The team can delete all the data from the tables where the job run number is equal to a specific value, then rerun and rereconcile.

Adding a feature like this makes it easier to detect when something changes in the source system. Then the team can fix the problem and work on understanding why this problem was not presented before the reconciliation.

David Marco

The data warehouse team should document and communicate each and every problem with the source system. The data warehouse team should then focus on those activities that do not involve the source system.

Since the data model for the data warehouse is subject oriented, the changes happening in the source system should not impact that area of the development effort. In addition, the data warehouse team should construct their data marts, a meta data repository, and error-handling mechanisms.

Larissa Moss

This may appear to be a communication issue within IT, but it is really a management issue for the business executives to solve. Too many times project teams are expected to solve problems that should really be solved by someone at a higher level who has the clout and authority to solve them. In this situation I suggest that person is the data warehouse business sponsor.

Giving the IT source system development team the benefit of the doubt, they are probably trying to satisfy their operational users by making these last-minute changes and by pushing forward as fast as possible to complete their project without regard to the data warehouse team's dependency on them. In that case, the business sponsor of the data warehouse team should discuss this situation with the operational users' business executives and the CIO. The operational users should be told by management (not by the data warehouse team) about the significance of the strategic data warehouse initiative. Management should also direct the operational users to ease off their own development team and to cooperate with the data warehouse team fully, even if it slows their own project. This lets both teams off the hook when they slip their respective schedules.

If the data warehouse is not seen as a strategic initiative in this organization, and if it is not supported by all business executives, then the sponsor and the data warehouse team have a different political problem. Unless the sponsor can get buy-in from the chief executive level of the company, situations like this may recur because there is neither a mandate nor an incentive for other business executives to cooperate.

If the source system development team is not driven by its own users, and if the lack of communication is really geared toward sabotaging the data warehouse initiative, the sponsor should talk to the CIO directly and ask for immediate correction of this situation. After all, this noncooperative behavior is more damaging to the objectives of the sponsor than to the workflow or the effort of the data warehouse team.

In any of these cases, it is the sponsor who should drive the resolution of the situation on the business side or with the CIO or both.

The worst possible situation for the data warehouse team would be if the sponsor were not willing to get involved, and if he or she kept putting pressure on the data warehouse team without helping it address the communication problem. Then the impediment to the data warehouse project is the sponsor (who is supposed to help remove roadblocks but isn't)—not the source system development team and its lack of communication. In that case, the data warehouse team members are truly working under an impossible situation because they are left to fend for themselves in the trenches.

Clay Rehm

For future reference, this is one of data warehousing's biggest cardinal sins. Do not ever build a data warehouse release based on a new or changing data source! Having said that, what should the team do now?

Establish a liaison between the operational and data warehouse teams immediately. This person must not already work on either team. Hiring a consultant who has nothing to gain from this project might be the best option. This consultant can be an unbiased third party who facilitates communication between the two teams on a *daily* basis.

Daily status meetings must take place until the problem is resolved. This meeting requires a facilitator, a scribe, and decision-making members from the operational team and the data warehouse team.

The data warehouse project manager must update the project plan that reflects reality. If the dates have slipped, it is important to deliver the bad news sooner rather than later.

If a change control process is not in place, management should freeze the data warehouse target *now* and implement the process immediately.

The project manager should communicate to all data warehouse stakeholders the status of the current situation. He or she should announce that there will be no firm data warehouse delivery date until the source is complete, unless there will be interim releases. This really is even more of a reason that change control is so important. Proper and honest communication is the most important part of developing a data warehouse. Project managers should tell the bad and good news now and do it often.

THE DATA WAREHOUSE VISION HAS BECOME BLURRED

When the data warehouse project began, the organization searched out the best practices in the industry and developed a strong set of data warehouse objectives. However, over the months and years, decisions were made and actions were taken that went counter to the initial objectives. Most of these decisions and actions were considered pragmatic and sometimes recognized as temporary, with the goal to eventually return to the initial objectives. What should this organization do?

Sid Adelman

The organization needs a champion to resurrect those data warehouse objectives, to explain their purpose, and to proselytize the advantages of making decisions that conform to those objectives. The champion needs to recruit believers who will support the objectives—especially people who will be involved in future decision making.

Joyce Bischoff

High-level management must be involved in validating the original objectives and setting today's objectives for the data warehouse, which may be quite different than the original set. After the current objectives are determined, they should be mapped against the existing warehouse, and the future strategy can be developed.

Douglas Hackney

The organization should compare the outcomes achieved so far against the mutually agreed-upon measures of success established by the team and the business stakeholders. In many cases, organizations set objectives that are little more than theory or grandiose pontifications impossible to achieve in any real-world scenario. If the pragmatic adjustments delivered incremental value to the business, relieved specific business pain, and met the parameters of the measures of success defined in the detailed scope statement, then the adjustments were appropriate.

Chuck Kelley

As the pragmatic and temporary decisions and actions were made, with the idea of returning to the initial objectives, someone should have documented what the decision or action was, why it was made, and how it will be rectified to move it toward the initial objectives. If that has not been done, it is time for the organization to define those objectives now. Only then will there be recovery.

David Marco

While it is critical to initially create a data warehousing vision, it is important to understand that the business's objectives will change over time; therefore this vision will continue to be refined as the data warehouse matures. On the other hand, it appears that some "temporary" modifications were made to the data warehouse and that these changes have impacted the original vision. In this situation the data warehouse champion needs to recommit this company to the original vision, and this person needs to create a committee that will enforce the best practices and then empower the committee members to make it happen.

Larissa Moss

This organization should reexamine its original data warehouse objectives. Objectives can change over time, and it's possible that the ongoing "pragmatic" and "temporary" deviations were indications of those changes. How an organization conducts its business and what information it needs for its decision-making process change over time, and the data warehouse objectives should be examined periodically to keep up with those changes.

However, if the pragmatic and temporary deviations in this case were truly veering off the stated objectives, and if the current data warehouse objectives are still the same as the original objectives, then the impact of having strayed from the objectives must be examined and addressed. The organization should develop a plan to replace any "temporary" fixes with more permanent solutions that meet the objectives.

In addition, the root causes for having to deviate from the objectives must be identified and addressed. For example, let's assume that one of the root causes is the impatience of users to follow a data warehouse methodology. In that case the users should be educated on the risks of not using a methodology; the methodology should be reevaluated to see if it could be streamlined; and development tools should be selected to speed up the process.

Clay Rehm

Strategic architecture and planning are obviously not in place. It is important to retain a continuous "vision" of where the data warehouse needs to be. Having said that, it is not easy to do. I am sure the data warehouse has changed hands and priorities. It may not be as important anymore since it is a "production" system in "maintenance" mode now.

The project manager needs to reintroduce the scope, requirements, and objectives. If these documents exist, he or she should update them. If they do not exist, he or she should create them. Documentation and visual diagrams are very powerful tools. Do not be afraid to use them.

The project manager should create a data warehouse advisory group (if one doesn't already exist) and have this group prioritize the objectives. The group must identify what must be done in the short term (tactical) and what must be done for the long term (strategic). The advisory group must include decision-making stakeholders of the data warehouse project, from both the business and IT worlds.

The project manager must present to the advisory group the history of the data warehouse's evolution. It is important that the decision makers know the history and the current state of the project. When determining the desired state, the group members must know where the project is now before they can get to where they're going.

In summary: Never underestimate the power of enterprise-wide architecture and strategic planning.

THE OBJECTIVES ARE MISUNDERSTOOD

The objectives for the data warehouse were never properly identified. The project is well under way but there is no method for judging whether the project will be successful. What should the organization do?

Sid Adelman

The organization should develop measures of success so it will know if the project is successful and so it can identify areas for improvement—there is always room for improvement with a data warehouse. Some examples of these measures appear below.

- The data warehouse is used. This requires the ability to measure usage; many access and analysis tools have this capability.
- The data warehouse is useful. A customer satisfaction survey could be the primary measurement vehicle.
- Performance is acceptable. Acceptable performance is relevant as perceived by the users, which means performance expectations must be managed.
- The data warehouse is cost justified. This requires measurement of the costs as well as the benefits.
- Managers are able to get more timely answers to their questions.
- The data is significantly cleaner.

Joyce Bischoff

As the saying goes, "If you don't know your destination, any road will get you there." There are at least two basic alternatives.

1. Go back and develop objectives. Modify the project plan to meet solid objectives.
2. After implementation, ask executives, managers, and users how the warehouse has benefited them and their work. Bring this information together into a single report that should spell out the strengths and weaknesses and provide an indicator as to the degree of success.

Jill Dyché

The project is well under way? What are people *doing*? How do they know what data to load? Or are they just using the "throw it at the wall and see if it sticks" method of data requirements identification? What are their transformation rules based on? Is there a data model, and if so, how did the modelers know what to model? And—I shudder to ask—are end-users involved?

I once worked with a telecommunications company whose data warehouse was "almost finished." Upon a bit of exposure to the project, it was clear that "almost finished" really meant "We're loading all the source system data we can get our hands on." The client had a good database product, a robust ETL tool, and some smart people on its team. Nevertheless, the project represented the well-worn "If you build it, they will come" mentality that has proven disastrous.

I say: STOP! Management should put a moratorium on development until a group of business people hungry for some data can be found. If this is the company's first data warehouse, then those users are definitely out there, particularly if the company is in the throes of customer relationship management (CRM), supply chain automation, or another strategic IT initiative. The data warehouse team should draft a clear, finite set of business requirements that can be solved by data, then go back to the project at hand and map what's taken place with what the requirements document says. Then the team should resume the project the right way.

The risk of continuing the project—particularly if it has progressed beyond ETL work—is that everything being developed will eventually be thrown away. Better to waste five bucks now than a hundred tomorrow.

Douglas Hackney

The data warehouse steering committee should immediately establish measures of success. It is critically important that the initial phases of the data warehouse project be measurable and be built to meet specific criteria established by the team and by the business stakeholders. The "build it and they will come" approach works for baseball fields in Dyersville, Iowa, but it does not work in data warehousing.

The committee should start by identifying business pain that can be addressed by the data in the source subject area of the system under construction. The group needs to differentiate life-threatening business pain from "this would be nice to have" pain.

Chuck Kelley

While moving forward with the development in an iterative environment, the project manager should work to strongly identify each of the objectives of each of the iterations. As time passes, the objectives will continue to be strengthened and understood.

David Marco

The project manager should examine what source data is being brought into the data warehouse and the types of reports planned for development. Then he or she should look for homogeneous groups (departments, lines of business, and so on) that would have a need for this type of information. The project manager should meet with any such groups to see if the data warehouse team can modify the reports or data to provide the groups with some value.

The project manager should make sure that the data warehouse team creates a subject-oriented data warehouse model. Making a subject-oriented model allows for tremendous data reuse among homogeneous user groups.

Larissa Moss

While the data warehouse project is still in progress, the project manager and the sponsor need to immediately develop clear objectives for the project. When the data warehouse project was originally approved, there must have been some justification for it. The project manager and sponsor should start with that justification and specify the financial impact of the business pain (for example, loss of revenue or excessive operating costs) that led to the approval of the data warehouse project. Furthermore, they need to describe the criteria for success, that is, what functionality or capability of the data warehouse is expected to eliminate or reduce the business pain—and how soon. In other words, what should be the expected return on investment? Once that has been established, the project manager and the sponsor need to review the data warehouse project scope and the delivery requirements to ensure that the project activities are in sync with the specific objectives they have just documented.

Clay Rehm

The goal at this point is to quantify what needs to be completed and what has been completed so far. The project manager must form a temporary

SWAT team to take the existing objectives and requirements and create understandable, testable, and accomplishable requirements from them. This will involve the time and energy of the business representatives to clarify and expand on vague requirements.

Using the existing project definition, scope, objectives, and requirements, the team should develop a new requirements document that is easy to read. It must have an approval section that allows the sponsors and development team a place to sign off. The document should also include a grid that lists each requirement and how the team plans to accomplish that requirement.

Bottom line: When gathering requirements, they must be understandable, testable, and accomplishable.

THE PROTOTYPE BECOMES PRODUCTION

A company developed a prototype so that the users and management could get a sense of what they would be getting. The prototype was never intended to become a production system, so the team gave little effort to cleaning the data, producing a workable database design, testing the prototype, or performing all that is necessary to deliver a high-quality product. Management said, "Great, let's roll it out to all the users now." How should the developers convince management that a prototype is not ready for production?

Sid Adelman

A prototype is a throwaway, a mock-up of the eventual product. In the case of a data warehouse, it usually has a small amount of data that has been carefully selected to show a capability but serves no useful purpose to help an organization make more meaningful decisions. The data in a prototype probably lacks integrity, is usually not current, and is often plain wrong. It's much like a movie set that looks fine from the front, but behind the facade there is no flooring, plumbing, electricity, roof, or anything else needed to make a building useful and usable.

Why would a company want to spend the time and money to develop a prototype?

Some companies develop a prototype to prove the concept of the data warehouse. This is akin to having to prove the concept of wireless transmission. As Michael Haisten, Vice President for Business Intelligence for Daman Consulting, has said, "We know it [the data warehouse] works." There have been countless success stories that can be validated without having to go to the trouble and expense of developing a prototype to prove the data warehouse works.

Other companies implement a prototype to get management buy-in. The idea is that unless managers can see a "working" data warehouse in their own organization with some of their own data, they would have no faith in whether or not a data warehouse would actually work. There are other ways to get management buy-in without the prototype exercise. Just to name a few:

- Have a query tool vendor demonstrate using some of the organization's sample data.
- Visit other installations that have working data warehouses.
- Attend conferences where case studies are described.

There is the possibility that unless managers see their own people implementing something, they will have no faith in their staff's ability to complete a project successfully. This could be the result of previous failures of the IT staff to actually deliver anything meaningful, on time and within budget. However, a prototype will not prove that these in-house incompetents can implement a robust data warehouse.

Still others want the prototype to help the organization evaluate tools. While the prototype may give some indication of the level of vendor service (vendors' service is usually excellent in the selling phase), a prototype rarely uncovers the warts found on most tools. Wart revelation usually comes after the databases get large, the queries get complex, and the really dirty and complex data has to be cleansed and transformed. These conditions rarely emerge while building a prototype.

And then other companies use the prototype to give the organization the experience it needs to build a data warehouse. In fact, building a prototype will provide some experience, some of which may be useful—but this experience could also be gained building some real and meaningful capability. A prototype does not provide the experience for the really difficult tasks that must be accomplished to deliver a data warehouse, such as handling complex and dirty data, designing and tuning very large databases, and dealing with unruly users.

Joyce Bischoff

Developers must cover themselves by putting their concerns in writing to all concerned parties. They should explain the impact of bad data, the lack of usability of the database design, the likelihood of large amounts of downtime due to lack of testing, and the probability of poor performance when the prototype is opened to large groups of users.

Douglas Hackney

The easiest route is to simply show management the dirty data in the prototype. Turning on a data warehouse system that you know includes dirty data is sure project suicide. You get only one opening night in data warehousing. There's no opportunity to work out the kinks off-Broadway. You'll get one chance to establish credibility. If you deliver a system with dirty data, the users will not risk their careers on it. It is highly likely that the system will be unused or underused and suffer the inevitable resulting loss of budget and resources.

Chuck Kelley

The good news is that it sounds like the data warehouse is a success. The bad news is it sounds as if the prototype was not built in an iterative manner. Each iteration shows the users new data. This is followed with cleaning the data, strengthening the database design, and testing the ETL process. Since it doesn't sound like the developers in this situation followed that iterative process, they are in a predicament—namely, trying to convince management that the prototype is not real. It should be noted that prototypes and proof of concepts commonly become production, so developers need to put into their schedules the items required to deliver a high-quality product.

For now, the developers should continue performing the tasks they are doing and build into their schedule the processes to phase in the tasks for the high-quality product, including a task to complete the cleanup. When completed, the developers should take down the data warehouse for a long weekend and put those modules into production, along with the appropriate code. Then they should work on the next item, and so forth, until they have achieved the high-quality product. And like every good IT group, the developers should learn from their mistakes and always treat the prototype and proof-of-concepts for data warehouses as items that will become production.

David Marco

It is important to explain to management that this prototype is just that—a prototype. It is not meant for production and will not be a solution for the business because of its architecture and data quality issues.

Larissa Moss

The data warehouse manager should definitely convince management that a prototype in the described condition is not ready for production! He or she needs to explain how the dirty data, the poorly designed database, and the untested application will not meet users' expectations when they start using the prototype. In addition, it would be a high risk to base critical business decisions on this prototype.

The data warehouse manager now has two choices: slam on the brakes and insist that the original project plan is followed, or try a new *release* approach with this set of users and management. Since the prototype appears to be an "almost functioning application," the data warehouse manager could point out that although this prototype cannot be implemented as is, it may not have to be thrown out entirely (assuming it has salvageable components). He or she can suggest that it can be used as an alpha or beta release by a few select users for the purpose of finalizing the data warehouse requirements. This will give the select users an opportunity to validate the requirements while the data warehouse team goes through another iteration of the prototype to complete the ETL process and the application and to tune the design of the database to avoid major performance problems.

Depending on the time pressure put on the data warehouse project manager, and depending on just how functional the prototype really is, he or she may also have to scale down the scope of the final application deliverable. In that case, the data warehouse manager will have to educate the users on the release concept of data warehouse applications. Unlike traditional development efforts for operational systems, which produce a fully functioning and finished system, the data warehouse is constantly modified and enhanced, that is, it is built in iterations. Taking this a step further, individual data warehouse applications can also be built iteratively. Therefore, a requirement from the users to deliver a completed data warehouse application is not even in their own best interest because they would give up the chance to evolve their own requirements as they go. It would also not be in the users' interest to deny IT the opportunity to evolve and revise the data warehouse environment so that the users get the most benefit from it in the most expedient way.

The release concept uses prototyping in a completely different way. Prototyping in effect becomes a methodology or approach for rolling out releases. In that case, the scope of each prototype would be very small, and the deliverable would be not the entire requested data warehouse application but a fully tested and fully documented stable *component* of the final application. With each release, more functionality and more data would be rolled out. With this type of development approach the users must expect and accept ongoing refinements (changes) to the databases and the applications. This is a drastic departure from a traditional development approach, and not all users will be comfortable with it.

In the end, the big lesson learned by the data warehouse manager from this situation is not to build any more functioning prototypes for this set of users and management unless they agree to the release concept and are willing to accept partial functionality.

Bottom line: Prototyping can be used very effectively as long as all stakeholders understand the purpose for the prototype, its limitations, and its life span.

Clay Rehm

The answer to this problem is stated in the question. It is up to the project manager to present the following facts to management.

- The prototype was never intended to become a production system.
- Little to no effort was spent on cleansing the data.
- Little to no effort was spent on designing a strategic database design that is flexible, scalable, and so on.
- Little to no effort was spent on testing the many scenarios that need to be tested to assure a high-quality product.

- Most importantly, little effort was spent on gathering user requirements that are understandable, testable, and accomplishable.

It is up to the project manager to document the facts in an easy-to-read document containing visual diagrams. The delivery of this news requires a strong project manager who is armed with the documented facts and has the support of the IT development management and team.

The project manager must send out the documentation to management, and after they have had time to review it, schedule and conduct a presentation to get approval on a project plan to analyze, design, develop, test, and implement the strategic solution.

A word to project managers: Manage expectations early. When presenting a prototype to management, be very clear that it is an example, not the final product.

MANAGEMENT DOESN'T RECOGNIZE THE SUCCESS OF THE DATA WAREHOUSE PROJECT

A data warehouse manager has now implemented three data marts but has been unable to convince management of the success of these efforts. What should the data warehouse manager do to show how successful these data marts are?

Sid Adelman

The data warehouse manager should start to measure the things that are of interest to management. If management cares about the productivity of the analysts, one measure could be the number of queries per day run by each analyst. If management cares about the timeliness of the information and if the data warehouse is able to deliver sooner, this improved timeliness can be measured. If management cares about the quality of the data, integrity and completeness can be measured. Each of these measurements should be reported to management monthly, highlighting the differences before and after data warehouse implementation.

Jill Dyché

The data warehouse manager needs to go back to the business users and ask them to quantify the value of the data marts, focusing on how the three data marts have increased revenues or decreased costs. He or she should convince management and business users to quantify and support such improvements, documenting them if necessary.

If "hard dollar" benefits can't be found, the data warehouse manager should have business users focus on key business initiatives that have been supported by the data marts and illustrate the before-and-after scenarios to show time savings, productivity improvements, or business success engendered by the data marts. Users should be able to complete the sentence, "If we didn't have this data mart, we would never have been able to. . . ."

Such an activity should be used as a learning exercise. The data warehouse manager might find that the data marts haven't been as cost effective as he or she expected. Thus such an activity can refine metrics for how the company chooses data mart applications in the future.

Douglas Hackney

The first thing the data warehouse manager should do is stop building data marts for IT and start building data marts for the business. By definition, if he or she cannot convince business management that the data marts are a success, then they are not a success. This is a classic example of IT-driven initiatives that are viewed as a success by the technologists but viewed dimly by the business. Data marts will never be viewed as a success by the business until the data warehouse team builds specific solutions to specific business pain. Often, data marts are built to fulfill the vision of IT. They're loaded with data, queries are run, and IT proclaims them to be a success. However, the business either didn't ask for them or doesn't have a use for them. So why should it be a surprise to anyone that the technologists cannot convince the business that the data marts are a success? Establishing mutually agreed-upon success criteria with the business prior to design and implementation will eliminate this problem.

Sean Ivoghli

Success of a data warehouse or data mart is determined by the benefit it provides to the business, not by the success in implementing the technology alone. If the data marts have active users, the data warehouse manager should capture the names of the users, the frequency of usage, the type of data used, and related usage data from the RDBMS or by using third-party tools. It would be even better if the data warehouse manager could quote the users on the value they receive by using the data marts. If there are no users, the project may be in trouble.

Chuck Kelley

While IT can tout the success of data marts, the data warehouse manager needs to find a member of each of the data marts business groups who can show the success of each. The data warehouse manager can call on those members as "expert witnesses" when making the case for success. He or she can focus on many areas to show success—saving time, finding new trends, reducing redundant reports, and so on.

Clay Rehm

As the saying goes, "Don't toot your own horn." If the first three data marts are as good as the data warehouse manager thinks they are, then the stakeholders and users of those data marts should be doing the marketing work. They should be telling their peers, coworkers, and management what a great system they have.

The next step is to talk to the prior users about performing road shows or demos to show how they cannot live without the data marts built for them. The data warehouse manager can help the users build these presentations with examples. The users should be able to say, "I don't know what I did before I had this data mart!"

If the data warehouse manager has created successful data marts, I assume he or she has built rapport and friendship with the users, so they would be happy to support the project. If not, the data warehouse manager has homework to do. His or her success depends on the success of the users and on his or her personal interest in the project.

CHAPTER THREE

Justification and Budget

Sometimes the accounting people act as if they think the orga-nization exists so they can keep books on it.

—Karl Albrecht and Ron Zemke

OVERVIEW

CFOs are notorious for demanding cost justification—that's their job. CIOs are often put in the position of having to justify the data warehouse before the company spends any money on it. Cost justification should be welcomed; it provides a basis for budgeting, the justification of staff, and the governance that determines project prioritization. Cost justification also ties nicely into measuring the project's success.

- *Budgeting:* Without cost justification, projects will always be in jeopardy. During future budget cycles, management will be looking for ways to reduce cost, and if there is no documented reason for completing the project, management is likely to forget the flush of excitement that accompanied the project's initiation.
- *Staffing:* Without cost justification, staffing the project with the right people may be difficult. By having some real dollar numbers to back up a request, management is more likely to accept the request.

- *Prioritizing:* Without a cost/benefit analysis, project prioritization is difficult, and management has little basis on which to compare projects other than a gut feeling that one is more important than another. Without a cost/benefit analysis, the line-of-business manager with the most power is likely to get his or her project approved. The project that is most important to the enterprise may never be implemented.
- *Measuring success:* By documenting the estimated costs and anticipated benefits, the company has a solid measure of success when the costs are not exceeded and the anticipated benefits are realized and measured.

Those people put in a position to justify the data warehouse are faced with a difficult task. There are questions about ROI. Will the data warehouse deliver the ROI that is expected with other capital investments? If it can't be expected to deliver an acceptable ROI, upper management is often reluctant to initially fund and continue to fund the maintenance of the data warehouse project. Most project managers have difficulty determining what the projects will cost. They often compute costs only for the initial implementation, with nothing budgeted for ongoing support and maintenance.

Tangible benefits are difficult to estimate, and any estimates are perceived with a jaundiced and very skeptical eye. Intangible benefits are usually dismissed as so much fluff, even though some of the intangibles, such as the reputation of the organization, are extremely important to senior management.

Every industry has applications that can provide tactical and strategic information to the key decision makers, so there is never a reason to embark on a project without cost/benefit justification.

Severe restrictions are often imposed on those whose job it is to justify the data warehouse. There are times where the improved productivity of the analysts cannot be considered because, since there is a policy that no one will be dismissed, there can be no cost reduction considered in the cost-justification process. Some organizations are tasked with the justification of the infrastructure needed for the initial implementation without the ability to spread the justification across all the intended projects and applications.

No one likes a bill, and department heads will fight to assign costs to any department but their own. It's always difficult to fairly allocate costs when the data warehouse has been developed for more than one department.

The justification for historical data—remember that one of the reasons to create a data warehouse is to perform trend analysis—is always difficult. The value of historical data, as it ages, becomes very difficult to determine and the cost of keeping the data grows since codes change over time; the farther back you go, the more difficult it is to reconcile the changes.

In the remainder of this chapter, we discuss solutions for six situations that relate to budget and project justification.

USER PRODUCTIVITY JUSTIFICATION IS NOT ALLOWED

Organizations usually fund and support a data warehouse only if the project can be justified by increases in revenue or decreases in cost. At United Amalgamated Consolidators, Inc., management will not sign off on productivity improvement cost savings since the company has a "no layoff" policy, and any personnel will have to be retained even if they have no work to do. How can a project manager justify a data warehouse along with the tools and other costs associated with it?

Sid Adelman

It's important to understand which battles to fight. In this case, it does not seem like any productivity improvements will be allowed to support a cost/benefit justification. The project manager has to find other areas of benefit. Depending on the organization, better decisions for marketing, distribution, inventory control, quality control, supply chain opportunities, and more effective customer control should be able to provide the revenue increase and cost decrease benefits needed to justify the data warehouse. However, the process of actually identifying the benefits and validating those benefits is a major task.

Joyce Bischoff

I have never seen layoffs as a result of increased productivity. The emphasis should be on the business benefits of the warehouse. For marketers, how many more solicitations can be targeted to specific groups of prospective customers? How much sooner will data be available for analysis? For insurance companies, how will more accurate claims analysis benefit the company? For hospitals, how can they identify the most effective treatments for certain health problems? After that information is available, which doctors do not use the most effective treatments and why? What is it costing the company *not* to have the information available for analysis in a timely fashion?

Douglas Hackney

Simply put, the project manager doesn't justify the project. Given these parameters, the project manager cannot lead the business and must wait until the business comes to him or her with a life-threatening problem that only access to integrated data can solve. When the business reaches a point where it is experiencing pain that can be solved by information, then the company should build a data warehouse system. You don't build data warehouse systems because everybody else has one or to enhance your résumé; you build them to address specific business challenges.

Sean Ivoghli

Data warehouses are frequently used to support sales and marketing organizations. Effective use of a data warehouse can result in increased cross-selling, improved customer segmentation and market penetration, enhanced customer relationships, better customer retention, and other similar results that boost the bottom line significantly. The amount of the impact would depend on the industry's sensitivity to marketing activity and how effectively the staff members apply their knowledge (from the data warehouse) to related sales and marketing activities. Data warehouses are also used to manage costs by eliminating unprofitable products, providing more accurate forecasting, identifying operational bottlenecks, and managing other nonhuman resources.

Chuck Kelley

Regardless of whether you have a "no-layoff" policy or not, user productivity is important to every organization. If we applied this same policy to hardware, then maybe this organization should not have a computer. After all, everything could be done by hand, and the computer will only allow an increase in user productivity. Increased productivity will decrease costs. As companies grow, if everyone becomes more productive, then there will be no need to increase staff. That will, in turn, cut expenses.

Let's say that a company sells tools to the public. A customer enters the store and buys a tool. Some trend analysis done within the data warehouse indicates that when a person purchases a third tool from the store, the next item he or she purchases is generally a toolbox. If the person at the cash register gets a note saying that this is the second or third tool purchased by this person, maybe the salesclerk could mention a special on toolboxes if the customer buys one now. This would increase revenue. Will it do it directly? No. But indirectly, and over time, the data warehouse will either decrease costs or increase revenues.

David Marco

I argue for pointing out "soft" ROI savings in this situation. If a company increases employee productivity by 20 percent and reduces headcount by 20 percent, that is "hard" ROI savings. If the company increases employee productivity by 20 percent and does not reduce headcount, that is "soft" savings. Soft savings are very important since they dramatically reduce the strain and associated costs ("hard" savings) of hiring new employees. In addition, "soft" savings help employees spend time on those activities that often slip due to lack of time, such as customer service.

Larissa Moss

This case seems to be less about the justification for a data warehouse project than it is about the justification for keeping staff employed with something worthwhile to do. The easiest and most worthwhile reassignment of displaced personnel is to the cross-organizational tasks of information asset management. Most companies currently lack an information asset management group, and if one does exist, it is on the IT side (known as data administration or data resource management). Information asset management is a business function, and it should be staffed with business people. An information asset management group is responsible for setting and enforcing standards for the collection, condition, definition, content, and dissemination of enterprise data. Those responsibilities include the following:

- Defining the meaning of the data
- Determining the owners of the data
- Setting data standards for the organization
- Establishing the business rules for collecting and storing the data

- Monitoring the domain (valid values) of the data
- Ensuring consistent usage of the data
- Setting meta data standards
- Understanding and capturing data relationships
- Creating (modeling) the enterprise data architecture
- Maintaining the source-to-target data mappings
- Maintaining the content of the meta data repository
- Resolving data disputes across business units
- Monitoring data cleanliness
- Establishing enterprise-wide data quality guidelines
- Reporting and resolving data quality infractions
- Leading the enterprise information quality initiative
- Teaching and mentoring data entry personnel
- Assisting IT in reusing already existing data and processes

The analysis techniques used to perform these cross-organizational information asset management tasks are easy to learn. If a data administration or data resource management group already exists, the displaced personnel can be added to that group. This would enhance the group's efficiency and effectiveness by allowing those employees to cover more business areas and more IT projects at the same time. If the above list of tasks is not sufficient to keep them busy, they can get involved with the actual data correction activities on the business side as well as IT, depending on their technical skills.

Bottom line: If it can be demonstrated that there is plenty of new work for the displaced personnel, the "no-layoff" policy should not stand in the way of including productivity improvement cost savings in the cost/benefit analysis.

Clay Rehm

If I were the project manager, I would start by reminding my management of the benefits of such projects. These are the times to be looking at long-term, strategic benefits and not just short-term tactical solutions. I would ask if the project could be done over time to possibly save money.

The organizational change management (OCM) benefits of the data warehouse project greatly outweigh the costs. Why? Because existing personnel will need to be trained to use the tools of the data warehouse and will learn how to be better analysts. Instead of spending their time looking for, gathering, and cleaning the data, they will spend their time using and analyzing the data. They will be looking for and finding anomalies—looking for areas of growth for the company, for example.

The data warehouse does not need new technology expenditures to prove its benefit. People tend to forget that the data warehouse is not about new software and hardware; it is about a new way of doing business. We as consultants have built plenty of data warehouses on the client's existing software and hardware. That wasn't new, but we created new methodologies, standard operating procedures, best practices, job descriptions, OCM changes—the list can go on. We provided new ways to model data and build database structures for ease of use.

The moral of the story: Find ways to improve processes without spending money.

HOW CAN THE COMPANY IDENTIFY INFRASTRUCTURE BENEFITS?

Management created a committee to make recommendations for the infrastructure needed for the data warehouse. The committee members must justify any expenditures for data warehouse tools (ETL, access and analysis, and so on). All the benefits the members have been able to identify have been soft-dollar benefits. What should the company do?

Sid Adelman

The hard dollars will be associated with the business projects and not with the infrastructure. The committee should identify, document, and communicate the hard-dollar benefits that will derive from the data warehouse, such as improved analyst productivity, improved customer retention, greater revenue per customer, better target marketing, and a greater share of the customer's wallet.

Joyce Bischoff

If a tool was the answer, what was the question? Too many companies think that tools are the answer in a data warehouse. Instead, a company should start with a small project that can be handled without additional tools. Tools provide only one means to an end, and many companies already have in-house tools, such as query and reporting tools, that staff can use for small projects. The ETL process for a small project can be coded manually and converted after the warehouse demonstrates success. In my experience, shops make more informed decisions about tools after they have had the opportunity to build a warehouse without them.

Jill Dyché

This company should undertake a comprehensive business discovery exercise that answers the question, "What is the need, pain, or problem that we can solve with data?" An effective business discovery exercise can eke out a range of unforeseen opportunities that can result in high-impact findings about the payback—both hard and soft—of information to the business.

If at the conclusion of the business discovery exercise the consultants or staff cannot find any corporate initiatives where detailed data can result in value-added business actions—and I've never seen such a case, but in principle it's possible—then a data warehouse is just not a good investment. In fact, it's the proverbial hammer looking for a nail.

Douglas Hackney

If the business is not willing to make the investment in the data warehouse infrastructure necessary to support and sustain the system, then the IT team should wait until such time that the business is willing to do so.

Sean Ivoghli

While soft-dollar benefits are an important component of a data warehouse cost/benefit analysis, most infrastructure investments have at least some hard-dollar justification. These are most easily obtained by comparing the purchase of these tools to the cost of developing and maintaining them in-house. The committee should start by defining the required functionality for the system. The members should identify the tools that would be purchased and the cost of developing other tools from scratch, mapping to each system requirement. In addition, they should consider the cost of maintaining and enhancing the software developed in-house and the productivity gains during development of the data warehouse when using automated tools. The infrastructure dollars should be compared to the product of person-hours and the hourly rate.

Chuck Kelley

Tools aid in the development and use of a data warehouse. These expenditures will almost always be soft dollars. These tools are like cell phones; their use may aid in the ability to increase sales with better communications, but that is a soft-dollar benefit. When companies want proof of hard-dollar benefits, the project manager must spend time explaining that the cost savings in terms of soft dollars are real—just as real as calculators for accounting, pads of paper for marketing, and spreadsheets for senior management. If this does not work, then the project manager should either do what he or she can with the tools the company already has (and forget the meta data) or consider that maybe the organization is not ready for a data warehouse. The data warehouse will change the way the organization does business. If the organization does not want to change the way it operates, then most likely the data warehouse will not help.

David Marco

One of two situations is occurring here. Either the data warehousing project is too small to validate the costs (software, installation, training, and upkeep) of using a tool, or the committee doesn't know how to define hard benefits.

Does a Retailer Need a Data Warehouse?

The CIO for a large retailer believes the company needs a data warehouse. The CFO (who still wears a green eyeshade) has questioned the need for a data warehouse and has challenged the CIO to state why any money should be spent on such an extravagant endeavor. What should the CIO do?

Sid Adelman

It's not IT that needs the data warehouse, it's the business. The driving force should come from a line-of-business manager who desperately needs to understand the customers' buying patterns, what's in the market basket, the profitability of different products, the profitability of products from different suppliers, and much more. The CIO should meet with the line-of-business managers, enlighten them on the possibilities available with a data warehouse, and educate them on what the competition is doing. These managers will then fight the battles with the CFO for the necessary budget.

Joyce Bischoff

The CIO should obtain a business sponsor who will fund the project. The goal is to identify the business benefits of a data warehouse and obtain company commitment based on the benefits.

Douglas Hackney

The CIO should pick a small, focused point of business pain that is politically meaningful and measurable and build a specific solution to relieve that pain. The system will demonstrate the value of data warehousing and provide tangible and material results that the CFO can evaluate.

Chuck Kelley

I suggest the CIO should become a salesman. Studies show that data warehousing provides an ROI, which is what the CFO is looking for. The CIO needs to do some intelligence work to find out the hot spot where the financial folks are having the hardest time. If the intelligence work does not uncover any good subject areas, then the CIO needs to go to marketing to find out what would be a big winner for marketing. The project needs to be small in size and time of development, but it will provide a big win for the overall organization. I would not use the words "data warehouse" but would come up with a different name, especially since data warehousing has been pinned as a problem. (Some people say it has a 70 percent failure rate, although I do not see that at all!) Once the right project is found, the CIO should invest some of the discretionary spending in the development of the subject area. Then the CIO must "sell" this concept and the win to everyone, including the CFO. The CIO should talk to each member of the executive staff to show each one what a great success the project is.

David Marco

In my experience, retail is one of the industry segments that spends the most money on data warehousing technologies (the other segments are banking, financial, insurance, automobile, and more recently, government). I recommend that the CIO in this situation follow a multipronged strategy similar to the process we used at Enterprise Warehouse Solutions when we had a very similar situation with a banking client.

First, the CIO should present to the CFO an overview of data warehousing. This presentation should provide the high-level fundamentals of data warehousing (what it is and what it isn't). In addition, this presentation should illustrate what other companies in the industry segment are doing. After giving the presentation, the CIO should ask the CFO for funding for a feasibility phase for a data warehouse. This feasibility phase should include a company assessment, a good project scope document, and high-level projections of project costs that together present a cost justification for the data warehouse. If the CIO does a good job on the cost justification, then the CFO should be on board. Remember, a good CIO knows how to sell a project.

Larissa Moss

The danger in the initiation of data warehouse projects by the CIO/CTO or other IT manager or group is that it is perceived by the business management to be a trendy and expensive technology playground with no apparent business benefit. In some rare cases, that is actually true. However, in most cases IT is simply aware of the information problems and solutions sooner than the business side because they are exposed to the problems on a daily basis. The task for the CIO/CTO is to communicate to the CFO and to other business executives the information problems, the current methods for correcting them, and the proposed data warehouse solution. This communication must include an itemized list of business costs or losses of revenue that are directly related to the existing information problems and the current process of correcting them. In addition, the CIO/CTO must be able to show how the data warehouse costs will be offset by the expected ROI. If he or she is unable to make a convincing case for increasing profits or reducing costs, the CFO has a right to remain skeptical.

Clay Rehm

It is up to the CIO to identify the business problem, how the data warehouse will solve the problem, and the ROI associated with building the data warehouse. It is completely appropriate to leverage other experienced resources (either internal or external) to help in this endeavor.

This is a perfect example of an organization that needs a data warehouse readiness assessment. The assessment's findings will provide the reasons why the organization needs the data warehouse, but more importantly the findings will provide the actions the organization must take to prepare for the data warehouse. It should be obvious that if the CFO is not on board, other executives may not be on board either.

The CIO must do his or her homework first and be able to present to the executives as well as other levels of the organization the benefits of a data warehouse. Building a data warehouse is such a political challenge (even greater than the technical challenges) that trying to build a data warehouse without executive and management support is quite possibly a career-limiting move.

I am a big believer in documentation and lots of it. The consultant hired to perform the readiness assessment must provide the documentation the CIO needs to present to any level of the company. The CIO must specify this documentation in the contract with the consultant. The documentation must provide examples of how other retailers benefited from the data warehouse. Benefits cannot simply be stated in terms of dollars saved or not spent; the documentation should also consider how the data warehouse identified possible customers and how those new customers contributed to the organization's bottom line.

What can the CIO tell the CFO about the competitive implications of the data warehouse? It is not a question of whether the company should have a data warehouse; the competitors all have one, so this company needs a data warehouse just to compete. In fact, the company cannot afford to not have one.

The CIO must use resources who have created data warehouses before to provide the relevant experiences, expertise, and information to the people to whom the CIO reports.

How Can Costs Be Allocated Fairly?

The sponsor of the first data warehouse project absorbed the entire cost of the data warehouse infrastructure. Now additional divisions in the company will be using the data warehouse—but these divisions do not want to pay for any part of the infrastructure. How should the costs be allocated and what should the sponsor do?

Sid Adelman

No one wants to pay more than they have to, but the initial sponsor is entitled to recoup some costs and allocate part of these costs to the other divisions. If the other divisions want to use the infrastructure, they will have to pay for it. A fair distribution of the cost (although no one will be happy with the allocation) could incorporate costs based on the volume of data, the number of users, and the activity of the users from each department.

Joyce Bischoff

It is important to build a data warehouse on a solid infrastructure foundation. Many shops have found it best to create a separate budget item for infrastructure costs and to allocate them across the company. This approach works best when there is support from top management.

Douglas Hackney

This political question should be addressed by the data warehouse steering committee. The technology team should avoid political issues and questions such as these at all costs. Questions about cost allocation, resource allocation, what to build, and what to build next are the exclusive domain of the data warehouse steering committee.

Sean Ivoghli

Many of my clients have struggled with this same dilemma. My experience has been that it is very difficult to take a direct approach to collect these costs. The following two approaches have worked for many of my clients.

1. Usually the existing data warehouse has many assets that interest other would-be users. As we all know, a data warehouse is a journey, not a destination. You don't just build one and move on. Data warehouses have ongoing development and maintenance costs. So one way for the first sponsor to recoup costs is to spread the ongoing costs across the new users.

2. Another way is to create data marts on top of the data warehouse for each user, which are really subsets of the data warehouse but segmented for security and customization purposes. The data marts can just be logical constructs of the semantic layer of the business intelligence (BI) tool, with some customization of the end-user reports. The

new users could be charged for the data marts in a way that recovers infrastructure costs.

Chuck Kelley

Charge-back is an essential part of any data warehouse project. Whether there is a formal charge-back mechanism in which the exchange of money occurs or an informal charge-back mechanism in which each group understands the costs incurred by using the data warehouse, there should be some sort of charge-back mechanism. We know that budgets will be cut from time to time, and it is important to know who is using the data warehouse and how much. It is also important that users understand what costs are associated with the data warehouse project to see if there is a benefit to its continued operation.

There are many charge-back mechanisms. Here are a few of the most popular.

- *Usage share:* Everyone pays for the usage percentage. If marketing uses the data warehouse 40 percent of the time, they are charged for 40 percent of the costs.
- *CPU and disk utilization:* Most operating systems today use this basic timeshare model (tracking CPU cycles used and inputs/outputs performed).
- *Flat fee plus a fee for each request submitted:* An amount that covers each of the requests made to the data warehouse adds to a flat fee associated with the infrastructure.

No matter which charge-back mechanism a company chooses, it is important that it fits the organization.

David Marco

The sponsor should go to executive management and either have the project budget increased to offset the costs of the infrastructure or have management convince (or require) the divisions to pay their fair shares.

Larissa Moss

In the past, each user paid for all the development costs of his or her own system. But a data warehouse is not a system, nor does it have only one user. Therefore, the charge-back mechanism of the past does not apply. Payment for data and for most infrastructure components must be separated from payment for the individual customized applications. An analogy may be that payment for interstate highways and tollbooths must be separated from payment for individual cars. Many cars use the same highways and tollbooths, just like many user applications use the same data and infrastructure components. We pay for the highways and tollbooths from taxes, that is, a collective fund, and for our cars from our own pockets, that is, personal accounts. Similarly, data and infrastructure components should be paid from a collective fund such as a corporate cost center or be allocated evenly across all business units like taxes; individual applications should be paid from personal accounts, that is, the cost centers of business units.

Many first-time data warehouse sponsors fail to address this issue until disagreements among business units break out. In other cases, there would have been no data warehouse project if the sponsor had not absorbed all costs. Either way, failure to institute a fair charge-back mechanism is a sign of lacking commitment from senior executives for a strategic enterprise data warehouse initiative. If the first project is a prototype to prove the feasibility and benefit of a data warehouse, the sponsor should negotiate a reimbursement plan for data and infrastructure expenditures with the chief officers of the organization. If the first project was conceived and developed for the sole benefit of the sponsor, and if the sponsor is not able to get buy-in from other line-of-business managers in terms of sharing the costs, the sponsor has two choices.

1. Claim the data warehouse as his or her own system and not share it.
2. Be philanthropic and eat the costs.

Clay Rehm

This is a difficult situation. The sponsor can remedy it by adopting one of the following options:

- Do not provide data warehouse access to the other departments until they pay up.
- The other departments may not want to pay because they do not know what the "infrastructure" is. This could be a matter of education. Teach them!
- Limit the entry of data from these other departments into the data warehouse.
- Shame the other departments into paying their share.

The next time the sponsor supports building a data warehouse, possibly at a different organization, he or she should involve other departments right away. By creating a development team user group across the organization and identifying tools that can be purchased once (such as ETL, BI, data cleansing, and so on), the cost can be allocated across the whole organization. The vendor may offer a volume discount.

The moral of the story: Plan ahead!

HISTORICAL DATA MUST BE JUSTIFIED

Users are asking for ten years of historical data. Not only will this require much more hardware, but the data warehouse team now has to reconcile all code changes for the last ten years. How can the data warehouse team justify all this historical data?

Sid Adelman

Make the users pay for those ten years. It's interesting that when the users who have asked for ten years of data see the potential bill, many of those users decide that two or three years of data are acceptable. The big cost may be not the extra disk and machine to support the ten years of data but the programming effort to reconcile the way data has been coded over the years.

Joyce Bischoff

Users always ask for more data than they actually need. Even the federal government does not require that much data. Tools on the market can analyze the actual usage of data on a table or column basis. Starting with a reasonable amount of data (one or two years), the project manager should use a tool to analyze actual data usage and determine the need for older data. Having this information at hand may help determine how often older data will actually be used.

Douglas Hackney

If having access to ten years of data is a valid business need, then it is inherently justified. We built a data warehouse system that had 28 years of transaction detail. While this was an onerous requirement from a technology perspective, it was a prerequisite of value from the business perspective.

Sean Ivoghli

Sometimes it is impossible to recover all the code changes going that far back. The more aggregated the historical data requirements are, the better off the company is. The data warehouse team members should determine the highest level of aggregation acceptable to meet business requirements. They should then look for other old reporting databases used to satisfy reporting needs over the years. With some luck, the team can find a lowest common aggregation layer that is acceptable to the users. Then the team should ensure that all the dimensions are consistent or can be categorized into consistent dimensions for the historical data that also make sense for current data. I would go after old reporting databases first because many of the buried operational data issues had been resolved there for reporting. The cost of cleansing, integrating, and storing high volumes of historical data will be easier to justify if the team brings them in at aggregated levels and from sources that have done at least some processing to prepare the data for reporting and analysis.

Chuck Kelley

If there is a requirement for ten years of history, then that is the justification. The users will need to be told about the cost associated for creating a data warehouse with ten years of historical data, and the users will need to approve the funding. As for the code changes, somewhere the changes have been documented (either in the code or in what the users work with now). This could be in some configuration management or change management system or in the actual code that produces the reports for users to look at today. If there was no data warehouse and users were allowed to continue to do their jobs the way they currently do, there would not be much reconciliation needed because of the source system changes.

If there are currently no systems that perform the functions that the data warehouse will perform (and this would be hard for me to believe), then time is needed to identify what needs to be done and then to build the ETL process to do it.

David Marco

It is important to understand that some companies actually need to keep all their data, regardless of its age. This is a common requirement for insurance companies. For example, if an insurance company writes a policy to insure a nuclear waste site, it may be 20–30 years before anyone discovers that Blinky the three-eyed fish is now living in the pond next door. Once Blinky is found, you can bet that the lawyers will be running to speak to the nearby residents.

The data warehouse team must determine how much historical data needs to be kept and the frequency that the users will be accessing that data. In general, I see the following access patterns for many companies:

- 75 percent of the queries access data that is no older than one year.
- 22 percent of the queries access data between one and two years old.
- 3 percent of the queries access data older than two years.

The decision about whether to keep data on DASD (rotating magnetic disk storage) or a lower-cost storage option should be based on the frequency that the data is needed and the required access time. With these access patterns in mind, I typically have my clients keep data that is older than two years in a lower-cost storage option, like near-line storage or tape. Rarely do the users mind waiting 24 hours for the data stored in these medias. If the users do complain about the response time, I make them cost justify keeping all the historical data in DASD. If it can be cost justified, then I'm willing to store all the historical data that way.

Larissa Moss

I suspect there is no charge-back or cost-justification process in place at this organization. The project manager should request the users to prepare a justification for their request for ten years of historical data. The users should itemize and estimate the dollar value for every benefit of having each additional year of historical data. At the same time the project manager or team should itemize and estimate the dollar value for the cost of adding and maintaining each additional year of historical data. In other words, there should be a comparison between benefits (in dollars) and costs for adding one year of history, two years of history, three years of history, and so on through ten years of history. This cost/benefit analysis should be presented to the sponsor who is funding the data warehouse project.

In addition, the project team should prepare the time estimates and project schedules for delivering each additional year of history. If the business value for storing ten years of historical data can be demonstrated, the additional time to deliver and maintain the data warehouse and the additional cost for more hardware and human resources should not be an issue. In many cases the cost/benefit analysis will show a diminishing rate of return after much less than ten years of historical data. As a compromise, a separately funded project could be launched to store ten or more years of historical data in a highly summarized fashion in a separate database with its own application.

Clay Rehm

First of all, it is up to the person or people who are requesting the historical data to justify the cost of getting it, cleaning it, integrating it, and reconciling it. This nontrivial task will involve the time and effort of many people.

If the requestors cannot convince the management (or the people who control the purse strings) to add this data, then apparently it is not worth adding. Historical data is very useful if it is accurate. If the data is not accurate, the data warehouse team will need to spend time fixing it, which may not be worth the time and expense of getting the data into the data warehouse in the first place.

Actually, I am surprised this contingency was never considered when building the first release of the data warehouse. Project managers should design data migration plans in the beginning phases of a data warehouse project.

Historical data can be justified because certain analyses (such as trend analysis) cannot be performed without it. The data warehouse has limited functionality without historical data.

Bottom line: Plan for the need to include historical data in the first release of the data warehouse.

No Money Exists for a Prototype

Nothing that IT suggests is taken on faith. Unless the people in charge of user management can see and experience a system, they are unwilling to believe it to be possible. All new systems are paid for by the business. The business is unwilling to fund the data warehouse without seeing it. However, the business is unwilling to pay for a prototype, and without a prototype, the business will not support any data warehouse activity. The CIO strongly believes that a data warehouse is needed for the business. What should the CIO do?

Sid Adelman

The desire for a data warehouse should ideally come from the business and not from IT. One of the most frequent justifications—perhaps not a justification at all—is that the competition is doing it. The CIO should be able to find one or more competitors that have implemented a data warehouse. Providing this information to user management should eliminate the need for the CIO to be the driving force.

Joyce Bischoff

The CIO should pay for a prototype but should do so only if an area of the business provides requirements. Without business support, there is no reason to build a warehouse, and the prototype will probably fail because it is not responding to a real business need.

Jill Dyché

First, let me say that whenever I see a CIO push any sort of technology, I get nervous. The CIO "strongly believes" that the business needs a data warehouse? What about the business users? After all, they're the CIO's customers; if they're not screaming for information, then what's the CIO's agenda anyway?

Moreover, it sounds as if the business users might be a bit cynical about IT's ability to deliver. The fact that they haven't "seen" a data warehouse in action and thus don't believe it can work sounds like a convenient excuse. After all, there are scores of software vendors who would *love* to come in and do a customized demo to illustrate the potential of data warehousing.

However, a proof-of-concept (POC) is more comprehensive than a demo and costs money. This is a danger sign any way you look at it: end-users don't see enough potential value in a data warehouse in order to fund it, and they're disaffected with IT's ability to demonstrate this value. Ironically, if the business users were to go out of house, an outsourcer wouldn't do a POC for free.

If IT has made mistakes in the past that have encouraged end-user cynicism, IT should consider absorbing the labor cost for an initial three-month POC activity. IT should convince a vendor partner to provide a loaner platform for the three-month activity to minimize its costs.

Before agreeing to this, the CIO and his or her staff should work with the business to codevelop a series of success metrics with the end-users. The business should clearly illustrate its expectations for the POC and define the criteria that must be met in order for it to be deemed worthwhile.

There should then be a clear agreement that outlines what happens if the POC is a slam-dunk. This holds both IT and the business users accountable for acting on the success of the POC and prevents renegotiation once the POC delivers on its promise.

Douglas Hackney

The CIO will need to demonstrate that a data warehouse is a best practice for the industry. Only by exposure to competitors' systems or to industry forums in which data warehousing is held up as a best practice will he or she gain the support of the business for a prototype.

Sean Ivoghli

The data warehouse is for the benefit of the business, not for the CIO. The CIO shouldn't do anything until he or she has sold the business on the values of a data warehouse. If the CIO could arrange to have the business executives visit with another company that has a successful data warehouse implementation, it might help the business see the value.

Chuck Kelley

The CIO needs to accept the fact that the organization may not be quite ready for a data warehouse. The CIO needs to find out what the problem areas are for each of the business groups. The CIO should then work to find someone in the organization who will support the development of a small prototype to show a proof-of-concept of the data warehouse. If the CIO cannot find anyone, then there are only two options left.

1. Find some discretionary money and develop a small prototype.
2. Accept the realization that the organization is not ready for a data warehouse and continue to work with the business groups, showing them how other organizations have used a data warehouse successfully.

David Marco

It is best when the business is driving the data warehousing project. Since this is lacking, the CIO should pitch to the business that IT will fund the prototype. All the business would have to do is work with IT on requirements and evaluate the prototype. If the business likes the prototype and wants to proceed with the project, the business should reimburse IT for the prototyping initiative. If the business decides not to move forward, then IT will absorb the costs. The CIO must make sure to keep the scope *very* limited and to set the business's expectations that the initial effort will be a prototype and not the final version of the system.

Larissa Moss

The CIO must be careful not to fall into the trap of "Build it and they will come." Data warehouses as IT initiatives have not worked for any company in the long run. Surely IT can build an application or a prototype to demonstrate data warehouse capabilities, but IT cannot develop a long-term, enterprise-wide decision support solution without the strong sponsorship of the business community. Having said that, the CIO can transfer his or her strong beliefs into a business case assessment. He or she can point out to the business community the loss of income or excessive costs incurred by the organization because of bad business decisions made in the past or because of an inability to make those decisions at all. Once the business users understand and agree with the root causes behind the existing decision support impairments, they will hopefully be more open to funding a prototype that can prove to them that their decision-making situation can be improved.

If that approach does not work for the CIO, the only other alternative would be to internally fund a very small prototype for demonstration purposes, which will have to be coupled with a business case assessment to justify further development costs of the data warehouse. Bottom line, if the members of the business community do not feel any pain, they will continue to be reluctant to fund something they don't believe they need. The CIO must turn that perception around by exposing the pain and showing them where (on the financial balance sheet) it hurts, followed up with a demonstration of how the data warehouse can solve that pain.

Clay Rehm

It sounds like the CIO has bigger problems than trying to convince the business that it needs a data warehouse. If the business users are unwilling to fund anything until they see it, I question the value of the data warehouse and the role the CIO is playing for this company. I also wonder why user management has not ousted the CIO.

Anyway, a way to win over the business without spending money is to present a prototype. Rather than doing it alone, the CIO should contact the top BI vendors to come in and demo their product in a "bake-off" contest, with the prerequisite that they must use the business's data. This can be a win/win situation—the business users can see how their data is used in a BI situation, and the winning vendor can land a contract with the client. The CIO doesn't spend any money and can show value to the business.

Additionally, the CIO and the complete IT staff must be customer focused. They must stop being so technology focused and show the business that they care and that they can provide solutions that the business needs.

In summary: IT must be in alignment with the business.

CHAPTER FOUR

Organization and Staffing

*If you're riding ahead of the herd, take a look every now and
then to make sure it's still there.*

—Will Rogers

OVERVIEW

Executive Sponsor

The executive sponsor is the person who needs the data
warehouse, usually the line-of-business manager who
recognizes the value of the decision support capability
of the data warehouse. The executive sponsor is the
primary driver of new requirements and should be
aware of how these requirements affect the schedule,
the budget, and existing accepted requirements. This
person provides budget and political support for the
project. The executive sponsor assures the availability
of business people who can articulate the requirements
and provide support throughout the life of the project.
The executive sponsor should also be the champion for
the data warehouse project and should promote it
whenever given the chance.

A politically strong, well-positioned sponsor with
an abiding interest in the success of the data warehouse
project is always a critical success factor. However, the
sponsorship and ownership of a data mart raise the

question of which department should ultimately hold responsibility for the project: IT or the line of business?

Help Desk Staff

Users will have problems. Therefore, user support is critical and must be planned for early in the project. If users are treated with sensitivity, they will be far more likely to ask for support and call the help desk. Users' interest in and use of the data warehouse should grow as they have successful experiences with it.

The help desk staff is at the heart of ongoing user support. Existing help desk staff may not be up to the task, and users frustrated with support may back away from using the system. User support is the first line of defense when the user has problems. Support people must be customer- or client-oriented and know that calls from users are not annoyances but the support staff's reason for being. Members of the help desk team must be knowledgeable about the tools, must understand the database structure, must know the data, and must be familiar with frequently run queries and reports. They must know the users' concerns and problems. They must have profiles of the users, knowing the power users and the more casual ones. The help desk staff must be patient and responsive. If time elapses between the report of a problem and its resolution, the staff must inform the users about solution attempts and progress. As for operational systems, an incident-tracking system should be in place.

User support staff should create and maintain a list of frequently asked questions (FAQs) and their solutions, possibly making the list accessible to users through the Intranet. Staff members should make extensive use of meta data to help train the users, inform the users about the characteristics of the system, and answer user questions. A large percentage of questions that come to help desks involve problems related to the timeliness of the data, the source of the data, or the users not understanding the meaning of the data. Most of these questions can be answered with meta data.

Some of the problems seen by user support relate to the update/load process, such as whether it completed on time and whether it ran successfully. These processes must be monitored, and any variance in availability or timeliness of the data should be communicated to the users. Other problems relate to performance. User support staff must have a feel for performance, monitor performance, report performance degradation to database administration, spot poor query techniques that could cause bad performance, and help the users write more efficient queries and reports.

Implementation Team Members

The biggest challenge to a project manager is recruiting and retaining the team that will implement the data warehouse. Good people are usually already working on other projects, and getting them transferred to the data warehouse project is very difficult. Hiring new people, even if they are skilled, requires extra time since the new folks need to learn where things are, who to talk with, and where the bodies are buried. Bringing in outside consultants and contractors has the same problems, along with issues of loyalty and the desire of some consultants and contractors to become wedded to the project and to the organization.

Entrenched empires often make it difficult for a project manager to control the resources necessary to make the project a success. Managers of database administrators (DBAs) often resist any attempt to have their DBAs report to anyone but their own department. The organizational structure that is appropriate for operational systems often does not work for a data warehouse organizational structure. The relationships within an organization and the reputation of people in key positions are part of the "soft" reasons a project succeeds or fails. Organizations are ready or not ready for the data warehouse depending on the available personnel skills, management commitment, and people interested in seeing the data warehouse succeed.

The debate continues to rage about how a data warehouse team should be organized, to whom it should report, and what roles and responsibilities the team members should assume. There is also uncertainty about to whom team members themselves, such as the DBA, should report. Very often, power and politics drive the decisions, and often these decisions are inappropriate and do not lead to an efficiently working team.

In the remainder of this chapter, we discuss eight situations related to organization and staffing and provide solutions for each.

To Whom Should the Data Warehouse Team Report?

A data warehouse manager has responsibility for the three data warehouse projects under development and the two already rolled out to the users. She is fighting to keep her department as a separate entity that reports to the CIO. However, a powerful application development manager thinks that the data warehouse team should report to him, and he is lobbying hard to make this happen. To whom should the data warehouse manager report and what recommendations would help her deal with this situation?

Sid Adelman

The standard answer is that the data warehouse manager should report to someone as high in the organization as possible. By reporting to the CIO, the data warehouse manager will be in a much better position to get the resources she needs, including DBAs, data administrators, network people, systems people, and security administrators. Note that this set of roles does not report to the application development manager.

However, the data warehouse manager should take care to not alienate the application development manager. Such an alienation could result in his trying to sabotage her projects. She will need his people involved in a number of ways.

Her involvement with the user community is critical to the success of all her projects. Pointing out the necessity for this involvement may be the best way to convince everyone that by putting the data warehouse team under the supervision of the application development manager, the data warehouse team would become more of an IT function and less responsive to the business.

Joyce Bischoff

The emphasis in a data warehouse project must be on the data and its flexibility for the future. From the perspective of application developers, the front end is given more attention than the data that provides the foundation for the warehouse. The warehouse group should have a strong data perspective and not report to an application development manager.

Jill Dyché

The answer to this question depends on several factors. One is how the company structures its other development efforts. Do end-user applications fall under the same development organization as back-office applications do? What about enterprise systems versus departmental systems? And strategic systems versus tactical ones? And why is the application development manager reporting to the CIO at all? He should report within the lines of business.

The real question here, though, is how the CIO views the data warehouse. If he or she views it as simply availing a handful of query applications, then perhaps having the data warehouse team report to the application development manager is okay. In such a case, the data warehouse manager should understand the quid pro quo—what the application development manager will do to improve the data warehouse's reputation and funding—before she agrees to the move.

However, if the CIO takes the "I" in the title seriously and understands that the data warehouse is a strategic business solution, he or she will make sure application development activities and the data warehouse group remain within separate groups that collaborate. The separation, as symbolic as it is organizational, signifies that the data warehouse is more than just a file server—it's an environment that will continue to warrant specific skill sets, technologies, and, most importantly, strategic value. If the data warehouse manager wants to continue reporting directly to the CIO, she should drive these points home. But the CIO's decision will be indicative of the long-tem support the data warehouse receives.

Douglas Hackney

The data warehouse team should report to the entity that is most neutral in the business management hierarchy. A data warehouse team that reports to the CIO will be skewed by the priorities of the technology organization and will build systems that are easy for IT to build and/or maintain. A data warehouse team that reports to the CFO will be skewed by the priorities of the finance group and will build systems and solutions oriented toward finance. An ideal reporting structure is one in which the data warehouse team reports to a COO, an executive vice president, or directly to the CEO management group.

Chuck Kelley

Assuming that the application development group focuses on the development of operational/transaction systems, the data warehouse team should be a separate group. The development life cycle, data models, database design, and other functions of the application development group and the data warehouse group follow different processes, and when the two groups are "fused" together, then one always loses the control needed to do the right thing for its applications. However, both groups need to work closely together because the data warehouse team needs to know about:

- When the operational/transaction systems change and what effects those changes will have on the data warehouse
- How data is passed from the operational/transaction system to the data warehouse, including any new requirements that might keep the data warehouse from getting the data (new backup/recovery schedules, new batch processing requirements, and so on)
- How changes in the data structures and data within the data structures will affect the data warehouse

David Marco

Data warehousing should reside at the enterprise level of an organization. An application development manager would not meet the criteria of enterprise level. If I were the data warehouse manager I would argue that if the application development manager owned the data warehouse, he would try to make the data warehouse exclusively target his application's requirements. This would make the data warehouse an independent data mart.

Larissa Moss

In my opinion the management and administration of any cross-organizational business initiative, like a data warehouse or customer relationship management, does not belong under the IT arm of the organization. It belongs on the business side. Data warehouse administration belongs under the CKO, who reports to the CEO. Development activities can be matrixed into that group or can be staffed by that group directly. If the organization does not manage its cross-organizational business initiatives on the business side, data warehouse administration must remain directly under the CIO. Under no circumstances should the data warehouse be treated like a system and moved under the authority of an application development manager.

A side note: Organizations at Capability Maturity Model (CMM) level 3, 4, or 5 recognize cross-organizational business initiatives as strategic enterprise architecture initiatives, while organizations at CMM level 1 or 2 typically do not. Depending on what CMM level this organization has attained, it may take a number of years for the data warehouse administration to be properly placed in the organization.

Clay Rehm

The data warehouse team should report to the person who best represents the business and keeps business interests at heart. Additionally, the best data warehouse development and support team is a hybrid team made up of business and IT resources.

The data warehouse manager must first identify whether the CIO is the best champion of the data warehouse. Why is this power play happening? Is the CIO not connecting with the business? The data warehouse manager should poke around to find out the true politics of this situation. Does the powerful application development manager know something the data warehouse manager doesn't know? She'd better find out now. If the data warehouse manager feels the CIO is the best choice, she then must approach the powerful application development manager to discuss his intentions. This requires an honest, tactful, and diplomatic discussion that does not put him on the defense.

The data warehouse manager should be ready to defend her position to others. She should explain her intentions and actions to the CIO. The data warehouse manager should be prepared to get powerful and influential users on her side in case she needs them.

The moral of the story: In life, you need to stand up for the things you believe in.

THE ORGANIZATION USES MATRIX MANAGEMENT

A company has created multiple core competency groups and loans out these skills as needed. One such group is the database administration group. The project manager is not allowed to hire a DBA for the project; instead, she must rely on the goodwill of the DBA manager to provide a skilled DBA when needed. This has not worked in the past since multiple DBAs were assigned during the course of development and the project lost continuity. In addition, the DBAs were not always available when they were needed. The project manager is about to begin another project. What should she do about this matrix organization?

Sid Adelman

The project manager needs to sell the idea of a core team, the bare minimum of skilled people she needs to report directly to her. Given the existing organizational structure, she needs to make a strong case to management to make this happen. The case should include her previous experience of not being able to get the DBAs when she needed them. She should point out the problems of the lack of continuity when different people were assigned and the resulting loss of productivity, extended learning curve, extensions in the schedules, and increased costs. The case should also include the best practices of organizations that have successfully implemented data warehouse projects. These best practices include creating teams that have DBAs, data administrators, ETL jockeys, business analysts, and query tool administrators who directly report to the project manager.

Joyce Bischoff

A skilled DBA must be assigned to the project on a full-time basis. It has been proven that the lack of available DBA time has hampered the progress of other projects within the organization, and this should not be allowed to happen again.

Douglas Hackney

An OLTP-experienced DBA is a poor choice for a DBA resource for a data warehousing project. Data warehousing has a completely different set of requirements in the DBA arena than operational systems. Data warehousing requires replication of data, the denormalization of data, and the adoption of many practices that are anathema to OLTP DBAs. The project manager should make the case that she requires a unique set of database management skills that exist only in DBAs who have data warehouse experience, and thus she needs her own dedicated, unique resource.

Sean Ivoghli

This situation points out the problem with matrix management. If the project manager can hire a qualified DBA into a programmer position on the team and convince the database administration group to give her "programmer" adequate DBMS permissions to create and modify objects on a test database with enough space, many of her problems will be solved. The project manager can use her own "programmer" to support development and use the shared DBA for moving things to production, performance tuning, and so on. If that doesn't work, the project manager should try to convince the sponsor to buy or lease a smaller server with enough DBMS licenses to support the project's development. Then the team can use that server for development and unit testing. The shared DBA would be available for system tests, migration to production, performance tuning, and so on. If the project manager can't accomplish that, she should become the assigned DBA's new best friend!

Chuck Kelley

I have not been a fan of matrix management because we all know that the best job gets done based on who oversees the workers. Since in this case the DBAs work for the DBA manager and not the project, their allegiance is to the DBA manager and not to the data warehouse. The project manager needs to get a service-level agreement with the DBA manager that says that the DBA group will provide one or two named people to supply the services. If no agreement can be made, then the project manager needs to raise the issue to management. She should explain why these DBA loans are not working and that either (1) the data warehouse project needs its own DBA or (2) it needs a fixed DBA team. If the management does not agree and forces the project manager to follow the core competency route, then she should document the problems that arise out of this situation and how they affect the performance of the team. Maybe she will be lucky and get a DBA eventually!

Larissa Moss

The project manager should insist on having a senior DBA assigned to the data warehouse project full time for the duration of the project. Her justification should be that the DBA is the chief designer of the data warehouse database and that he or she must also assist the ETL and access and analysis lead developers in designing their respective applications. The DBA is therefore on the critical path, which means that the project schedule will be affected if he or she is not available when needed.

Database design is crucial to data warehousing and should not be performed on a part-time basis. It also should not be performed by programmers, unless those programmers were DBAs on their previous jobs. If management still doesn't accept this justification to free up one full-time trained and skilled DBA for the project, the project manager should adjust her project plan to reflect anticipated delays, similar to those that have been caused by unavailable DBAs in the past. These types of delays will undoubtedly cause slack time for the remaining team members as they wait for the DBA's participation. The reason for this slack time should be explained to the sponsor. Hopefully the sponsor will support the project manager's position.

A side note: In my experience, DBAs are too often underused in their capacity as expert database designers and are too often treated like "glorified clerks" subservient to the programmers. In a number of organizations DBAs are expected to execute data definition language, which is often poorly "designed" (created) by programmers, and to maintain those poorly designed databases without the authority (and allocated time) to redesign them. This is not only frustrating to the DBAs but also costly to the organizations.

Clay Rehm

Partially dedicated resource allocations rarely work very well. Not only are people you need not available when you need them, you have to retrain them each time you need them. This hurts the project, it hurts the users' perceptions of the support of the project, and it hurts the overall development time line.

The project manager must be realistic and account for the DBA's unavailability in her project plan. The project plan time line will lengthen due to this unavailability. When upper management questions the project manager (they will), she must be able to provide the facts.

This environment is called a data warehouse. It is not called an ETL warehouse or a BI warehouse. And it is not called a data warehouse for nothing. To have proper support and coverage, the data warehouse support team must have at least one dedicated DBA. The support team *must* have dedicated resources that are experts of the data. Period.

The project manager must realize and believe that the matrix management organization will not work, and then she must go on a crusade to defend that position. If the data warehouse is really as important as the users think it is, the project manager must give the users a chance to join the "cause" to recruit full-time data expertise.

In summary: A data warehouse must have dedicated data experts on the team.

THE PROJECT HAS NO CONSISTENT BUSINESS SPONSOR

The organization has a policy of constantly rotating managers. The business sponsor who started with the project has been reassigned and now has no interest in the project. The new business sponsor is not familiar with the data warehouse or the project. She also has different views about what is important. This will probably lead to changes in the scope of the project. The project manager feels concerned about this change in sponsors. What should he do?

Sid Adelman

It may already be too late, but the project manager should have identified, as one of the critical success factors, the need for the same sponsor for the duration of the project. The project manager should have asked for a dispensation of the policy of rotating managers.

Given a new sponsor, it's critical to connect with her and gain her acceptance of the scope agreement. If the new sponsor does not accept the scope agreement as signed by the previous sponsor, it's appropriate to develop a new agreement with a different schedule for delivery.

Joyce Bischoff

The project manager should work with the new business sponsor and change the scope as needed. If this means that funding must be increased, the new sponsor must understand the need and respond.

Douglas Hackney

Rather than taking direction from a specific individual, the team should build the data warehouse project to satisfy a set of requirements set by a data warehouse project steering committee. The committee works with the team to define a detailed scope statement that delineates exactly what will be built, for whom it will be built, what data will be used, and, to the extent possible, what technology, time line, and so on will be involved in the project. By providing a committee with whom the team can communicate, the project will have much more continuity than if the team were relating to a specific individual in this high turnover environment.

Chuck Kelley

The first job of the project manager is to sell, sell, sell. There is a constant need to explain the data warehouse and how it adds value to the organization. The project manager can sit down with the new business sponsor and show how the data warehouse adds value and how the project is proceeding according to plan. Having a strong business case in place helps strengthen the project.

Now, the real question is, "Who is the data warehouse champion from the business groups?" This person should not be someone who will be rotated throughout the business. It should be a senior executive who has some pull in the organization. If there is no such data warehouse champion, then the project manager needs to find one. If none is available, then maybe this organization is not quite ready for the value that a data warehouse can add.

David Marco

The project manager needs to work with the new business sponsor to capture her requirements for the data warehousing. These requirements need to be balanced with the previously captured requirements. While capturing these requirements the project manager must address the situation of the rotating business sponsors with the existing business sponsor.

Larissa Moss

This is a classic problem when business executives do not treat data warehousing as a cross-organizational business initiative. It appears that the data warehouse in this organization is treated as "just another system," or put another way, as a "pet project" of one sponsor or another. Not only will this approach lead to changes in the scope of the project, but over the long run it will most likely also lead to stovepipe data marts—one for each sponsor.

The project manager has two choices: He can either change direction and instruct his team to march to the beat of a new drummer, or he can try to recruit a different sponsor.

1. If the project manager decides not to challenge the new scope and direction set by the new sponsor for the project, he should at least try to convince the new sponsor to become the permanent champion for the data warehouse initiative. Together they should try to convince executive management to let the new sponsor remain in that position until the end of the project so there will be continuity from this point forward.

2. Recruiting a different sponsor is politically more risky and could possibly result in political suicide for the project manager. Whether or not he should take this risk depends on:
   - How much the new scope of the project deviates from the original scope
   - What the business justification was for the original scope as opposed to the new scope
   - How powerful (or not) the new sponsor is in the organization
   - How many allies the project manager has (if any)

Assuming that a business case assessment was performed before the data warehouse project began, the project manager can use the original business justification to persuade or pressure the new sponsor not to change the scope and direction of the project. However, if the new sponsor does not care about the justification for the old scope and appears not to have a compelling justification for the new scope, the project manager could step out on a limb, find a more suitable sponsor, and take his case to executive management.

I do not recommend that the project manager become the sole martyr for a data warehouse cause. However, this course of action may be warranted given the right set of circumstances, as outlined below.

- The new sponsor's decision to change the scope and direction of the data warehouse project appears to be frivolous and self-serving without solid business justification, *and*
- Executive management has a reputation for being reasonable and will likely accept the project manager's justification and request for a different sponsor, *and*

- Other influential users (including the more suitable sponsor) strongly believe that the current scope and direction of the data warehouse should not be changed, *and*
- Those other users are willing to support the project manager and agree to present the business case to the executives of the organization as a team.

Hopefully the decision of the executives would be to accept the project manager's request that the more suitable sponsor be assigned to the data warehouse project. If the executives take any other position or action, the project manager is obviously out of a job.

Clay Rehm

The project manager should have sufficient documentation in place to be prepared for any new user or sponsor. There is never too much documentation!

The project manager should be proactive and initiate a meeting with the new sponsor before she calls one with him. He should build a rapport and become the sponsor's friend. He will not accomplish this during the first meeting, but it will happen gradually over time. That is why project managers enter the data warehousing field—to accept a challenge and to make the business people happy.

The project manager should be prepared to spend additional time with the new sponsor and document the goals of the data warehouse. He should start a formal change control process now to alert all stakeholders of the change in scope and the change in the project plan. I suggest starting anew, possibly even with a new project name. The project manager should become known in the business as someone who negotiates win/win situations, someone who cares and actively listens to the users' problems.

Bottom line: Always be prepared and always keep the sponsor happy.

Should a Line of Business Build Its Own Data Mart?

The staff members of a sales unit need the capability of a data mart. They have asked IT to build it for them, but the request is low on IT's priority list. The sales line-of-business department has neither the expertise nor the inclination to build a data mart on its own, but it does have the budget. What should the sales department do?

Sid Adelman

This is not an ideal situation. A better situation would include a major commitment from IT, but absent that commitment and interest, the sales department can buy the expertise from a consulting firm that can build the sales data mart. Assuming that IT will still provide the infrastructure, the project will still require some involvement and commitment from IT. However, if IT does not want to be involved at all, an application service provider (ASP) could supply the necessary infrastructure.

Joyce Bischoff

Since the line of business has the necessary funding, the sales department should consider hiring a consulting firm to build the warehouse. It is critical, however, that IT have some involvement. The IT manager would be well advised to work with the consulting firm to ensure that all IT standards regarding hardware, software, data, and processes are followed.

Jill Dyché

The sales department could wait for IT, which could take a long time. Alternatively, sales can try going it alone, which invites the building of a stovepipe system that might not conform to the standards that IT has established, let alone allow sharing the data with other parts of the organization. This risks the creation of yet another legacy system. The fact is, business ownership of business intelligence applications is an increasing reality, and IT can either fight it or ensure that business intelligence development gets done the right way.

The ideal, of course, is for the sales department to collaborate with IT. This means understanding the company's data standard, business rules, tools, and platforms and adhering to them. Failing the regular availability of IT staff, the sales department can engage consultants to construct requirements for the new data mart, as well as technology selection metrics and a project plan.

In the meantime, the sales department should establish regular head-check sessions with IT to ensure that the development process is valid, that milestones are agreed on, and that the data and functional requirements identified don't already exist elsewhere in the company. IT should provide a dedicated team of experts to corroborate the sales department's plan. Depending on its resource availability, IT might even provide specialists to help the sales department select consultants, build the project plan, and approve the business requirements document.

However the two organizations choose to work together, IT should make sure that the sales department has the resources it needs to leverage existing data models, ETL scripts, meta data, and other enterprise-level IT resources whenever possible. This includes giving key developers within the sales data mart team access to data on an enterprise data warehouse, so that the sales data mart becomes a dependent data mart rather than a standalone system.

Douglas Hackney

The sales department should contract with an experienced consulting firm to implement an architected data mart. One of the criteria for success for the project should be the ability of this data mart to fit into the overall architecture of the organization, if one exists. Another criterion for success should be the knowledge transfer from the consultants to members of the sales department and the IT team.

Sean Ivoghli

If the need is urgent and IT does not have the resources to get the job done on time, then the sales department should look into hiring a consultant to do the job. If the team chooses to hire a consultant, he or she should adhere to IT development standards and provide adequate documentation and knowledge transfer so that IT can support the system.

Chuck Kelley

If the need for a data mart is high enough, there are only two options.

1. IT could modify its priorities by accepting the money from the sales line of business and putting a team into place (either by hiring new people, using current employees, or hiring contractors) to build the data mart. This is the best option.
2. The sales line of business could hire a consulting company to build a data mart. This option will most likely cause the most problems since

IT will have to spend time with the consulting company, providing extracts of source systems and answering questions about the data.

Using either option, the sales line of business needs to have a data warehouse champion role defined to keep the project running. The champion must be someone high enough in the organization that he or she can make decisions (sometimes by edict) if the success of the data warehouse is a goal.

David Marco

I assume that the sales department has already tried and failed to get the priority of the data warehouse raised on IT's radar. Since the sales department doesn't have the necessary expertise but does have the budget, I suggest partnering with a qualified, consulting vendor to construct a quality data warehouse.

Larissa Moss

It appears that the sales department is caught in this situation because the organization either did not prioritize its data warehouse projects properly or is not ready for a planned and phased data warehouse implementation.

Here are some questions the project manager should ask.

- Are the members of the sales department aware they will be adding to the existing DSS spaghetti chart if they build their own stovepipe data mart, thereby violating the organization's data warehouse strategy (if one exists)? Hopefully, the answer will be "No."
- The larger question to ask the CIO: Should IT, the sales department, or any other department be allowed to add one more stovepipe system to the thousands of systems already being supported by IT, thereby making the integration for the data warehouse even harder? Hopefully, the answer will be "No."
- The ultimate question for the CEO, CFO, and COO: Does the organization want to keep expanding a nonintegrated IT environment, which is incredibly expensive to maintain and from which it is almost impossible to extract consistent information? Hopefully, the answer will be "No."

The point is that the sales department's situation is a much larger strategic management issue, rather than just a tactical staffing issue, because the real question is "What is the data warehouse strategy in this organization?" Is the data warehouse supposed to be a new integrated, shared, and reconciled decision support environment, or is it considered to be just a new way to build applications? If the latter, then the organization is not engaged in data warehousing because the sales department will not be the only department to build its own stovepipe solution. On the other hand, if the data warehouse is considered to be a new integrated, shared, and reconciled decision support environment, the organization must make the commitment to sufficiently staff up to build this new environment.

- The organization must establish and staff a data warehouse administration department to coordinate and manage the data warehouse development work, whether the work is performed by a dedicated data warehouse team, by IT staff matrixed to the data warehouse department, or by consultants.
- The data warehouse department must be given a head start to establish at least some of the infrastructure, such as standards, policies, and rules the developers should follow.
- Most importantly, the organization must create a governance policy to prioritize the applications for the various departments, so that another situation like the one the sales department is facing can be avoided.

The sales department and IT should resolve these strategic issues with executive management first, before tackling tactical implementation issues. If executive management decides that the sales department requirements are so great that the department cannot wait its turn, the executives may change the priority of IT projects. If the priority of the sales department is raised but there is insufficient staff to build an integrated data warehouse solution, the executives may ask that a stopgap solution be implemented right away. In that case, the sales department, IT, and executive management are all accepting the price for this stopgap solution: an integrated data warehouse solution will have to replace the temporary fix later.

Bottom line: Controlling and allocating corporate resources—which extends to setting priorities on projects (operational and decision support) and staffing them—is usually a strategic business function, not the function of one line of business or IT alone.

Clay Rehm

The sales department members need to perform a quick readiness assessment first to determine whether they are ready to build *and* maintain a data mart. This assessment must include analysis of the business, the technology, the politics, and the sales department. Just because the sales department has the budget, does it need a data mart? What is the purpose or reason for the data mart? The assessment will identify whether the sales department really needs a data mart and will determine whether this is the right time to build one.

If the sales department members are ready, they must determine whether the department has any internal talent to help design, develop, and maintain a data mart. Even if they think they do, they should hire a consultant to design the data mart with the following directions:

- Follow an enterprise data architecture.
- Reuse data, tools, and processes from existing internal data warehouses.
- Use conformed dimensions.

The sales department should make sure business needs are captured in a requirements document. There are three main criteria for each requirement: that it be (1) understandable, (2) testable, and (3) accomplishable.

If I were asked to build the data mart, the sales department would need to prove to me that it really needed a data mart. The department members would have to prove to me that they know what business problems they plan to solve with the data mart.

In summary: Just because you have the money doesn't mean you need to spend it. Spend your money wisely.

THE PROJECT HAS NO DEDICATED STAFF

A company has tasked a data warehouse manager with the management, development, and support of an enterprise data warehouse that crosses multiple divisions. This manager has almost no dedicated staff; he must rely on pulling business and IT people from each line of business as he needs staff on the project. These people are often not available, especially when he needs them. Important meetings are unproductive when key personnel cannot attend. This has caused major delays and wasted time for those who did attend the meetings. Sign-offs have not taken place on time, and many decisions have had to be delayed. What should this data warehouse manager do?

Sid Adelman

It seems that the division personnel this data warehouse will support have little interest in the project. The lack of interest might also stem from the line-of-business managers not having much interest in the project. This usually means they don't see much benefit to their divisions. If they don't see the benefit, they will not support the project, and the data warehouse manager will not get cooperation from their staff.

A few questions come to mind.

- Who is the sponsor of the project? If it truly is a cross-division enterprise data warehouse, hopefully the sponsor is the CEO or COO.
- Has management communicated to the troops the importance of this endeavor? Sometimes executives have a vision but are the only ones who know about it. Management must communicate the vision.
- Has management defined and communicated to the stakeholders the benefits of the data warehouse? People need to know why this is a good move for the organization.

Joyce Bischoff

High-level business sponsorship and commitment are the keys to the solution. If there is a business justification for the project, the business sponsor and data warehouse manager must ensure that adequate resources are available. The following questions should be addressed:

- Have the business objectives of the project been clearly documented?
- Has the project been funded?
- Has the data warehouse manager identified project resources and ensured their availability?
- Were personnel resources assigned to the project for specific amounts of time? If so, why are they not available? Are managers of the project personnel on board with the project?
- If personnel resources are unavailable, is it possible to bring in consultants to supplement the staff?

The data warehouse manager should stop the project until the organization has resolved all the above issues.

Douglas Hackney

The data warehouse manager should reduce the scope of the project to a manageable size, given whatever dedicated resources he can secure. Only by demonstrating the value of integrated data through the delivery of small, incremental phases will the data warehouse manager enlist the support of the business sufficiently to accomplish a broad, cross-divisional scope. Dedicated resources are a prerequisite for success in data warehousing, especially in large-scale implementations.

Sean Ivoghli

IT development projects that require significant design and development and have deadlines cannot be successful without dedicated staff. This especially applies to data warehouse projects. As we all know, IT projects are full of peaks and valleys with issues and activities. This is caused by changing requirements, miscommunications, unpredictable technologies, mismanagement, unrealistic deadlines, and other risk factors. In addition, the inability of the human mind to manage and focus on multiple complex issues and tasks at the same time makes it impossible for shared team members to focus on the data warehouse project and manage their tasks efficiently. This explains why the data warehouse manager finds himself competing with other meetings and other managers' expectations.

I have seen this type of team structure implemented many times for data warehouse projects. It usually results from a lack of commitment from management or a lack of understanding of data warehouse projects. In the latter case, some inexperienced managers think that since data warehouses use data from multiple sources and business operations, then the best way to set up a project is to have shared staff from various groups. Such managers also figure that this is the best way to squeeze every last bit of work out of IT staff and increase productivity. I have never seen this structure work properly. In fact, it usually fails for these types of projects. Not only does the data warehouse project fail, but other projects also suffer from reduced participation and distraction of shared staff. The first thing the data warehouse manager needs to do is to convince the sponsor(s) of the project to get him a dedicated team. If that doesn't work, he should look for another job.

Chuck Kelley

The senior management staff must be committed to the development of a data warehouse. Without it, situations like this will occur. In times like these, there needs to be an internal look at the organization to see if the organization is ready for the data warehouse.

If I were the data warehouse manager, I would get each person on the business side to make a commitment for two hours each week, always on the same day and same time. For example, I would ask Mary Marketeer to meet with the team and me every Wednesday at 9:00 A.M., and during those times I would try to learn about and document all the issues that Mary and marketing brought to light. Then on other days, I would try to get worked into her calendar on an as-needed basis. Without this commitment of time, I think it will be hard to complete the task assigned.

David Marco

The data warehouse manager should clearly document all these issues (no dedicated staff, lack of staff availability, and so on). Then he should have a good, old-fashioned, sit-down meeting with the project sponsor. If the project sponsor believes that the project is important, then dedicated staff members are required. If this project is not as important as the other things those people are working on, then the project should be delayed until resources can be fully allocated. By clearly documenting all the issues in a professional and direct manner, the data warehouse manager will create a good communication vehicle and will properly protect himself from misplaced blame.

Larissa Moss

The symptoms of not getting adequate staff or user involvement point to an enterprise data warehouse solution that is looking for a business problem. The data warehouse manager should concentrate on identifying the business problems that the data warehouse will solve. One of three situations may exist.

1. If the business problems exist and are recognized by at least one business executive, the project manager should ask that executive to sponsor a

business case assessment study. Together they should conduct a study of the business problems and prepare a business case report that itemizes the problems with their associated costs to the company. The costs can be either excessive operating expenses or lost revenue caused internally or externally through competitive pressure. In either case, the business case report must show how the data warehouse will eliminate or reduce the problems and how soon the return on investment will be realized if the necessary staff were available when needed. It is then up to the business executive sponsor to force the issue of staff availability and participation.

2. If the business problems exist but are not recognized by the business community, the data warehouse manager could launch a crusade of exposing the problems to gain support for a data warehouse solution. This could be a slippery road for the data warehouse manager for political reasons. Some business executives may feel threatened by the exposure and may try to squeeze out not only the data warehouse project but the data warehouse manager as well.

3. If no business problems exist, the data warehouse manager should find a more worthwhile project. Many data warehouse initiatives sponsored solely by IT never gain sufficient user support and thus flounder.

Clay Rehm

Management has not prioritized projects and tasks for business and IT. Everyone is working on multiple high-priority tasks, and the people who scream the loudest for staff time will get that time (or they'll get it because of their relationships with key people).

It is obvious that the key personnel do not think the enterprise data warehouse is important; otherwise they would make time for it. The data warehouse manager must take matters into his own hands and make the data warehouse important. He could demonstrate a prototype of what he thinks the final solution will be. He could tell users that if they do not get involved, he will deliver a close replicate of the prototype!

Is the organization ready for a data warehouse, especially an enterprise data warehouse? Most likely it is not. A readiness assessment by an unbiased, experienced data warehouse consultant is required.

There are times in your life when you must question the things that are happening to you or are being imposed on you. Just because someone decides that something is a good idea does not mean that it is appropriate for everyone. In this scenario, the data warehouse manager has been asked to do something that has been set up to fail. I am always up for a good challenge, but when the cards are stacked so unfavorably, the challenge cannot be accomplished. This situation is a great opportunity for a data warehouse manager who likes a lot of visibility, for someone who can tackle the impossible, who has the energy and creativity to actually wake up each morning and say, "I can do this!" It is important to note that this role will be stressful and exhausting. This is not something just anyone can do.

Assuming the data warehouse manager has overcome the feelings of doubt, he has to ask himself, "What are the goals, the assumptions, and risks? What support do I really have from the people who are asking me to accomplish this task?"

Once he has conquered the pangs of anxiety and the realization that this is not a dream (nor a nightmare), he should write an easy-to-read document that explains the current state of the project. This document must include the problems encountered on the project (for example, the lack of dedicated staff and the subsequent effects on the project). Once completed, he should ask a peer to review the document for readability and content. Then the data warehouse manager must present this document to management. The executives must understand the situation and provide alternatives. The data warehouse manager must develop a detailed project plan (a schedule with a work breakdown structure) and distribute it to the people who will be working on the project. He should individualize the project plan so the team members can see how the plan affects them positively.

If the data warehouse manager still can't get the time from key personnel, he should take them out for breakfast, lunch, or dinner. Or he could take them out golfing on a weeknight or on the weekend.

How can the data warehouse manager get people to come to meetings?

- Serve donuts and beverages.
- Keep the meetings short.
- Send out agendas ahead of time.
- Always have a facilitator and a scribe.

- Never stray off the agenda (the facilitator will manage this).
- Conduct one-on-one sessions instead of group meetings to get or communicate the needed information.

The moral of the story: Communicate reality and get the priorities straight.

THE PROJECT MANAGER HAS BAGGAGE

The project manager reports to the data warehouse manager. The project manager comes from the IT side of the organization and is not well liked or respected by the business people, who do not answer his phone calls or respond to his e-mail messages. What should the data warehouse manager do?

Sid Adelman

The data warehouse manager should dump the project manager. It sounds like he cannot be rehabilitated. The project needs a manager who is liked and respected by the business people. Otherwise the important connections will not be made, communication won't happen, and the project will fail.

Joyce Bischoff

The project manager should be replaced. The project manager must be highly respected by both the IT and business communities if the warehouse is to be successful. The data warehouse manager should consider assigning a project manager from the business community with an assistant project manager from the IT side of the organization. This would emphasize that the project is a business project and not an IT project.

Douglas Hackney

The data warehouse manager should find a project manager who is more user-oriented. The required attributes are intelligence, flexibility, and business orientation. Everything else can be taught.

Sean Ivoghli

It is critical for the project manager to have good rapport with the users. If the data warehouse manager has a good relationship with the users, he or she should investigate the reason why the project manager is disliked. If people dislike him because of his lack of integrity, incompetence, or behavior issues, the data warehouse manager may want to consider not using this project manager. If the users give reasons other than those (reasons that can be resolved with some intermediation), and the data warehouse manager believes in the project manager, then the data warehouse manager should actively campaign to increase the project manager's popularity by supporting him, making him look good, and helping him mend relationships with the users. If that is not possible but the data warehouse manager still wants to go with this project manager, then I would advise hiring a very senior business analyst for the project with a strong industry background, a solid understanding of technology, and an attractive personality. The data warehouse manager could use this person as the main liaison to the users and have the project manager manage the project on the IT side.

Chuck Kelley

If I were the data warehouse manager, I would meet with the business people to discover the reason for the problem. It could be a personality conflict, a communication problem, or simply incompetence. If I felt this was a personality conflict or communication problem, I would want to determine what could be done to help overcome the problem. If I felt the problem was the project manager's incompetence, I would work to help the project manager improve or I would replace him with a more suitable person.

David Marco

If the project manager is a "weak" employee, I would move him out of the role. But if he is a good employee, I would sit him down and talk to him about the issue. I would make sure to illustrate the specific traits causing the problem. After this talk I would need to decide whether this personality problem is correctable or whether I should choose another qualified project manager. If I had a good replacement I would move the original project manager to another data warehousing project under a different line of business. If he is the only option I have, then after my talk with him I would talk to the business people who have a problem with him and try to bury the hatchet.

Larissa Moss

The first question that comes to mind is "Why did the data warehouse manager select a project manager who is disliked by the business community?" There are two possible answers: (1) the data warehouse manager did not know that the project manager was disliked, or (2) the data warehouse manager had no choice in the selection of the project manager.

If it is the first case, the data warehouse manager should investigate and understand why there is such dislike of the project manager. Usually there are two sides to every story, and airing both stories through non-hostile communication channels can sometimes mend disagreements if some misunderstanding between the two parties originally caused the problem. If it turns out that the project manager has a habit of making self-serving, inappropriate decisions or in general has a belligerent personality, he should simply be removed.

If the data warehouse manager is faced with the second scenario, where he or she had no choice in selecting the project manager, it is safe to assume that he or she also has no authority to remove the project manager. That points to a bigger problem, namely that the data warehouse manager has responsibility without authority. The data warehouse manager needs to change that situation if he or she does not want to get stuck in other no-win situations in the future. The data warehouse manager needs to clearly identify his or her own role with all its responsibilities and authorities and negotiate with his or her superiors the conditions for accepting the job. If the data warehouse manager is not given any authority over selecting who reports to him or her, the data warehouse manager should look for a more gratifying position elsewhere.

Clay Rehm

The data warehouse manager must meet one-on-one with the project manager and assess his communication skills. Is he bitter, angry, confrontational, condescending, depressed? Does he not speak in business terms? If the data warehouse manager believes this is not a communication skills problem, then he or she needs to get to the root of the problem. The data warehouse manager must survey specific business people one-on-one only and determine why they do not like or respect the project manager. The data warehouse manager must get to the root of the problem and not just the symptoms. Which of the following seems to apply best to the project manager?

- He just doesn't know his job yet, but he can be taught.
- He will fail on the job regardless of any additional training.
- He doesn't care (the worst case of all). If he doesn't care about his job, tasks, or career, it will be extremely difficult to remedy this situation while he remains the project manager.

The data warehouse manager should ask the project manager's permission to review examples of his e-mails so the data warehouse manager can provide mentoring and coaching on communication style. The data warehouse manager should consider hiring an unbiased third party who specializes in coaching and can effectively provide input on personnel problems.

I strongly recommend an open forum if both sides will accept it, but there should be no negative consequences as a result of this meeting. What does this mean? The data warehouse manager should call a meeting attended by the project manager and the people who do not respect him, then let everyone speak candidly! If the problem cannot be fixed, the data warehouse manager should consider the cost of not meeting the project time lines compared with the cost of replacing the person in question.

The business people who aren't responding to phone calls or e-mails are acting very childishly. Regardless of the situation, everyone needs to maintain his or her professionalism.

Bottom line: Be proactive; get your personnel to play nice together or replace them.

NO ONE WANTS TO WORK FOR THE COMPANY

A company has allocated sufficient money to hire the people needed to complete a particular project. In fact, the pay scale for positions within this company exceeds that of the region and even the rest of the country. The project desperately needs everything from business analysts to database administrators. However, this industry has been vilified in the press and by some leading government and health officials. Recruiting agencies have been beating the bushes to no avail. What should this company do?

Sid Adelman

It seems like the only option is to bring in some hired guns. Consultants and contractors are more easily lured since they know they will be leaving after the project ends and they may be able to conceal their activities from friends and family. However, the company should make sure the consultants and contractors document everything, including the decisions they make. It would be best to automate as much as possible. Automated processes have no conscience.

Joyce Bischoff

From a long-term perspective, the company needs to upgrade its image using public relations techniques. Management should encourage IT personnel to become involved in professional organizations and make contributions to these organizations whenever possible. The company should also send personnel to attend conferences and practice networking with their peers. Higher visibility of the IT people will make the company seem more worthwhile to others in the field.

Douglas Hackney

The company will have to accept the higher costs associated with using consulting resources for the construction of the system. It is unlikely that the company will be able to recruit and retain the full-time staff resources necessary to design and implement the system. Management should focus its efforts on recruiting and retaining resources sufficient to maintain the system once it is built.

Chuck Kelley

If the company cannot find anyone to work on the project as employees, the company should contract with consulting firms. For the most part, consulting firms will accept the work as long as the money has been appropriated. The company may need to approach a smaller consulting firm. The consultants may require an advance on expenses, but that would be better than not building the data warehouse. Although the company will not fulfill the employee head count, at least the project will move forward. Then, who knows, maybe the company will be able to hire some of the consulting firm's workers once they see that the company is not full of bad guys after all. One bit of caution—management should make sure to get in writing exactly what it will pay for. Some projects outsourced to contractors have never been finished, which has been costly to the organizations.

David Marco

I recommend rethinking and reworking how the company presents itself to potential employees. If this reworking did not solve the problem, I would recommend one of the following remedies.

- *Outsourcing:* Most firms that specialize in outsourcing have very limited knowledge of data warehousing. In addition, outsourcing is a long-term commitment that poses many challenges.
- *Partnering with a consulting firm:* Finding the right vendor is the key.
- *Hiring consultants:* This could be a good option; however, the company's bad reputation still creates issues.

Clay Rehm

This company has two parallel tasks: (1) to start a marketing campaign to announce that it is "okay to work for us," and (2) to retain contracted talent. The contractors can get the project started while management recruits employees. As the employees trickle in, there must be a plan in place to transfer the knowledge from the contractors to the new employees.

The moral of the story: Keep moving forward.

THE ORGANIZATION IS NOT READY FOR A DATA WAREHOUSE

The organization's lack of readiness for a data warehouse plays out in limited technical skills, reduced staff availability, lack of motivation, political infighting, assassins, a CIO who's ready to retire and doesn't want to take any risks. . . . The business neither wants the data warehouse nor has the money or the inclination to participate in any data warehouse endeavor. What should the newly appointed data warehouse manager do?

Sid Adelman

This is clearly a situation that isn't going anywhere. There is zero chance the data warehouse could be a success. The newly appointed data warehouse manager should go back to his or her manager, explain the impossibility of success, and ask for another position in the organization.

Joyce Bischoff

If the new data warehouse manager cannot obtain commitment for work under his or her responsibility, he or she should look for another job, either inside or outside the company.

Jill Dyché

The first thing the data warehouse manager should do in this situation is to stop using the term "data warehouse." He or she should stop talking about the data warehouse project and reassign the data warehouse project team. The data warehouse manager should remove the term "data warehouse" from the job title. In short, he or she should put data warehousing on the back burner.

This company has a lot of shoring up to do, and the improvements needed will do more than just help the company prepare for its data warehouse. Staff education, technology improvements, and organizational streamlining can benefit many other business initiatives besides data warehousing. These fixes should take place not in order to prepare for data warehousing but to foster improvements for the company's long-term health.

This in turn will prevent the eventual data warehouse from being saddled with, or even blamed for, the cost of improvements that preceded it. In other words, supplementing employee skill sets, upgrading software, implementing management changes, and even hiring and firing employees will ultimately save the company money and incite a host of benefits, data warehouse or no data warehouse.

Only after some of these basic improvements have been made should a data warehouse project be launched. And if they're not made? Then launching a data warehouse is like sweeping a dirt floor: a well-meaning gesture but a futile one.

Douglas Hackney

The data warehouse manager should find another job. This is a no-win, no-chance scenario. Plenty of companies both want and need data warehouse solutions. This data warehouse manager would be much better off researching opportunities at another firm rather than banging his or her head against the wall at the current firm.

Sean Ivoghli

I don't know of very many competitive industries where companies can't benefit from a data warehouse of some shape or form. It seems as if this company's management doesn't have a vision. The benefits of any data warehouse need to be recognized by the business first. Therefore, the data warehouse manager should seek a visionary in the upper management of the business who would become a champion to the project. A good place to start is with the person who hired the data warehouse manager and then work up the corporate ladder. Why did they hire the data warehouse manager? Who in the organization thinks they need a data warehouse, and why? Once the data warehouse manager finds a sponsor at an influential level of management, they should work together to build a vision that clearly demonstrates the benefits of a data warehouse. A good idea is to see what the competition is doing. Then they should develop a business case and present it to executive management along with the vision. If executive sponsorship cannot be obtained, the data warehouse manager can still look into justifying a smaller data mart project with benefits for a department or a single business unit. Once successful, smaller data mart projects can be noticed by upper management and can evolve into full-scale data warehouse projects with benefits for the enterprise.

Chuck Kelley

This situation requires a major sales job. Virtually every organization, whether public or private sector, needs a data warehouse. The data warehouse manager should start by talking to different groups within the business to find out where the problems lie. The data warehouse manager should express where the data warehouse can help and why the organization needs one (for example, the return on investment, the ability to expand into new markets, or other ways the data warehouse can help the organization fulfill its objectives). If this doesn't help and the data warehouse manager wants to do data warehousing, then maybe dusting off the ol' résumé is in order.

David Marco

Mark Twain is commonly credited with writing, "Never try to teach a pig how to sing. You'll waste your time and annoy the pig." If the CIO is ready to retire but won't be retiring in the next 12 months and doesn't want to take any risk, the data warehouse manager will have a better chance of teaching a pig to sing than changing the CIO's mind. The data warehouse manager should continue studying data warehousing, get as much training as possible, and then circulate his or her résumé.

Larissa Moss

The data warehouse manager needs to find out why he or she was hired or put into the role of a data warehouse manager. He or she needs to talk with the person who conceived that position to find out the intended purpose. Maybe that person did not understand what a data warehouse is but thought it was the right solution for a problem. The data warehouse manager needs to find out what that problem is and what the appropriate solution for it is.

If the solution does not require a data warehouse, the data warehouse manager has the choice of redefining his or her position and working on an appropriate solution or resigning from that position. If a data warehouse is the correct solution, the data warehouse manager could enter into an uphill struggle of educating the company on data warehousing, or he or she could take the easy way out and resign from that position. Having been down this road many times before, my personal advice is to take the easy way out.

Clay Rehm

The problem is pretty clear. The organization is not ready for the data warehouse!

The data warehouse manager should document the reason the data warehouse was proposed. He or she should find the current project definition, scope, and requirements and then collect and further document the "what, who, why, when, and how." The data warehouse manager should present this documentation to the management and users. At the same time, the data warehouse manager should hire an outside firm that specializes in data warehouse readiness assessments. This firm should perform the assessment and present the findings to users, management, and IT. The consultant must present his or her findings to the data warehouse manager first for a reality check. If the consultant does not identify the issues in order to sugarcoat and get the gig, the data warehouse manager should give the consultant the boot and try again. Company staff members may argue that they have the expertise to create a data warehouse project. Why hire consultants? Even if the in-house expertise exists, management will not respect or hear staff members since they work at the company and thus must not have the expertise, management thinks, because otherwise those people would be consultants!

Like everything else in life, data warehouse projects fail due to poor or nonexistent communication. The data warehouse manager should identify the client culture in writing and share it with everyone, listing the steps necessary for the team to work together effectively. Each team member must participate in a personality profile. A written agreement should document the project's acceptance.

If the data warehouse manager is really serious about the project, he or she must hire an independent consultant or consulting firm that has successfully designed, developed, and sustained data warehouses—and has references.

If all this fails, the data warehouse manager should run! (Well, maybe walk.) The manager should look at this as passing up the biggest challenge of his or her life!

Bottom line: Never attempt a project for which the users are not ready.

CHAPTER FIVE

User Issues

With the customer as the reference point, priorities become easier to set.

—Mary Walton

OVERVIEW

Users are sometimes called end-users, clients, knowledge workers, or business analysts. Sometimes they are statisticians or staff working for management, tasked with creating and delivering reports in exactly the format desired by senior management. Without users, a data warehouse has no reason to exist. However, these users are usually impatient to get the information they need to support their work. User departments often vie to make their projects first in line. The user department must be more than just involved in the data warehouse project; they must be committed.

Not all users are created equal. There is great variation in how much the users know about computers, in how much they know about the data, and in how willing they are to use new tools. Power users are much more likely to write their own queries and more willing to experiment with the tools and go where no other users—or only a few—have gone before. More timid users are unlikely to write their own queries. The appropriate model for these users is canned, prewritten queries they can launch with just the entry of a few

109

parameters, such as a region number or an amount range. The training for each group of users should be tailored to their needs and their propensity to learn and try new things.

Users and user liaisons identify what data they need, how timely it should be, and where the data originates. The users specify what information they need and in what format. They determine the need for historical data, including the periods and how far back to maintain the history.

With the help of data administration, users provide the business definitions. These definitions are in the terminology of the business, not in IT terminology. These definitions should be stored in a meta data repository and should be available to anyone running a query or receiving a result set or report. Many organizations are putting the definitions on their intranet giving accessibility to these definitions throughout the organization. The author of the definition and the last date of update would be available along with the definition. Data administration must keep the definitions current; they perform the mechanics of the updates. The currency of the content is up to the business stewards of the data. They are the first to know of changes or updates to the business.

Users are responsible for determining who can access the data and at what level of detail. Access may be given for summary data but not for the detail. The users are responsible for identifying the domains (valid values) of the data. Users know whether summary data is adequate or whether they need to access the detail data. In a number of cases, users have thought a summary would be enough, but once they saw the summary, they realized they needed the detail to understand what made up the summary.

Users are in an excellent position to validate the quality of the data as they review their reports. Data quality problems are sometimes uncovered by IT—if IT has a proactive quality program. Users should be sensitized to looking for data quality problems and reporting them to IT. It's not enough to just identify the data as "junk"; users should report all suspicious dirty data. Users should be closely involved in certifying the initial population of the data warehouse. The certification process alerts IT to data errors, especially as a result of transformation errors. Certification also increases user involvement and buy-in for data quality. We should all know by now that even if an application program has generated a report, the report might still be incorrect. The users hold the responsibility of validating the accuracy of all reports. Users know what to expect and are well suited to write test cases. If the data is much different than expected, the users should investigate further.

Users are often involved in identifying the transformation rules and the cleansing rules for the extract/transform/load process. Users specify code transformations (for example, 01/02/00 becomes 02012000), indicate what to do when mandatory fields are blank, inform IT about which records are invalid and should be dropped, and so on.

Depending on the organization's charge-back policies, the users are often responsible for paying the bill. They may be charged for the use of machine resources, IT personnel, consultants and contractors, and software related to the data warehouse. Be aware that the ways people are charged often drive their behaviors and interactions. Charge-backs can have a self-regulating effect on how resources are used, or the charge-backs can cause aberrant and counterproductive behavior. Charge-backs should be tailored to generate the desired user behavior and should not result in unhappy users. Carefully consider any plans for charge-backs to avoid unintended consequences, such as users not using the system to its full potential.

While rarely explicitly stated, users have expectations about the quality of the data, and those expectations are almost always unrealistically high. Often the users have been unable to articulate all their requirements and appear not to know what they want. This can frustrate the data warehouse team, leaving its members unsure of which way to proceed. When users do not like the access and analysis tool, there is always a problem. In many instances, the users have a negative impression of data warehouses, an impression often based on bad experiences with an access and analysis tool. When the business also does not support the project, this raises some interesting points about how the data warehouse was sold and whether this is even the right set of users for a data warehouse.

In the remainder of this chapter, we discuss solutions for six situations related to users.

THE USERS WANT IT NOW

An organization has a corporate culture that fosters "siloized" business units with IT implementations that are not integrated with each other. However, the multiple business unit sponsors want their data in the data warehouse, and they all want it now. It's obvious that not all the sponsors can be satisfied at once. What should the data warehouse manager do to avoid angering any of the business unit sponsors or causing them to run off and develop their own data warehouses?

Sid Adelman

The company should establish a business advisory board, which is sometimes called a steering committee. This board would consist of representatives from the business, not from IT. They would make the high-profile business decisions and determine which applications have the most value to the business and which should be developed first. More importantly, the steering committee takes the heat off the data warehouse manager.

Joyce Bischoff

The company should form a data warehouse advisory committee representing various business areas. Members should be high-level executives who can evaluate the various requests and determine the best sequence of activity. The committee should establish a foundation of naming conventions, meta data, and warehouse standards before or during the first project. Without the processes for ensuring best practices, inflexible silo data marts will probably be constructed.

Douglas Hackney

Each of the business unit sponsors should be a member of the data warehouse steering committee. The steering committee should establish the build-phase priorities for the data warehousing team.

Sean Ivoghli

The data warehouse manager should begin by finding out what base metrics each user group is interested in and ranking them in order of their significance to each business unit. Then he or she should figure out what the most common and most valued (for business analytics) base metrics are across the enterprise. Based on the capabilities and budget of the team, the data warehouse manager should scope out a first phase that delivers the base metrics that would deliver the most value to the most people and then start analyzing the requirements for those metrics for each business unit. Different business units will have different perspectives on each base metric, and each unit will have its own derivations and calculations needed from the base metrics. The different business perspectives will define the dimensions needed in the data warehouse as well as the grain of the metrics.

Chances are that the first phase will have to bring in each base metric at or close to its atomic level in order to satisfy many business units. The atomic level contains all the dimensions that everyone needs, so the project team can build aggregates from there. The project manager should choose to deliver only as many metrics as can be delivered by the deadline. "Sales amount" is usually a great candidate for a base metric that could satisfy many needs across an enterprise.

The users in some business units won't be completely happy because they'll want more metrics than are available in the initial phase, but most users will become more patient once the data warehouse team has delivered some initial value. From that point onward, the data warehouse manager should use the same utilitarian (maximized benefit for maximum numbers) approach in future phases unless a business unit has more clout or becomes more of a contributor or champion. In that case, the data warehouse manager should use his or her better judgment to serve the best interests of the project and the company.

Chuck Kelley

The data warehouse manager should ask the head of each of the business units for the funds to create that unit's warehouse. The data warehouse manager could put together a team of folks to build each of the environments. The major requirement to attach to the teams is that all data requirements must be fed through a centralized data group responsible for making sure that each of the dimension structures are complete to support each of the business units. This will allow each group to build separately while also allowing for an enterprise-wide view of the data.

David Marco

I would gather the business sponsors together and create a data warehousing steering committee. The first task of this committee would be to create a project time line that would show each business sponsor when he or she would receive data. It is important to make sure that sponsors are not left out of this process.

Larissa Moss

There will be little difference in outcome if the business unit sponsors run off to develop their own silo warehouses or if IT is forced to either quickly shove all the data into one database or develop multiple silo data marts in a hurry to pacify the sponsors' self-serving needs. A data warehouse initiative is not about self-serving needs. If the sponsors don't understand that and the chief officers of the organization don't support it, there will be no true data warehouse initiative at this company, no matter what management calls the decision support projects. Using newfangled data access and data analysis technology does not a data warehouse make! If the organization is truly not interested in an integrated, shared, cross-organizational decision support environment, that is, a data warehouse, then it does not matter what the "data warehouse" team does. The result will still be adding more islands of automation—end of story.

However, if the organization—at some level—*does* want an integrated, shared, cross-organizational decision support environment, the data warehouse manager must find the person with that vision. Together they should identify the business problems caused by the current silos and extrapolate future problems that may be caused by adding more silos under the guise of data warehousing. Many books line the shelves these days demonstrating the enormous costs of maintaining redundant and inconsistent data as well as maintaining the redundant processes to create, maintain, and reconcile that data. Many more books are written on the tasks and techniques for moving away from decision support silos to an integrated data warehouse environment. Once the difference between the two environments is understood and accepted, an assessment and a cost justification should be prepared for moving the company from a siloized environment to an integrated environment.

The case must then be made to the highest executive level in the organization for conceptual buy-in to move the company away from the siloized environment. Equipped with that buy-in, the data warehouse manager and the person with the vision must meet with all business unit sponsors and prepare a cost justification for each of their information needs. These cost-justification reports, along with an overview of what data warehousing is and what it is not, should be reviewed with all business unit sponsors. An attempt should be made to reach a consensus for prioritizing the sponsors' needs. If that fails, the cost-justification reports should be taken to the highest executive level in the organization for prioritization.

The executives in the organization must be actively involved in setting the new decision support direction for the company, establishing a governing body for data warehousing, and communicating with business unit sponsors. If buy-in cannot be obtained from the highest executive level in the organization, that is a clear indication that the organization is not ready for data warehousing.

Clay Rehm

This effort requires the work of a highly skilled project lead who can communicate well and get people motivated and excited. This project requires a strong person who can bring the business unit sponsors together in a room and convince them to create the right solution so that these leaders do not go off and do their own thing.

There are many things the data warehouse manager can do:

- Develop an enterprise data architecture approach.
- Establish standards for conformed dimensions and enforce those standards.
- Implement a virtual enterprise data warehouse when it's appropriate.

To accomplish these items, the data warehouse manager should assemble a data warehouse scope/planning/requirements team. This team is responsible for gathering requirements across each silo in a quick yet somewhat thorough fashion. This team needs very good communicators and people who are respected throughout the organization.

The team can take a rapid application development (RAD) approach to designing the enterprise data architecture. This requires the skill and grace of logical data modelers who do not get hung up on theory and can quickly identify common data elements across the enterprise. Also, when identifying the common or conformed dimensions across the enterprise, these modelers must be ready to resolve conflicts and differences of opinion when business units do not agree on terms such as "product" or "customer."

If it becomes necessary, the compromise is to agree that there is both a "marketing product" as well as a "product."

The data warehouse manager should take the approach that the team will not be able to build the grand, theoretical enterprise data warehouse. Instead, the data warehouse manager should consider that if each business unit creates its own data warehouse, how can data, meta data, tools, and processes be shared among them to create a virtual enterprise data warehouse?

The moral of the story: Take the time to do quick, thorough, common-sense strategic planning while delivering tactical fire-fighting solutions.

THE BUSINESS DOES NOT SUPPORT THE PROJECT

The IT department of a company hired a consultant to build a data warehouse. The business does not support the project, but IT tells the consultant to keep working even though the business side is making plans to oust him. What should the consultant do?

Sid Adelman

If the business doesn't want the project, it's not going to happen. The field of dreams is just a dream. The consultant may build something, but if the business users don't want it, they will not come. The real answer depends on the consultant's level of integrity. A reputable consultant will walk away. A disreputable consultant will perform some tasks, cash the checks, and provide very little work of value to the client.

Joyce Bischoff

Projects without business sponsorship are rarely successful. The consultant should discuss the problem with the IT managers and encourage them to open conversations with the affected business areas. The consultant could use this avenue to try to obtain joint sponsorship of the project. If the IT managers insist that the project move forward, the consultant's contract will probably force him to keep working.

Douglas Hackney

The consultant should meet with a representative of the business to try and resolve the issues. If a solution cannot be found, then the consultant should resign the account.

Sean Ivoghli

The consultant should try to find out why the business users do not support the data warehouse project. Are they unsupportive of the in-house IT department or the consultant? In either case, the consultant should try to convince the users that he has the experience to make even the worst IT department successful. But to do that without upsetting the IT department, he should consult the IT group on his strategy for winning over the business unit. During the course of the project, the consultant should let the IT group take credit for his accomplishments and help mend the relationship between IT and the business users. That creates a win/win situation that everyone can feel good about.

If the users just don't support the project, then the consultant really needs to revisit the business case and win the users' support before continuing the project. The team shouldn't take the "build it and they will come" approach unless at least one business group is sponsoring the project. If no one can win the sponsorship of the target business group, then the consultant should try to win support from other business groups. IT sponsorship alone is not enough. Without business support, the project will fail, even if the consultant develops a technological miracle.

Chuck Kelley

The consultant needs to talk more with IT to understand why the business has a problem with the project. If IT cannot or will not provide the information, then the consultant needs to meet with the business users to understand the issues. If that cannot or does not happen, then the project is probably a lost cause. The consultant should continue working on the project as requested by the IT staff (no use burning bridges with them!) for as long as he believes the company will pay him, and he should do as much as possible to resolve the problem. It may be a lost cause, but giving a valiant effort to support the group that hired him is the best thing the consultant can do.

David Marco

The first mistake is that the consultant was hired by IT without the blessing of the business. I would confront the business side of the house to sell them on the value of the data warehousing project. If this doesn't work it may be time to gracefully end the project, before the official ousting occurs. The business may be against the consultant just because IT hired him.

Larissa Moss

The consultant should cut his losses, protect his reputation, and get out as soon as feasible. This is assuming that all attempts to explain and reason with the business users have been exhausted and the animosity is irreversible. Cutting his losses does not mean that the consultant should walk out in the middle of a contract. That would ruin his reputation. But it does mean minimizing any further investment in the engagement that does not directly and necessarily contribute to a "successful" conclusion of the engagement. If IT hired the consultant, the contractual obligations are to IT. The consultant must fulfill these obligations as best he can.

If there are means to renegotiate the contract for an earlier conclusion for the benefit of all involved parties, the consultant should pursue that option. If the contract is based on time and material and not on a fixed bid, it should provide for a cancellation period. The consultant should investigate the option of canceling the contract. Continuing to work in an environment that is irritating the business users is at best extremely frustrating and uncomfortable to the consultant; at worst it can permanently damage the consultant's reputation, not only with other clients but also among colleagues in the industry. "Sticking it out" can be more damaging than ending the engagement prematurely but amicably.

Clay Rehm

There is no way a data warehouse project can succeed without business representative support. If the project team cannot articulate the goals of the business, the consultant shouldn't even start this project; he would be wasting everyone's time. So, the consultant can ask himself, "How can I get the business to support the project?" The business needs to be shown the importance of this project. This will take a strong, charismatic leader who can speak well and knows the business as well as the field of data warehousing.

The consultant should call a meeting of both the business executives or representatives and IT and tell the truth. The company is not ready for a data warehouse. The consultant should tell them that he does not feel right making money on a project that is destined to fail. Before calling that ever-important meeting, he should create an agenda—and then follow it. This type of group meeting works because it shows the credibility of the consultant, and it uncovers whether the internal IT and business areas can actually work and play together. It may take the consultant to play the mediator and facilitator role.

In summary: Be honest from the beginning and identify critical issues early and often.

WEB-BASED IMPLEMENTATION DOESN'T IMPRESS THE USERS

IT delivered a Web-based application. Unfortunately, the users did not notice or appreciate the advantages of the Web-based implementation. They expected this implementation to work as fast as a client-based system and to be very easy to use. The users were not interested in participating in system development and testing. How can the project manager sell the advantages of Web-based delivery to the users?

Sid Adelman

This situation has two issues: (1) the users' response time expectation and (2) their lack of interest in the project. One of the major failures of data warehouse projects is unfulfilled user expectations, and performance expectations are often a problem of unrealistic expectations. If response time is critical to the users and the Web implementation cannot provide adequate response time, the Web approach should be reevaluated. Should this application have been on the Web? Are the benefits justified? Are the clients impressed enough with those benefits to justify it not being a client-based system? If the benefits are there, then the project manager should market those benefits differently and in a way the users will accept. If the benefits are lacking, the project manager should take the application off the Web and make it as easy to use as possible.

Regarding the users' lack of involvement in the project, it seems that the users were not properly sold on the project in the first place or that the project agreement (where the users' responsibilities were clearly defined) was not taken seriously.

Joyce Bischoff

It sounds as if the IT group has delivered a poorly designed Web-based system without user advantages. Users should have been involved from the start in defining business benefits and designing the screens and processes to ensure satisfaction. If there are few business benefits, there is probably no justification for the project. If the system is slow, a performance review could be conducted to identify the potential for improved performance, but it may be a waste of time under the circumstances.

Jill Dyché

So who decided to deploy Web-based functionality without checking in with the users? Who established the performance metrics? Who released the application without prototyping it and getting end-user sign-off? Show me a development team that deploys an application—Web-based or not—without making the end-users its stakeholders and I'll show you a development organization with a new piece of shelfware.

The failures here are insurmountable: lack of business requirements, lack of a value proposition, lack of end-user buy-in, and lack of expectations management. The project manager should institutionalize business requirements, project hard and soft ROI, obtain end-user sign-off, meet with management to nail down realistic investment and delivery expectations, and then try again.

Chuck Kelley

IT must not force the choice of tools on the users, but the users must choose what tools best fit their needs. IT needs to allow the users to continue to use the client-based systems and to charge back to each of the business users appropriately. Next, IT should build a large number of reports that provide the data that many users want to see and provide it using the Web-based delivery tool at a much lower cost. This will help migrate users to the Web-based environment.

David Marco

This situation suffers from two issues. First, it seems clear that the business users have fairly sophisticated front-end requirements and were expecting a client-based system. Unfortunately, IT did not bother to properly gauge the users' requirements. Second, the business users did not buy into the project. They were unwilling to participate in either the development or the testing of the data warehouse. It sounds to me like the business didn't really want a data warehouse and that the IT department went out on its own to construct one.

To sell the advantages of Web-based delivery to the users, I recommend some user education courses on data warehousing. In these courses it would be important to note that most if not all of the front-end tools are Web-enabled; Web-based delivery is much less expensive and requires less training.

MANAGEMENT REJECTS MULTIDIMENSIONAL TOOLS AS BEING TOO COMPLEX

A team designed a data warehouse for multidimensional analysis, but management thinks the end-user tools that permit such analysis are too difficult to use. The business did not recognize that since multidimensional analysis by its very nature is significantly more flexible than traditional access and analysis, the tools to take advantage of its benefits are equally more complex. The complexity could have been addressed with additional training, but management rejected the requirement for additional training. Management has now rejected the multidimensional tools on the grounds that the users would never want to learn how to use them. How can the data warehouse team salvage the multidimensional tools?

Sid Adelman

The project manager must recognize that not all users are created equal. There are power users as well as users who can't find their keyboards at high noon. The project manager shouldn't try to force a tool on the latter users. They will not accept a tool that they find too complex. As some people in the company use the multidimensional tools, the associated buzz will generate interest and subsequent usage by a larger and larger number of users.

Joyce Bischoff

Maybe the multidimensional tools should not be salvaged at this time. Business users should have a strong say in the selection of tools for analysis. Many successful warehouses have been created without multidimensional tools. After the users are more comfortable with a warehouse environment, multidimensional tools may be considered once again.

Douglas Hackney

The question should not be how to salvage a tool but how to implement a proper solution to the specific business pain. This is a very common example of a team of technologists picking a tool and implementing it rather than focusing on the specific business problem that needed to be solved. If the system were solving life-threatening business pain, there would be no problem getting the users to use the tool, regardless of how complex it was. The project manager should focus on the business needs first and then apply appropriate technologies to meet those needs. The project manager should not set out to implement a tool or technology just because the technology team members believes it is sexy, cool, or would look good listed on their résumés.

Sean Ivoghli

Despite the dream of "enabled" users and enterprise knowledge workers, it is very common for complex analytical tools to be rejected, even with training. Most corporate users of data will still prefer simple reports to a complex analytical platform. Most of them will be happy enough just to have easy access to the reports (via the Web). If the company has an analytical platform that does not allow for the distribution of simple, static, or semi-static reports, then management should probably consider creating a position within each user group that is in charge of business data analytics. This person would live with the users but be a strong data analyst and an expert at using the tool. This person can both create reports and help the users create their own reports. Adoption of these tools may be a lengthy process, but if the users are not using the tools, then they are not using the data warehouse, which could then become endangered. One way or another, the project manager must find a way to get the users to derive value from the data warehouse, even if he or she has to initially spoon-feed them. This suggests that "fishing" for data with analytical tools has proven to be too technically challenging for many would-be users of information and that there is probably a good case for creating "information analytics experts" and embedding them among the business users in order to facilitate the consumption of information.

Chuck Kelley

The problem is that the team designed the data warehouse for a single-tool environment. The data warehouse should be designed to be flexible to feed any tool environment. Multidimensional tools are somewhat more complex than other tools to build but not necessarily more difficult to use. Most multidimensional tools can be made to look like their less complex siblings, so I would use that approach to try and salvage the tools.

David Marco

One of two situations is occurring. First, not all organizations are ready for the tools they need. Data warehousing is a rapidly growing field, and there will come a time when such organizations will be ready to enter it. Second, it is possible that the multidimensional tool was poorly implemented. One of my clients had users who greatly disliked their multidimensional tool; however, when we reviewed this tool's implementation it was absolutely terrible. It appeared to have been installed with minimum tailoring for the client.

Clay Rehm

Sometimes the users do not know all the answers or know exactly what they want. Their moods can change, the business cycles can change, and management resources change. Whatever the reason the tools were rejected, the project manager *must* reintroduce this concept to the users and provide appropriate and thorough training. Rolling out tools without a user-friendly interface or proper training is a sure way to drive users away, never to return.

Before trying to reintroduce the multidimensional tools, the project manager should have an unbiased third party determine whether there are other things possibly wrong with the data warehouse. Are the business requirements being met? Was the data modeled correctly? Are there data quality problems? Are the tools not being used because of political reasons? For example, is the person who selected the tools not respected in the organization? A qualified data warehouse consultant can help answer these questions in a few short weeks.

Bottom line: Invest the time upfront identifying the true problem before dismissing the users' needs or giving up completely.

THE USERS HAVE HIGH DATA QUALITY EXPECTATIONS

The business users have been led to believe that the data they will be seeing will be complete, accurate, and very timely. They came to that conclusion since no one indicated anything to the contrary. What should the data warehouse team do to reset the users' expectations to the reality of what they will be getting?

Sid Adelman

The late Mayor Daley of Chicago was fond of exhorting his followers to "Vote early and vote often." The same should be said for setting user expectations. Users should never be allowed to leave a meeting with overblown expectations for schedule, function, performance, availability, or data quality. Users need to understand which data will be accurate, complete, and timely and which data will not. Some organizations store indicators of quality in their meta data so that users will know what they are getting.

Joyce Bischoff

Users need to understand that the data in the warehouse can be no better than its source. Although it is possible to transform existing data to a common standard, this will not correct the problems with basic data quality. Again, the completeness of the data will depend on the completeness of the source data.

It is up to the data warehouse developers to ensure that the timeliness meets user expectations. If not, either the design is poor or expectations are unrealistic. Improved communication is vital.

Douglas Hackney

Inadequate expectation management is the leading cause of data warehouse project failure. Successful projects require endless repetitive communication, expectation management, and marketing. In this case, the data warehouse team members must take immediate action. They must have one-on-one communication with the users to clearly communicate exactly what the system will contain in terms of data completeness, data accuracy, and timeliness.

Chuck Kelley

Whether or not they were led to believe anything about data quality (in many cases IT does not say anything about it), many people believe that data warehouses, by default, are complete, accurate (perfect), and timely. And data warehouses should be. But they are not. The cost associated with cleaning that "last" record is quite high. The data warehouse team needs to start *today* defining what the data quality of the data warehouse is. *Today*, the data warehouse team needs to understand the issues that result from not having clean data and the cost associated with cleaning that "last" record. The team must develop a strategy and plan to show the users what they are going to get, when they are going to get it, and what the next steps are. The data warehouse team needs to meet with the users as often as it is feasible to reiterate this plan. Finally, the team needs to look forward to see if other similar issues will arise and then start preparing for them *today*.

David Marco

It will be important to educate the users on the quality or lack thereof of their data. Every company within the Global 2000 has data quality issues. Most of these companies have severe quality issues.

It is vital to capture the specific data quality statistics directly in the meta data repository. This information can then be provided directly to the business users on their data warehousing reports (see Figure 5–1 for an example) or in a separate report.

These data quality statistics should be captured during the ETL process of the data warehouse and its data marts. Throughout this step the data warehouse team should be trapping and counting the records that are in error. If the current ETL process does not have this functionality, then the company needs a new data warehouse architect since the current person is not qualified. Many companies do capture these data quality statistics; however, most keep the statistics just for the current data warehouse load run and then delete this vital information, which is the wrong thing to do. These data quality statistics need to be loaded directly into a meta data repository. Then these statistics will be stored and time-stamped in the repository so that the system's data quality can be defined, tracked, and measured over time. You cannot measure what you cannot define, and you cannot improve what you cannot measure.

Larissa Moss

Involve the users on the project—full-time if possible—as soon as possible. The more the users are exposed to all the source data analysis tasks, dirty data discoveries, discussions, and problem resolutions, and the

2001 Monthly Global Sales Report				January 7, 2002
Month	Product Category	Sales $ (in thousands) U.S.	Sales $ (in thousands) International	Sales $ (in thousands) Total
December	TV	22,101	10,200	32,301
	VCR	11,190	4,300	15,490
	Cellular Phone	12,190	7,193	19,383
	Digital	4,002	1,301	5,303
	Micellaneous	1,209	670	2,079
November	TV	42,000	22,200	64,200
	VCR	21,190	9,878	31,068
	Cellular Phone	28,193	12,198	40,386
	Digital	8,901	2,901	11,802
	Micellaneous	2,730	1,530	4,260
October	TV	70,100	22,950	103,050
	VCR	31,900	4,378	46,778
	Cellular Phone	41,700	7,193	59,250
	Digital	20,000	4,301	7,700
	Micellaneous	4,850	2,870	7,700

Data Quality Tracking Statistics
8.4% of the dollar value was not loaded.
1.7% of the records were not loaded.

Figure 5–1: Example of a data quality statistics report. From *Building and Managing the Meta Data Repository* by David Marco. Copyright ©2000 David Marco. All rights reserved. Reproduced here by permission of Wiley Publishing, Inc.

more they participate on the project, the more comfortable they will be with the development approach as well as the final deliverable.

IT has shielded the users for decades from data quality problems, many of which were created by the very same users who now have unreasonable expectations about data quality. Some users create data quality problems "unknowingly" and quite "innocently." For example, users are often frustrated with IT's backlog of change requests and resort to "solving" their own data needs by misusing fields or inventing cryptic values to represent a business rule or copying data into their own private files and manipulating it. They do not always realize the problems they cause for IT and other downstream users, and even for themselves, with their so-called data solutions. They do not realize it because IT has always managed to reconcile and maneuver through their creative data solutions. Since users from many departments have their own private data solutions, the overall condition of the data sources is not universally understood by all users. As a result, users are now surprised that data quality is such a big problem. Shielding the users from their own bad habits must be stopped, and they must get immersed in the projects along with IT, especially since the users are the ones who will have to provide guidance for the cleansing process.

Clay Rehm

Uhh . . . tell them?

Why won't the data be complete, accurate, and very timely? Do the data warehouse team members not have confidence in the data and the data validation procedures, or are the team members under a very tight time line? Whatever the reason, if the expected results will not be delivered (and not just data quality but any part of the data warehouse), the project manager should tell the users the truth immediately. He or she should even consider providing education on how the process of data movement works. When presenting the data warehouse to the users, sponsors, stakeholders, whomever, the project manager should show visual diagrams of the current state, the desired state, and how the warehouse will evolve from the current state to the desired state. He or she should make sure to speak to the challenges as well as the benefits.

The moral of the story: When presenting bad news, do it as soon as you find out about it.

THE USERS DON'T KNOW WHAT THEY WANT

An organization with unforgiving users is attempting a data warehouse. It has become very difficult to get the users to articulate what they want or even why they would want a data warehouse. What should the data warehouse team do?

Sid Adelman

A proof-of-concept could be used to get them interested and to get them thinking about what they want.

Stories about what other organizations in this industry are doing with the data warehouse will often get the users interested and focused on specific applications.

Joyce Bischoff

The data warehouse team should ask top management from the business areas to define the business objectives clearly. The average user may be unaware of business advantages that are possible with a data warehouse. If the business is unsupportive of the project, it will be a waste of time and money. The team must either obtain a business sponsor or cancel the project.

Douglas Hackney

The team members should not initiate a project until they have identified specific business pain that is politically meaningful, measurable, and sustainable and that can be relieved by tabular data. If the organization simply is not ready for a data warehouse, the team should be put on hold and the issue revisited quarterly until such time as the business meets these criteria.

Chuck Kelley

Well, I think this is a problem. First, the data warehouse team needs to develop a group of users that can act as "construction consultants" responsible for helping the team define the requirements. Most users are not sure of what they want until they see something. Data warehouse environments need to be developed in small iterations where the users are constantly seeing new and improved data delivered at their doorstep in a maximum of three-week increments—even if the first iteration has only four measurable facts with four dimensions upon which the users can look at those measures. The team should set up specific times during which the users can provide feedback to the team about the data's accuracy and presentation. Each iteration builds on what has already been done or starts a new area for analysis. Trying to do everything at once will only cause unforgiving users to become more unforgiving. The team wants them involved during the whole process.

David Marco

Prototype . . . prototype . . . prototype. My consulting organization had a very large insurance client that brought us into its data warehousing initiative. The client had previously spent three years and $4.2 million and was still in the design phase of the application. It was clear to me that the end-users were not going to articulate their requirements. Therefore we

cancelled all the design meetings and built a prototype. From this prototype we selected a small target subject area for the data warehouse and in
four months had it up and running. The lesson here: A good prototype
can go a long way.

Larissa Moss

The data warehouse team members should do their homework. If users
don't know what they want, it may indicate one of two situations: (1)
there is no business problem and the users are currently receiving all the
information they need on a timely basis, or (2) there are so many business problems that the users don't know where to start. Therefore, the
first thing the team members should ask themselves is whether they are
building a data warehouse in search of a business problem or whether the
data warehouse really has justification.

If there is justification but the users do not know enough about data
warehousing to recognize it as a solution to their information problems,
the data warehouse team should launch a data warehouse education
series. This should cover discussions of specific business problems as well
as missed business opportunities, the concepts and objectives of data
warehousing, and data warehouse reporting and querying capabilities,
including demonstrations of some tools. The data warehouse team
should then select the most critical business problem with the most willing sponsor for the project. One of the sponsor's responsibilities should
be to take on the role of spokesperson and champion for the data warehouse team and promote it to other business areas. Hopefully, other users
will get data warehouse fever over time.

Clay Rehm

A user who does not know what he or she wants does not necessarily have
a character flaw. IT must reach out and use an iterative process to understand what is needed. IT must get to know the business and get into the
users' heads. By the way, the project plan must accurately show that
requirements gathering will not happen in one day.

(If you are a user and you are reading this—sit down right now and
diagram or document your current business rules, systems, and processes, and diagram or document your desired-state business rules, systems, and processes. Your IT staff will love you for it. Also, don't try to

learn IT; use the time you have to try to understand your business better and what you, your subordinates, and your leaders need in order to be successful. Pass this information on to your IT contacts.)

Does the data warehouse team have appropriate business analyst resources that understand the business, have the respect of the business users, and can translate business terms to technical people and technical terms to business people? If the answer to any of those questions is no, the project manager must recruit a business analyst for the team. A good business analyst is a good communicator, both written and verbal. A good business analyst really understands the business.

If the team members are still having problems gathering requirements, they should consider whether they are

- Collecting existing systems architecture, topology, and data flow
- Collecting existing business processes
- Documenting desired-state business processes using visuals—data flows, process flows, functional flows, and so on

If these suggestions fail, it may be time to perform a readiness assessment. This can be accomplished by an experienced data warehouse professional, whether an internal or external consultant. The goal of the assessment is to determine whether the organization or users are really ready to build a data warehouse.

Would it be possible to demonstrate or prototype something first? Assuming the data warehouse team members know the business, they can take the data they know and create "dueling" prototypes—different versions—to see which one gets the users more excited. I find it is easier to shoot at something that exists instead of trying to create something new.

The data warehouse team should help the users by understanding their business and finding creative ways to articulate that understanding back to the users.

CHAPTER SIX

Team Issues

The greater the loyalty of the members of a group toward the group, the greater is the motivation among the members to achieve the goals of the group, and the greater the probability that the group will achieve its goals.

—Rensis Likert

OVERVIEW

The data warehouse is built not by a single individual but by a team. The makeup, skills, attitude, leadership, and harmony of the team spell the difference between success and failure. The single most important job of a project manager is recruiting and retaining a team that works well together. The roles of the individual members should be well defined, and all team members should feel comfortable in their roles.

The previous experiences each member has had with the other team members is probably more important than any other single factor in predicting how well the people on the team will interact. The respect the members have for each other must be real and cannot be dictated by the project manager. One of the biggest risks to any project manager is having team members who have poor attitudes, bad work habits, or incompatible skills. These people should not be accepted on the team, even temporarily—a temporary assignment may outlast the project manager's tenure. His or her job is not to rehabilitate dysfunctional team members but to implement the project. The project manager should reach a clear understanding with his or her boss about what the job really entails. The boss will be successful only when the project manager is successful, so the boss should support the project manager's efforts to build and sustain a strong team, including the choice to dump team members who could hurt the project.

Team Goals

The team needs to have common goals. For example, while a primary goal of the DBA is a good database design, the overall team goal of a successful implementation must be foremost in everything the DBA does. A terrific database design is wasted if the users don't use the data warehouse. The team members should develop a set of common goals with the users, and the team members should post these goals above their workstations and constantly review the goals to be sure everyone is working toward a common objective. Some examples of specific goals appear in the list below.

- Provide knowledge workers, suppliers, and customers with the tools to make more informed decisions that will result in higher productivity, lower cost, higher-quality products, and shorter time to market.
- Improve the quality of data so that reports are legible, integrated, and summarized.
- Unlock data from the legacy systems.
- Provide better access to and delivery of data.
- Make available more flexible information from multiple sources.
- Increase data consistency.
- Satisfy the diverse needs of a broad range of users.
- Provide the metrics of performance, usage, and user satisfaction.
- Provide access to integrated data.
- Enable users to obtain a historical perspective of the data.
- Deliver information in a more timely manner.
- Ensure data quality and integrity.
- Eliminate many production reports.
- Minimize requests for new reports, particularly ad hoc reports.
- Minimize the effort previously required to reconcile inconsistent reports.

An overall goal of a data warehouse is to deliver to the users a system that has the following characteristics:

- Very high-quality data
- High availability
- Good performance
- Flexibility
- Data integrated from multiple sources
- Easy expandability when incorporating new data
- Low risk
- High user acceptance
- Cost justified
- Ability to deliver the data warehouse in a reasonable period of time
- A set of capabilities that provide a significant and positive impact on the organization

Incentives

Significant rewards given to the whole team provide an incentive that often breaks down differences and disagreements among the team members. Large bonuses given to specific team members can cause resentment and animosity toward the recipients. Significant bonuses (for example, one month's salary) at milestones and at project completion can help forge a very effective team.

These bonuses also provide incentive for the team members to remain on the project. The last thing a project manager wants is for key individuals to leave before the team completes the project. This doesn't just mean leaving the organization; good people are always in demand from other parts of the organization.

Consultants and Contractors

Consultants are major players in the data warehouse arena. They assess the situation, give advice, help plan the implementation, and sometimes provide the complete implementation. They have varying degrees of influence which, when overly powerful, can often create problems with the existing IT staff. This can be very demoralizing to the existing employees since they are unable to significantly influence the process and direction of the data warehouse project. Consultants have been known to misrepresent their ability to rescue a data warehouse organization and its project from an impending failure. Consultants often appear to be overly optimistic. Organizations must assure themselves of the consultants' capabilities.

Consultants and contractors can make a significant contribution to a data warehouse project, but the question is how best to use them and their expertise. Organizations also need to know how to make the best use of a budget for consultants and contractors.

When consultants and contractors have been allowed to do all the work on a data warehouse themselves, they end up being the only ones who know the system. If they leave, the organization is left with employees who have not been allowed to learn the system. The documentation is rarely adequate for helping the employees fully understand the system. Contracts often include a section on knowledge transfer to the full-time employees, but consultants often ignore these clauses. Inadequate schedules can become a reason for bypassing the knowledge transfer part of the agreement.

Many organizations outsource all or part of their IT operations. In such a situation, the data warehouse manager must still consider whether to outsource the data warehouse. If he or she decides not to outsource the project, the question becomes one of how to go against the organization outsourcing standard and represent to management that the data warehouse should not be outsourced.

In the remainder of this chapter, we explore eleven situations that deal with team issues and consultant issues.

A Heat-Seeking Employee Threatens the Project

The company has a very bright, hard-working person in IT who dearly wants to bring in a beta release (code that is not generally available) from his favorite vendor. If he doesn't get his way, he either will leave or will be less than supportive of the project. This beta code would be used in the data warehouse implementation. What should the project manager (the employee's boss) do?

Sid Adelman

The project manager should not allow the inclusion of any code critical to the project that has not been thoroughly tested and used in production by other organizations. The project manager needs to change the mind-set of this heat seeker, perhaps with a bonus system that includes as conditions the success of the project and a reduction of project risk (both of which would be compromised by beta code).

Joyce Bischoff

The project manager should bring in the beta release and allow the IT person to support it on a time-available basis. However, the beta release should not be used for the warehouse implementation until the beta code has been proven to be successful.

Douglas Hackney

The project manager should explain to the employee that he can use the beta code in a laboratory in an experimental fashion to explore its potential uses for future releases, but the beta code cannot and will not be used in a production release of the data warehouse.

Sean Ivoghli

The project manager should not compromise the success of the project to appease the employee's infatuation with immature, bleeding-edge technology. Data warehouse projects are inherently saturated with technology risks due to the requirement for integrating different technologies from different vendors. Introducing any beta release software into the mix creates significant additional risk. I would look into what makes the bright IT person tick and why he is pressing for this technology. Is he bored with the tools he is currently using? If so, maybe he would get excited about using some other, more proven, new technology. If that didn't work, I would try to convince him to wait until the software is mature and the bugs are worked out. If this vendor is a popular one, that shouldn't take long—perhaps just a phase or two down the road. If I couldn't appease this person some other way by giving him something else that he needs, and if he isn't mature enough to recognize the value of efforts to reduce risk, I would consider that it may not be as big a loss as I might fear to lose him in the long run. Being a team player is a very valuable attribute of any developer.

Chuck Kelley

The project manager should ask, "Would I consider the introduction of beta code on an operational system?" If a hard worker wanted to put unproven software into your bread-and-butter reservation system, would you allow that, even if the employee threatened to leave? I doubt it. The question in the situation posed above centers around what type of software is involved. My assumption is that the software is ETL. I doubt the database or end-user access tool would be involved in this type of question.

The schedule must be the driver. If the schedule allows sufficient time for testing beta software, then I would be inclined to allow for testing of the code, but I would make it clear that the schedule must be met either with or without the beta code. I would require agreement between the heat-seeking employee and the rest of the team that he will not slow down anyone else's schedule because of the use of beta software. I would set a cutoff date after which he could no longer use the beta release if it gets in the way of the project schedule. And lastly, I would make an agreement with him about the risks he would incur (up to and including his dismissal) if he did not follow the schedule.

David Marco

I would allow the employee to bring in the code and run his own testing of it. I would meet with him to define the criteria that the code will need to pass in order to be included in the data warehouse project. If the code didn't pass all the testing criteria, I wouldn't accept the use of the beta code. The key is defining the criteria up front, before the employee brings the beta code into the project. This way I would have his support at the onset.

Clay Rehm

If I were the project manager, I would ask myself, "Which is more important: to keep this employee or to deliver a successful data warehouse?"

It is important to keep good people around, especially if they have positive attitudes, work hard, accept extra assignments, take the initiative, and provide solid results. The most important quality I look for is someone who gets along with the business users. I like someone who can build a rapport with the users, building a solid relationship and getting to know what they really want and need.

As his manager, I would have a candid discussion with him to determine what drives him. Is it that he really believes in the vendor product, or is it that he gets credit and visibility from being the one who chose the product? I would discover his motivation—why is this vendor his favorite?

Did the vendor send him goodies? Does he really know the differences between the vendors? Does he know his stuff?

I would also look into whether our company has incentive plans. If the tool this employee picks makes the project a success, will he be compensated as a result? If the product fails and hurts the project, will there be serious consequences to him that are written in the contract that I, he, and the legal department signed? I would call his bluff—is he willing to bet his career with our company on this product? Would he be willing to get fired or demoted because he believed so firmly in this product, even if it does not work?

As a project manager, I would determine what is best for the company and resolve how the employees can meet those needs and have their interests met at the same time.

MANAGEMENT ASSIGNED DYSFUNCTIONAL TEAM MEMBERS TO THE DATA WAREHOUSE PROJECT

A project manager has been given a team composed of members who are unskilled and unmotivated—generally the dregs of the company employees, those whom other managers did not want on their teams. The project manager has been asked to do the best she can. What should she do?

Sid Adelman

With this type of team, the project manager has no chance to succeed. It's time for her to have a heart-to-heart talk with her boss about success. Assuming the boss will be measured by the project's success, he or she needs a reality check. The boss needs to understand and believe the futility of attempting a project with such a nonperforming staff. The project manager should ask for the authority to choose her own staff.

Joyce Bischoff

There are several alternatives the project manager could try.

- Schedule training classes to bring skill levels to the necessary levels.
- Allow selected individuals to attend data warehouse conferences.
- Augment the staff with enthusiastic consultants who will transfer knowledge to the team.

- Arrange visits to other companies that have enthusiastic teams and successful data warehouses.
- Provide articles and materials to team members regarding data warehousing and discuss the articles at team meetings.

If all else fails, the project manager should explain to management that this team does not have the basic qualifications needed to build a warehouse. If management will not replace the unmotivated employees, the project manager should cancel the project.

Douglas Hackney

The best bet is to pair these resources with proven, experienced data warehouse consultants who can both deliver some incremental value to the business and educate the team members, to the extent possible. Given normal turnover and attrition it will be possible to build a valid and viable data warehousing team over the course of several iterations.

Chuck Kelley

The biggest thing the project manager can do is to try to motivate the team members. Maybe an offsite group meeting will allow them to build relationships and motivate them to work as a team. The team can be evaluated by seeing how well the individuals get along with each other. Next, the project manager can put in place an incentive structure. Bonuses can mean either money or deadline parties. For one project I worked on, we held a team party once a month during the first three months of the schedule. After that, the party occurred when we met certain major deadlines. While this is hard to do with a data warehouse project since the deadlines may come at a more rapid pace, the project manager could institute other types of incentives.

Alas, there are times when management will not be willing to do this. Then the project manager needs to understand why these folks are the dregs of the company. When I coached soccer, I was once given a team of kids whom no other coach wanted. They were largely new to the sport and undisciplined, and some were unmotivated (their parents made them do it). So I decided to develop the team by making soccer fun and by using incentives to change their mindsets. I would apply this same principle to this data warehousing situation.

David Marco

Unskilled employees can be trained; however, motivation is another matter. I would first analyze each person to gauge whether he or she is unmotivated because of treatment received in the previous department or because he or she is unmotivated by nature. An employee who is unmotivated by nature won't likely change, and the project manager needs to cut the person loose.

Larissa Moss

The best the project manager could do is to replace these unskilled and unmotivated dregs with a high-powered SWAT team, but she obviously is not in a position to do that. Her second-best solution is to get on a different project. If that is not an option either, the project manager must understand that she is accepting the position of being a psychologist, mother, mentor, and babysitter in addition to being the project manager.

In order to get her dysfunctional team functioning, she has to understand the psyche and motivation of every person on the team. She will have to spend hours "therapizing" the team members into wanting to work as a high-powered team, which starts by getting them excited about learning new skills. Not having the right skills is not the problem here; not having the desire to learn new skills is. If the project manager can get her team members to acquire new skills, she will have to continuously mentor them and reassure them that they're doing a good job. In addition, she must be prepared to referee petty problems among team members and deal with other work-related or family problems her team members may have.

Realizing her predicament, I hope this project manager will reconsider her first two options: to remove either the current team or herself from the project. After all, management does not seem to value her or the data warehouse project much if the executives expect her to function with an unskilled and unmotivated team.

Clay Rehm

The project manager should run! Or she could look at this as the second-biggest challenge she might face (second to the situation in which IT is the project's assassin; see Chapter 1).

The project manager must get to know her team before doing any-thing else. She could take each team member out to lunch or visit each one on a weeknight or the weekend to find out why he or she is not moti-vated. Maybe someone close just left or died, maybe his or her living con-ditions are not good, maybe he or she is going through a divorce.... The project manager should find out what skills each team member currently has and what skills he or she wants to have. What do the team members really want to do? They may be unmotivated because they have been passed over on promotions or never received the training they were promised.

The point is, before giving up on the team, the project manager should really find out what the problems are for each person. Each team member has a different story, and it needs to be heard. The project man-ager could enlist the help of a peer or even hire a professional coaching mentor to provide assistance. This will be very time consuming, so the project manager should expect to spend some very long weeks on this process. If I were the project manager, I would ask someone to conduct one or more personality profiles (such as the Myers-Briggs Type Indica-tor [MBTI], the Birkman Method, the Communication Profile [DISC], and the Personal Interests, Attitudes, and Values inventory [PIAV]) of each team member to determine his or her best work style, strengths, and weaknesses. For this effort to be successful, the project manager must also be a coach, a mentor, and a teacher.

When preparing time lines and scope documents, the project man-ager should take into account that she does not have the people in place who can deliver. She must extend the time lines to include training and education of the team and the time she will spend dealing with people issues, coaching, mentoring, and teaching. She needs to bring onto the team a good resource to use as an example for the others, so the schedule must also include time to find a high-quality person and bring him or her up to speed. The team must be trained before starting the project. The project manager must create and maintain a training plan for each team member. Education is vital; the project manager should start sending her team members to appropriate training immediately.

I would encourage the project manager to watch movies like *Hard-ball*, *Mighty Ducks*, and others that show how a ragtag team that has no expectations of ever winning can actually win while the players learn valuable lessons along the way. If it is important to keep each team member, then the project manager must take the time to identify his or her work style; is each one a "don't know," a "can't do," or a "don't care" type of person?

The moral of the story: Don't give up on anyone until you have really tried to make things work.

MANAGEMENT REQUIRES TEAM CONSENSUS

Management wants everyone on the data warehouse team to get along and wants consensus from the team members before making any moves. One or two team members always disagree with the project manager or the rest of the team. This has seriously delayed making decisions and moving ahead with the project. The project is now in jeopardy of slipping. What should management do?

Sid Adelman

First of all, management should understand that while total consensus is a great idea, it is not appropriate for moving a project along expeditiously. Management needs to understand that if schedules are important (and you can bet they are), someone needs to be given the authority to make decisions. These decisions should be made after consultation with specific team members who have knowledge of the situation and are versed in the technical reasons for going one way or another. However, the team members and management should understand that consensus is not the goal—delivering a high-quality product on time and within budget is.

Joyce Bischoff

The project manager must be strong enough to make a decision and stick with it. After all the discussions and consensus building, if the dissenters are obstructing progress, the project manager should remove them from the team.

Sean Ivoghli

The approach of "it takes a village to make a decision" does not work for IT projects. Someone who is qualified needs to take charge and lead. In a data warehouse project, that person is either the project manager or the data warehouse architect. It is better to make decisions and take action than to do nothing. Of course, the company must use a project manager or data warehouse architect who has adequate experience and a good track record. Yes, mistakes will be made. They always are; but they can also be corrected. The biggest mistake is to do nothing. In this case it seems as if the project manager lacks either the appropriate experience or leadership skills. He or she can make up for a lack of experience by hiring an experienced data warehouse architect. However, if the project manager lacks leadership skills, he or she shouldn't be a project manager.

Chuck Kelley

I am a firm believer that we cannot all just "get along." If we all got along, there would be no challenge—no working outside the box. These important challenges keep us from doing what we always did before.

In this case, the data warehouse champion within management *must* step in and settle the consensus. *Consensus* does not mean *unanimous*. The project manager needs to work for consensus but has a job to complete. Slips in schedules and increases in budgets should cause the champion and management some heartburn. If not, then maybe the organization will not see the benefits of the data warehouse enough to complete the implementation.

David Marco

I would sit the two problem children down and have a very clear discussion on the ramifications of their actions on the project. Then either they will change their ways or I will have them rearranging desks in our Siberian location.

Larissa Moss

Since the project manager and the business sponsor have the ultimate responsibility for the data warehouse project, it is in both of their interests to set the rules for the game. If management by consensus has been tried and failed (as it always does), the sponsor must protect his or her interests by convincing management to give the project manager and the sponsor the authority to make the final decisions.

As an interim solution and a means to convince management that team consensus is neither necessary nor desirable, a short brief could be prepared by the project manager and the business sponsor listing the issue, the opinions, and the final votes—just as the Supreme Court does. After one or two such exercises (to give management the benefit of understanding the concerns behind the dissenting votes), management will hopefully be convinced of the impracticality of team consensus. Hopefully the executives will trust the project manager and the sponsor from that point forward to make decisions that are in the best interest of the company without requiring lengthy justifications or team consensus.

If management is not comfortable with that solution, external consultants may be called in as the tiebreakers. However, this solution is not only pricey but will also further solidify any feelings the project manager may have of being considered untrustworthy or incompetent.

A third alternative is to bring in an organizational development consultant to evaluate the situation and provide his or her expert recommendations to management. If the project manager cannot convince management of the ludicrousness of management by consensus, maybe the organizational development consultant can.

Clay Rehm

It is easier to be critical than to be creative.

The solution to this situation is simple. One person must listen to all input and make the final decision. Successful projects rarely have too many cooks in the kitchen. Successful projects require a strong leader who is not afraid of failure, embarrassment, risk, and so on. The role of the project manager can be compared to the role of the U.S. president. Neither is intimately involved with details, and each relies on other people to present the facts he or she needs to make the tough decisions, right or wrong.

The project will be successful only if management puts one individual in charge, someone with authority and accountability. This high-stress, high-risk position needs to provide value and benefit to the person in charge. Additionally, management must enforce a new policy: any team member who challenges decisions must either provide documented, factual, alternative solutions or keep quiet and refrain from bad-mouthing the decision makers. There must be negative consequences for the bad apples.

Project managers need to be strong; they hold the positions they do to make the tough decisions. They need to start making them.

PRIMA DONNAS ON THE TEAM CREATE DISSENSION

A project manager was able to sell management on the need to have very bright and talented people on her team. She handpicked almost all of her team members, and to the dismay of their previous managers she was able to get these folks transferred to her team. Most of these people were the stars in their departments and were used to setting direction; their managers and coworkers alike accepted their recommendations with little comment or disagreement. Now the project manager has found these folks to be not only stars but also prima donnas who don't like accepting ideas from other stars. These stars disagree so much that they are unproductive. What should the project manager do?

Sid Adelman

The project manager's job in this situation boils down to the following three tasks.

1. *Develop a common set of goals embraced by all team members.* The team members must clearly know the goals and objectives of the project, and the members must all aim at achieving those objectives. The objectives should be measurable, such as the delivery date, the level of data quality, the function delivered, the tangible benefits achieved, and, most importantly, the happiness of users actually running queries and reports.
2. *Develop an accepted process for airing positions, evaluating those positions, and making decisions.* The strong differences of opinion must be voiced, but the discussions and evaluations should not jeopardize the success of the project. The rule must be that after a decision is made, that's it; there is to be no more time spent on continuing to reevaluate the facts and the decision.
3. *Build a team spirit.* The project manager can encourage a team spirit by offering common rewards for achieving the objectives of the project. This means that individual team members should not be singled out

for praise. The rewards should go to everyone on the team, and these rewards, if possible, should be substantial. T-shirts are nice, but bonus money carries more weight.

Joyce Bischoff

The project manager should take the following steps.

1. *Schedule team-building exercises and, possibly, a social event.*
2. *Be very objective in defining issues and alternatives, clearly identifying the contentious issues and the alternative solutions.* The project manager should ask the whole team to identify the pros and cons of each alternative, with no constraints on what is accepted. This is best handled in a group meeting but may be handled through written documents that can be consolidated and reviewed at a project meeting. In my experience, the ideal solution usually becomes obvious when all pros and cons are clearly stated in a reviewable format and the team has an open discussion.
3. *Project members who are unable to be team players should be replaced.*

Douglas Hackney

The project manager should leverage the organizational development or human resources group to resolve these conflicts. I have found offsite workshops facilitated by neutral parties to be particularly effective. Bringing in an industry expert whom the majority of the team respects to arbitrate some disputes may also be effective.

Sean Ivoghli

The problem is not that all the team members are stars. The problem is that they all want to be the leader and the most valuable player of the team. Stars come in many shapes and forms. Some are quiet, competent performers. Some are vocal leaders. Some are creative visionaries. The problem here is that the personalities of the team members are not compatible enough to produce the desired result. The project manager should clearly define the roles and responsibilities of every team member. There should be no doubt about who is responsible for what decision. Although she should encourage collaboration, she should also make the team members aware of their roles and make it clear that their performances will be measured primarily on their abilities to perform their responsibilities and to do so in the given team environment. Troublemakers should be reprimanded or, if their behaviors don't improve, replaced with better team players.

Chuck Kelley

Working with stars is one of the most horrible experiences. The project manager must stroke their egos while continually trying to move the project forward. One thing I would do is bring in an organization development specialist to help the members of the team become a team. These "touchy-feely" folks are great at helping people understand motivations. These things do not happen overnight—it will take time to make the stars work as a team, and each team member must be willing to change. If they cannot find a way to work together, then maybe the project manager needs to transfer some of the stars to another project to make the team more cohesive.

David Marco

Everybody on a project team has to play a role. This includes the project manager. At the beginning of a project I make sure that everyone is keenly aware of their roles and the hierarchy of the team. As the old saying goes, there is no "I" in "team."

Clay Rehm

The project manager must determine which stars she can live without. She should figure out who has skills in different areas and get rid of the overlapping talent. She especially needs to get rid of the negative resources. The project manager should bring in a consultant who has experience with data warehousing and bring in junior people who are ready to provide good ideas even if they don't have experience.

The project manager simply doesn't have the time to deal with this kind of immature and unprofessional behavior. Each team member will demand attention; therefore not all of them can work on this team. She should keep on the team only the people who want to make a difference, who want and like to work with users, who honestly want to build a system for the users and not for their own résumés.

Bottom line: As a manager, do not tolerate negativity and egos.

TEAM MEMBERS AREN'T HONEST ABOUT PROGRESS ON ASSIGNMENTS

The members of a data warehouse team did not want to look bad, so they weren't forthcoming about the statuses of their assignments. This meant that other team members who depended on the completion of those assignments were themselves delayed. In addition, the project manager was unable to accurately represent the status of the project to management. How can the project manager convince the team members to accurately reflect their progress on assignments?

Sid Adelman

There must be some history here of needing to look good. There must have been rewards, or more likely punishment, for representing anything but wonderful successes. If the norm is to give only good news, the project manager shouldn't expect the team members to suddenly change. They will need to feel comfortable telling the truth, and it will take some time to build their trust. It may help to restrict the individual members' status reports to only your team.

Joyce Bischoff

Status reports may not always be honest. In this situation, the project manager needs to sit down with each employee and perform a detailed review of the current status of each deliverable. It is also helpful to print a PERT (Program Evaluation and Review Technique) chart showing the dependencies of each activity. By highlighting all completed activities and displaying the PERT chart at project meetings, it becomes obvious who is holding up progress. The chart can also be displayed on a wall outside the project manager's office so that everyone can see it. In my experience, this method usually has a positive effect because no one wants to look bad.

Douglas Hackney

This behavior will not change without consequences. Unless and until the project management team implements consequences for inaccurate reporting, this activity will continue. A graduated scale of consequences should be implemented, with removal from the team being the ultimate consequence.

Chuck Kelley

I think a good project manager needs to work with each team member to have a constant understanding of where that member of the team is in terms of progress on assignments. Rather than relying on status reports and weekly reports, the project manager should feel comfortable talking to each team member as an individual to learn how the team member is doing with assignments and how the project manager can help. For example, the project manager could ask how the team member solved a particular problem. This can give the project manager a handle on what is happening.

No one likes to feel that "Big Brother" is watching him or her, but the project manager is responsible for delivering a quality product, on time and on budget. The project manager needs to build an environment where the team members feel comfortable giving bad news, knowing there will be no serious repercussions. In fact, having a worse repercussion when team members provide inaccurate status reports is important in the team environment. To move a project forward, a project manager needs people who ask for help when they need it. The project manager in this scenario should try to instill in each team member the idea that "If you haven't figured it out in one hour, you should ask someone." Then the project manager can know what is happening with each member of the team.

David Marco

When an assignment is falling behind and other people are expecting it to be completed, the problem becomes highly magnified. I always tell my employees that there are only three things that will get them into trouble with me: (1) a lack of motivation, (2) dishonesty, and (3) an attempt to hide a problem. I always tell my team members that I will not be upset with them if they are doing the very best they can but are still falling behind. On the other hand, I remind them, if I don't know they are falling behind, I cannot do anything to make sure that the overall project time lines are not impacted. Bad news only gets worse over time.

Larissa Moss

It appears that this data warehouse team is organized in a traditional way: team members are assigned certain tasks and are expected to work on these tasks individually until the tasks are done and can be handed over to the next person. This is the wrong team approach for data warehouse projects.

In a SWAT team or think tank approach, the work performed by team members is self-regulating and not dependent on anyone's honest status reporting. Every member of the SWAT team, including the project manager, shares equally in the responsibility of planning, assigning, performing, controlling, and reviewing tasks. The SWAT team meets every day to review which team members are performing which tasks and to discuss any problems discovered or resolved. Therefore, everybody on the team automatically knows the status on a daily basis. Problems and solutions are discussed, proposed, tried, and reviewed by the entire SWAT team as they come up. If a team member falls behind on an assigned task, it is known immediately because the team as a whole is responsible for discovering and resolving problems and for helping each other with assigned tasks. There is no handing over of a work deliverable after a task is completed; only the "lead hat" is transferred from one team member to another while work on that deliverable is continued seamlessly.

Clay Rehm

The project manager must educate the team on the importance of communication, no matter if it is positive or negative news. How can the project manager do this? He or she could schedule an initial meeting with the whole team on the impact of communication, using examples of how not telling the project manager makes the project manager and the whole team look bad. He or she should tell the team members, "If we are not communicating, we do not look to the client like a solid, well-oiled team."

Starting immediately, the project manager should require each team member to submit a detailed, written weekly status report. If the deliverables are not produced, it is up to the project manager to ride herd on the team member for the report or to understand the reason it is not done. The project manager has no control over people's honesty. However, the project manager has the unique opportunity to influence people's lives in a positive or negative way.

If deliverables are not done right the first time, they will just have to be done again, which can cause further frustrations and delays. I believe in the "three strikes" method. I give each person three chances to improve or

I let them go. This may sound harsh, but when working in a professional environment with high stakes, there is no excuse for wanting anything less. I don't agree with keeping people around who are not productive—the people who work hard at not working! Project managers shouldn't even think twice about removing such employees from the project.

If he or she hasn't done so already, the project manager should hire a project management assistant to manage the update of the project plan and to check up where everyone is each week. This person will keep the project plan up-to-date and will follow up with team members on tasks. The assistant would bring the concerns and issues to the project manager to resolve.

In summary: Project managers should not tolerate team members who do not communicate.

A CONSULTANT OFFERS TO COME TO THE RESCUE

The data warehouse was built years ago and can no longer satisfy the needs of the business. A large consulting organization has convinced management that consultants can bring order out of chaos and solve all the data warehouse problems. What should the CIO do?

Sid Adelman

The CIO should be careful; the consultants might lull the company into believing they really can solve all the data warehouse problems. It's wise to be skeptical of any such representations. Real life is not like that. We are no longer children who believe in the Easter Bunny. The CIO should consider the cost of not having the data warehouse for some period of time if the consultants do not deliver. The CIO should also determine how failure will affect the reputation of the business. The CIO should ask the consultants how they plan to go about fixing all the problems and then evaluate their solutions, capabilities, and commitment to the CIO's organization. The CIO should ask the consultants to back up the proposal with specific and substantial written guarantees in the event the consultants cannot solve all the data warehouse problems.

Joyce Bischoff

First, the CIO should identify all the problems and develop a plan for solving them. He or she should bring in a team of experts to perform a detailed evaluation of the data warehouse. The result should be a set of recommendations the CIO can then review. Without such an assessment, it is unlikely that any consulting firm will be successful.

Douglas Hackney

First, the CIO should be very wary of the economic model used by large consulting organizations. In many cases, project leaders are rewarded and receive bonuses based on the number of people who can be placed at the client site. Second, the CIO should be wary of one-size-fits-all solutions mandated by the consulting organization's methodology. Thirdly, the CIO should be wary of hardware and software vendor relationships with the consulting firm. The firm might try to sell the CIO unnecessary tools and technologies that are part of an incentive package contained in the relationship between the consulting company and the hardware or software vendor. Finally, the CIO should insist on knowledge transfer. Large consulting companies are well known for cooking fish dinners but not well known for teaching clients how to fish.

Sean Ivoghli

The CIO should use internal staff members to identify the inadequacies of the data warehouse. Their loyalties are (or should be) with the organization. Once the CIO has identified the problems, he or she should try to find the reasons behind them. The CIO should itemize and prioritize the issues and then issue a request for proposals (RFP) to find a consulting firm to help with the solutions. If possible, the CIO should avoid using consultants to identify the problems since their interests lie in providing more services. If the CIO does use consultants to identify inadequacies, the CIO should make sure the consultants know that they (or any of their partners) will be disqualified from participating in the RFP. The CIO may want to make an exception to this approach in the case of a candidate consultant with whom the CIO has worked enough to have faith in the consultant's integrity. Even so, the CIO should make sure to involve the employees in the process as much as possible.

Chuck Kelley

First, I would ask for a fixed-price contract. If the consultants know all the problems, then they can solve all the problems at a fixed cost. I would put a clause in the contract stating that if the consultants miss deadlines, the rest of the work will be paid for at a discount rate.

I doubt that the large consulting organization can see more problems than the CIO can. This is similar to an issue a customer of mine had. This consulting organization spoke with the senior management staff members and told them to rewrite the application to use state-of-the-art, bleeding-edge technology. The consultants said they could do it for $2 million. I told the CIO to accept it as a fixed-price contract, but the consulting organization ran. There was no way to do the job for that amount.

David Marco

Larger consulting firms tend to struggle in their data warehousing initiatives. Often these groups bring in the fresh-out-of-college, "Mongolian horde" developers. This type of approach is not going to be successful. I would recommend that the CIO create a data warehouse center of excellence (COE) comprised of people (internal and external) who truly understand how data warehousing projects need to be conducted. The people involved in the COE would then check on the work done by the large consulting company and ensure that the consultants had the correct skill sets and performed the work properly.

Larissa Moss

Not all consultants are created equal, and one size (of consultant) does not fit all problems. In order to pick the right consultants for the job, the CIO must understand the original goals of the data warehouse and why the data warehouse has outgrown those goals. Is it because of scalability problems, outdated technology or tools, the wrong database design, a corrupted database, dirty and unreliable data, or long ETL and maintenance cycles?

The CIO should review each individual consultant's background and determine whether his or her expertise really fits the problem. After the consultants have been made familiar with the problems, the CIO must ascertain whether the consultants understand the root causes for the company's data warehouse problems and whether they know how to correct them. To determine that, the consultants should be asked to describe how they resolved a similar situation at another company. That company as well as others that have been clients of those individual consultants (not the consulting firm as a whole) should be called for references.

A note of caution: Large consulting firms have been known to send their high-powered senior consultants to close the deal and then turn the actual work over to their rookie hires, who are often little more than trained beginners on one or two popular products.

Clay Rehm

There is a good chance the consultants can bring order to the chaos and solve the data warehouse problems. So how can the CIO find out if they can? He or she should hire someone who has solved such problems successfully many times before and even has had failures.

When evaluating data warehouse consultants, the CIO should take the following steps:

- Review their methodology.
- Review their references.
- Actually see what they created before by visiting the sites of previous clients.
- Ask what their deliverables will be.
- Ask about their estimated time frames and costs, focusing not on price comparisons but on how realistic the consultants are when estimating project schedules and budgets.
- View examples of documentation from previous projects.
- Give the consultants opportunities to show what they know about the business and the business problem(s).

An assessment is always in order and should be expected. A realistic assessment can be completed in four to eight weeks. The CIO should expect a detailed document to come from this assessment, one that does not sugarcoat anything. If the consultants don't tell it like it is, the CIO should consider using someone else. Consultants are extremely helpful, but the CIO must do his or her homework and research to find the right fit for the organization.

THE CONSULTANTS ARE RUNNING THE SHOW

The new CIO came from one of the big consulting organizations and brought three of his lieutenants with him. These lieutenants now hold the important positions in the IT organization. All the data warehouse project teams report to one of these managers. This manager has contracted with his old organization for consulting help for the new data warehouse project. The project manager has been asked to work with these consultants, who seem to have an inordinate amount of power and influence over the data warehouse project. In fact, the consultants have seriously undermined the views and positions of the project manager. The bills are piling up, and it looks like the project will be way over budget. What should the project manager do?

Sid Adelman

The project manager needs to decide if he or she is willing to take a second seat to the consultants. There is no way the project manager will ever be able to convince management that he or she should have the primary authority on the project, and if the project fails, the project manager is sure to catch the blame. If the project manager is unwilling to accept a secondary position with little authority and decision-making capability yet the potential for shouldering all the blame, it's time to get off the project and do something else.

Joyce Bischoff

The project manager should sit down with the consulting managers and the IT manager who has responsibility for the project and review the current status and costs. Projections of future costs should be made with the involvement of all interested parties. The project manager should make sure that management understands what it will cost if things continue as they have been. He or she should try to convince the consulting firm to provide a fixed price for completion of the project. A decision can then be made regarding the future of the project.

Douglas Hackney

The project manager should seek new employment. This is a no-win, no-way-out situation. The new CIO will continue to surround himself with cronies and will protect them from their mistakes and provide cover for the excessive billings of the resources they bring in. It is not unusual for there to be a financial kickback arrangement between the ex-consultant CIO and his lieutenants and the contracted consulting organization. It is better for the project manager to get out while he or she can, with dignity and integrity intact.

Sean Ivoghli

With this kind of politics and relationships all the way up to the CIO, the project manager has three choices.

1. Join the party. (He or she doesn't have the political clout to do anything about this.)
2. Look for another job. (His or her position may be endangered anyway.)
3. Find an ally on the business side and start fighting back. (This is risky, but if the project manager is at the end of the rope and feels righteous, this could be his or her only choice.)

Personally, I wouldn't waste my talents on an organization that doesn't appreciate them. Plenty of companies would love to have an experienced project manger who cares about what he or she is doing.

Chuck Kelley

First, it should be made very clear who is responsible for the acceptance of the project. If it is the project manager, then the project manager needs to make sure that he or she has the authority to make the decisions. Without authority, responsibility is a problem waiting to occur. If the project manager doesn't have decision-making authority, he or she should make sure that the new CIO understands that if the project manager has no authority over the project, there is no guarantee of success.

If the CIO agrees to give authority to the project manager, then the project manager needs to keep track of every decision that is not followed or overturned by either the CIO or one of his lieutenants. The project manager should provide a weekly, bimonthly, or monthly status report of all these items and forward it to the CIO along with commentary about the effects of those decisions on the overall possibility of project success. If there are several such issues and success is in jeopardy, then dusting off the old résumé may be high on the project manager's list. If the CIO does not agree to give the project manager authority and continues to make the project manager the responsible party, then the project manager should definitely pull out that résumé. He or she is headed for disaster.

David Marco

The project manager must clearly document the situation that will occur with the data warehousing project. The project manager will not be able to change the direction of the CIO. Therefore the project manager should either update his or her résumé, move to another project, or do the best job he or she can (while continuing to document the situation) until a new CIO comes into the company. The project manager should keep in mind that the average stay for a CIO is 18 months, so the likelihood of the CIO and his lieutenants leaving the company is fairly strong.

Larissa Moss

Assuming the project manager has already voiced his or her concerns about the budget and the schedule, and assuming those concerns have been repeatedly rejected or ignored by his or her manager as well as the consultants, it would be futile for the project manager to seek remedy from within IT. The project manager must either get the business sponsor to become his or her ally and support his or her position or the project manager should leave the project so as not to go down with the sinking ship and possibly even be blamed for it.

If the sponsor is a respected senior business executive with a strong commitment to the project and a willingness to be involved, the project manager should approach him or her with the budgetary and scheduling concerns. The sponsor could arrange for a meeting with the CIO, the consultants, and the project team to hear all views and positions. The sponsor could even hire another independent consultant for advice on a particular issue that is in dispute. Bottom line: Without support from an influential business executive, the project manager has two choices: go along with the program or quit the project.

Clay Rehm

There is nothing wrong with the fact that the consultants have power and influence—in fact, that's what they need to get through the inordinate amounts of red tape at most companies. However, if the consultants ignore the views of the users and project manager, then for whom are the consultants building the data warehouse?

The project manager needs to document everything that has been done to date:

- Project definition
- Scope statement

- Requirements document
- Design document
- Weekly status reports
- Updated project plan

The project manager should conduct a working session with the consultants to review the goals, objectives, and scope of the project and determine whether the consultants are on board. The project manager should identify and document the areas in which the consultants' views differ from the organization's views.

The project manager should demand from the consultant manager a resource plan of how many resources of each type are required and for how long. With support from his or her manager, the project manager should contact the consultant manager and require that he or she produce weekly status reports from each resource working onsite.

The project manager should ask him- or herself these questions.

- Is each consultant resource adding value?
- Are the consultants moving the project forward or are they just cashing in?
- Does each consultant resource have a client counterpart? If not, why not?

After documenting the facts, the project manager should schedule and conduct with management a presentation of those facts, without any emotion and without looking like an "anticonsultant." The project manager should be prepared to handle any questions asked by management.

Even if the consultants are in charge of the project, the project manager should conduct regular reviews of the goals, scope, and requirements for reality and sanity checks.

THE CONTRACTORS HAVE FLED

A data warehouse was built three years ago. None of the contractors who developed the system have remained, and the meager documentation is poor and out of date. The data is dirty, and there are no controls for data integrity. The users are unhappy with the existing data warehouse. A new data warehouse manager has been given responsibility for all the data warehouse activity in the organization. What should this data warehouse manager do?

Sid Adelman

The data warehouse manager must determine whether the existing system can and should be salvaged. A few questions must be answered.

1. Are the users using the existing system?
2. Are these users dependent on the system?
3. How dirty is the data? What are the problems related to data quality?
4. Which pieces of the system can be salvaged, if any?
5. Where are the problems? What is their impact?
6. Are the problems political, perceptual, or technical?

After answering these questions, the data warehouse manager is in a position to generate a plan of action and to create a set of recommendations to management to either fix the system or to discard it and start over. An easy decision rests on questions 1 and 2. If the users are not using the system and are not dependent on it, throw the system away.

Joyce Bischoff

The data warehouse manager should perform a data warehouse assessment to determine its strengths and weaknesses. Also, he or she should consider performing a data quality analysis. The reports should contain an evaluation of the current situation, recommendations for correcting weaknesses, and the rationale behind the recommendations.

Douglas Hackney

The data warehouse manager should strike out on a fresh course, not to fix what is broken but instead to identify fresh opportunities to add value to the business with integrated data. The data warehouse manager should clearly rebrand the new initiative with a different name and positioning from the old data warehouse. He or she should start small, stay targeted, and make sure to deliver a solution for someone who is politically meaningful within the company.

Chuck Kelley

One thing a good data warehouse manager does is plan for all types of contingencies, no matter how low their probability of occurrence. The disappearance of all the contractors is one of those low-probability items that will happen on occasion.

This data warehouse manager needs to place a hold on all new development, continue with the production environment, and put together a plan to create the required documentation. Next there needs to be some analysis of the data quality and integrity. Once all of this has been done, the data warehouse manager can develop a plan for the future. The biggest issue facing the data warehouse manager today is to get control of the data warehouse, and following the steps above is a way to start to capture that control.

David Marco

Obviously a good meta data repository would greatly mitigate this situation. For this case I assume that a meta data repository was not constructed three years ago. Since this is most likely the case, I recommend that a good data warehouse assessment be done on this system. The purpose of this assessment would be to decide whether the data warehouse can be salvaged and is worth the effort. If not, the data warehouse manager will need to start a new data warehouse initiative.

Larissa Moss

The first thing this data warehouse manager should do is a thorough assessment. This assessment should analyze the following items:

- Original data warehouse requirements for functionality, data, tools, access
- Data warehouse project plan used (if any)
- Data warehouse design for database(s), ETL, access and analysis
- Methodology used (if any)
- Documentation produced (if any)
- Roles and responsibilities of internal staff (if any)

After the assessment, the data warehouse manager should perform a gap analysis to answer the following questions:

- Which of the original data warehouse requirements are being satisfied? Which are not?
- Which pieces of the current data warehouse design are appropriate and effective?

- What documentation exists? What shape is it in?
- Who on the internal staff was involved in the project? What do they know?

Once the data warehouse manager has a good understanding of what was required, what was delivered, and where the holes are, he or she needs to prepare a plan for bringing the data warehouse back on track. This plan should include the steps listed below.

- Prepare an assessment report outlining the findings, issues, and recommendations.
- Organize a well-balanced staff of business analysts, systems analysts, DBAs, and programmers.
- Create a list of prioritized activities for correcting current deficiencies (from documenting to redesigning and recoding).
- Prepare a cost justification for the prioritized activities.

The data warehouse manager must negotiate the plan with the business community to secure approval and funding for his or her strategy and then go to work.

Clay Rehm

This situation presents a fun and exciting challenge, and the new data warehouse manager must be able to view it this way. If not, the wrong person has been assigned to this task.

The new data warehouse manager must first document (in writing and visual diagrams) the current state of the data warehouse, including all the positives and negatives. The data warehouse manager should investigate and document how the environment looked before the data warehouse was built three years ago and locate the original scope statement, work order, requirements, project plan, and so on.

The data warehouse manager should then document and diagram the desired state of the data warehouse by interviewing existing management, users, and support staff. This process includes identifying the current business problems.

With the help of an internal or external data warehouse expert, the data warehouse manager should determine what can be built and what time lines to set. He or she should create a plan that presents the evolution from the current state to the desired state. The documentation must include diagrams that show the evolution over a period of time, mapping out each step of the way. The manager should make sure the desired state design incorporates enterprise data modeling and architecture. He or she could hire temporary workers to assist in the updating of all the documentation of the current system and processes.

When the data warehouse manager has completed the documentation exercise, he or she should present the findings to upper management. The goal of this presentation is to get additional funding to fix the data warehouse so it can function at the desired state needed for the organization to be competitive.

Bottom line: Look at this tough situation as an exciting opportunity for growth and learning.

KNOWLEDGE TRANSFER IS NOT HAPPENING

An organization's executives planned to bring in a consultant to help with the first implementation of a data warehouse and then to have internal staff continue development after being trained by the consultant. The consultant assured the client that knowledge transfer was part of the package, but since the schedule became tight, the consultant has not had time to transfer his knowledge to the organization's employees. The employees, relegated to performing menial tasks, are learning very little from the first implementation. How can the executives ensure that knowledge transfer does take place?

Sid Adelman

To quote movie producer Samuel Goldwyn, "A verbal contract is not worth the paper it's printed on." It's one thing for the consultant to give verbal assurances; it's much more important for those assurances of knowledge transfer to be in the contract with identifiable measurements that support the fulfillment of the contract. The project plan should have included tasks for knowledge transfer and should have allowed time in the schedule for knowledge transfer for the tasks for which the consultant had primary responsibility and for which the client was supposed to learn how to perform the task.

Joyce Bischoff

The executives should discuss the problem with the consultants. If there is no time in the project plan for knowledge transfer, it may be necessary to expand the assignment to ensure that the staff will be properly trained.

Jill Dyché

The answer to this question depends on the contract between the company and the consulting firm. If the contract is a standard time-and-materials agreement with a 30-day out clause, the company should consider firing the consulting firm and cutting its losses. There is no reason to be held captive by any vendor, and since the firm has not established knowledge transfer as a success metric, the company's staff members will inevitably have to educate themselves about the system. Better to do this sooner than later.

If the contract with the consulting firm is more complex and involves severe financial penalties for early cancellation, then the company should examine its contract and implement a service-level agreement with the consulting firm. In other words, new success metrics for knowledge transfer, ongoing staff training, and regular status reporting—including stand-up reviews by the consulting firm's partner or account manager—should be instituted pronto.

Looking ahead, the company should also examine its standard contract so that it is not beholden to a chosen vendor and is never placed in the position of relinquishing control of a project. The contract should be revised to include hard and documented metrics for ongoing knowledge transfer. Then a new consultant—one prepared to live by these contractual terms and willing to assume the in-progress work of the predecessor—should be engaged.

Douglas Hackney

First, the executives should ensure that a knowledge transfer plan is in place. Specific seminars, classes, and mentoring sessions should be discreet portions of the project plan. Capability expectations should be clearly defined for each team member, and progress plans for these team members should be part of the regular project reporting package.

Second, the executives should be realistic in their expectations. A B-grade player is not going to turn into an A-plus rock star in three to six months. Additionally, as noted in the scenario, when crunch time comes, education and mentoring are usually sacrificed on the altar of due dates. The executives should work with the consultant to review and modify the knowledge transfer plans as the project progresses. The company will most likely need to make some sacrifices in order to achieve the desired delivery dates. As these activities slip, they should be added to the tasks for the next iteration.

Sean Ivoghli

The executives should integrate and pair up the staff with the consultants on the development team. Documentation and knowledge transfer should become part of the weekly deliverables. The executives must allow the consultant reasonable time to perform these tasks; then the consultant has no excuse to leave the project without completing knowledge transfer. Unfortunately, tight deadlines and project emergencies usually prevent executives from allowing for knowledge transfer. Knowledge transfer is valuable. Anything of value comes at a cost, in this case, time. When people start realizing that, there will be more knowledge transfer.

Chuck Kelley

The executives should include as part of the contract a contingency that a sufficient amount of money will be withheld until the knowledge transfer has taken place. Some of the knowledge transfer can occur after the data warehouse goes live. Someone working through the next phase with the staff can provide that knowledge transfer. It should be understood that not all the knowledge transfer will occur during the first phase. I believe that if an organization wishes to enter into a relationship that includes knowledge transfer, it should be done in multiple phases.

- *Development phase:* The consultant does most of the major work; the staff members provide assistance and look over the consultant's shoulder.
- *Watchdog phase:* The consultant looks over the shoulders of the organization's staff members and provides any assistance necessary.
- *Release phase:* The consultant is on call for any assistance required. This may be a monthly or weekly review but does not involve the day-to-day activities.

David Marco

The first step is to find a consulting company that truly wants to transfer knowledge. A good consulting company should have a written methodology, with narratives and templates. This methodology must be specifically designed for data warehousing and not a general IT development methodology. Also, the project plan must be built with knowledge transfer in mind. For example, time needs to be allocated for training courses and for the increased time it will take to teach the client personnel how to build a data warehouse. I believe strongly in having a client partner for each consulting role. The job of the client partner is *not* to watch the consultant do the work. Instead, the client partner should share in the completion of each task. This is when true knowledge transfer occurs.

Larissa Moss

Knowledge transfer takes time, and that time should be reflected in the project plan. The organization can avoid another similar situation by examining the consultant's project plan. Knowledge transfer can appear in one of two ways on the project plan.

1. For each major project activity, create and estimate separate tasks for knowledge transfer, and assign them to the mentors (consultants) as well as the staff members to be trained.
2. Add an additional adjustment factor for knowledge transfer to all final project task estimates for all resources.

If the knowledge transfer adjustment factor is embedded in the final estimate of each task (option 2), it is more difficult to validate whether or not enough time is allocated for knowledge transfer unless *all* adjustment factors are well documented. Most project management tools have built-in adjustment factors for skill-related, project-related, company-related, and personal activities (vacation, illness, and so on), but they do not have a separate adjustment factor for knowledge transfer. In that case, one of the other available factors must be increased by a sufficiently large margin to cover the time needed for knowledge transfer. This margin must be documented outside the project plan tool. In either case, knowledge transfer must be part of the estimating calculation; it must be documented and verifiable.

Clay Rehm

A two-step approach to building a data warehouse is best.

1. Let the experts build the first release while the client watches and participates. Either hire consultants or use internal staff members to design and build the first release. Stay out of their way, providing business knowledge, requirements, and input when they need it. Since the first release is so critical, it needs be done correctly and on time by people who have done it before. Knowledge transfer is very important, but not as important as a successful first delivery. If the first release is not delivered successfully, then knowledge transfer hardly matters since the data warehouse project most likely will be shelved.

2. Once the first release is done, after it has been delivered on time, at or under budget, and is doing what the scope agreement said it would do, then and only then let the experts educate, watch, and participate.

How can the executives make sure the knowledge transfer is happening? Report cards. That's right—just like grade school. The expert (teacher) must develop a report card for each team member (student). The report card must contain sections to track the job description, the normal tasks that role would play, what is expected in that role, and the gap analysis— how is the student doing? Is he or she learning? Can he or she take over when the expert leaves? What additional training does the student need before he or she can take over?

The experts must build the first release on time and under budget. They should focus on the second and subsequent releases for knowledge transfer.

HOW CAN DATA WAREHOUSE MANAGERS BEST USE CONSULTANTS?

A data warehouse manager has the assignment to design and build a data warehouse infrastructure complete with standards, methodology, and tools. He has the mandate and the budget (although not unlimited) to bring in new tools along with consultants and contractors as needed. How should the data warehouse manager bring in consultants? For which jobs and for how long? How should he most effectively use consultants and contractors?

Sid Adelman

Consultants should be brought in to help (to *help*, not to do all the work themselves) build an architecture, help establish data warehouse standards if none exist, recommend a data warehouse methodology, help develop a project plan and a project agreement, and help the client select tools.

Contractors should be brought in when the client lacks specific skills and when those skills are necessary for the successful completion of the project. In the process, the contractors should teach those skills to client personnel assigned to the project. The data warehouse manager should make sure client personnel are in place to act as catchers for the skills.

Joyce Bischoff

It is difficult to finalize standards and purchase tools without some idea of the mission and strategy for the data warehouse. Initially, the data warehouse manager should bring in a small group of consultants to define the warehouse mission and strategy and develop a first draft of a project plan with cost estimates and personnel requirements. At that point, a decision can be made regarding the adequacy of the budget. If necessary, the scope of the project may require adjustments. After the scope is finalized, the data warehouse manager should bring in a team of consultants to begin work on various aspects of the project.

Jill Dyché

This data warehouse manager is actually in a pretty good position. Although his budget isn't huge, he nevertheless has a clean slate and can establish a healthy precedent for how to best engage consultants.

The optimal scenario here is for the data warehouse manager and his full-time staff to do two things.

1. Develop a project plan that details the development tasks necessary. The data warehouse manager and key staff members should then determine which of the project plan's tasks are one-time-only tasks— for instance, building a specialized load program that extracts data from the enterprise resource planning (ERP) system. These tasks usually require finite and specialized skills that don't mandate staff training and are optimal work for temporary, skilled consultants.

2. Develop a skills matrix. The skills matrix lists individual roles and necessary skill sets in a grid that provides a way to track which roles or skills need fulfillment, as shown in Figure 6–1. Such a skills matrix can be complex or simple, but its goal should be to illuminate weaknesses in existing expertise. These are the holes consultants should fill.

Data Administration for Marketing Data Mart

	Local Development Team	Corporate IT	Tech Support Department	External Consultant
Understanding of customer data from the billing system.	○	●	○	○
Knowledge of customer billing data model.	○	●	◉	○
Experience documenting data transformation rules.	◉	●	○	●
Acquaintence with internal billing systems terms and SMEs.	◉	◉	○	○
Logical data modeling expertise.	●	●	◉	●
Knowledge of standard metadata tool.	◉	◉	○	◉

● = *Known Resource*   ◉ = *Available Resources*   ○ = *Unknown/Must Locate*

Figure 6–1: Sample skills matrix for data administration for a marketing data mart. SMEs = subject matter experts. Reprinted from Dyché, Jill, *e-Data: Turning Data into Information with Data Warehousing,* Fig. 6-3, © 2000 Addison Wesley Longman, Inc. Reprinted by permission of Pearson Education, Inc.

An ancillary advantage of performing both of these activities is that they foster a sense of ownership among full-time staff members, who can often become intimidated or threatened by the arrival of senior-level consultants. Having the team involved in determining the best use of consultants maximizes the chances that, when the consultants come on board, full-time staff members will feel as if they were stakeholders, not victims of the decision.

Douglas Hackney

The best approach is one focused on knowledge transfer and leadership. The data warehouse manager should start by hiring as many A-level, full-time team members as possible. He could fill in the capability gaps by using experienced consultants paired with less-capable players and by using lower-cost, technology-specific tool jockeys for implementation of specific technologies. The data warehouse manager should engage a senior-level consultant to provide overall leadership, project management mentoring, best-practice implementation, and milestone reviews.

Chuck Kelley

The data warehouse manager first needs to make an accurate assessment of each person's skill set to determine what skills are needed. Next he needs to define what a consultant is and what a contractor is. A *consultant* is someone who provides expertise and can be an advisor or a deliverer of tasks. A *contractor* is a person who provides the delivery of tasks. The advisor consultant works on a periodic basis (typically one to three days a week) to see what is happening and to help reshape or redirect the project if it goes off course. The amount of time needed is determined by how well the development effort goes. The delivery consultant is an advisor as well as a person who delivers specific tasks. For example, the delivery consultant may be someone who delivers on the task of the data model. His or her periodic time basis will be higher at the beginning of the project, dropping off to an advisor role during the middle to end of the project.

A contractor has the day-to-day tasks to deliver. The contractor might be responsible for building the ETL process or for overseeing the DBA functions. Clear, concise tasks need to be defined to manage the contractor.

Identifying what is needed within the team allows the data warehouse manager to find the right talent at the right time to make the project successful.

David Marco

The data warehouse manager needs to conduct a gap analysis on his staff to identify his team shortfalls. Once he has defined the gaps, the data warehouse manager needs to decide which of these project roles will be temporary and which will be permanent. He can fill the temporary roles with consultants. Initially he can place consultants in the permanent roles, until he can hire or transfer employees onto the project.

Larissa Moss

The data warehouse manager has to determine three things before he can decide how to spend his allocated budget on consultants and contractors to build the data warehouse infrastructure.

1. *Are there infrastructure components already in the company that can be used or modified for the data warehouse?* If some infrastructure components already exist in other parts of the company and if they can be adapted to data warehousing, they should be reviewed and the necessary modifications should be identified.

2. *Does the company have staff with the required infrastructure skills (standards, methodologies, and so on) that can be made available for the data warehouse either temporarily or permanently?* If the company already has internal staff with the needed infrastructure skills, the data warehouse manager should try to have at least one staff member made available to work on or supervise the data warehouse infrastructure activities, even if only on a temporary basis. In that case, the data warehouse manager can get by with hiring a few contractors who have the necessary skills to perform the activities under the direction of the "borrowed" internal staff member.

3. *In what area of infrastructure is there no expertise in the company?* If there are no existing infrastructure components in the company and no internal staff members with infrastructure skills, the data warehouse manager will have no choice but to hire a high-priced consultant to set up the data warehouse infrastructure.

Note: Hiring contractors and having them work under the staff's direction is a lot cheaper than hiring consultants. Contractors are hired when the company has a shortage of skilled workers. The company tells them what needs to be done, and the contractors perform the work. Consultants are hired for their expertise when the company has none. They tell the company what needs to be done and charge accordingly. With a limited budget, the worst situation for this data warehouse manager would be to have to hire both consultants and contractors to establish the data warehouse infrastructure.

Clay Rehm

First of all, before deciding which consultants to use, the data warehouse manager should evaluate what each consultant has done on past projects. The manager needs to see demonstrations, methodology, documentation, project plans, references, and so on.

Second, does the manager have a good rapport with the consultants? Not with the consulting firm's sales or marketing force, but the people who will actually do the work? Many times the consultants' sales folks oversell a job just to get it and end up bringing in subcontractors to fill positions. The data warehouse manager should meet with the people who will be assigned to his site and make sure he is comfortable with them. He should review their résumés and interview the consultants, asking them about their experiences.

The consultants must be able to show a documented methodology and templates of deliverables from prior projects. If they do not have these kinds of things, the data warehouse manager should not consider hiring them.

Early in the project, the manager could consider doing a personality profile of each member of the client and consulting teams to identify each person's communication style, strengths, and weaknesses.

Once the data warehouse manager believes he has selected the right consultants, he should assign them to perform a readiness assessment. It is important to make sure the organization is really ready to build a data warehouse before spending any more money on the project. If the data warehouse manager picked the right consultants, they will provide an honest assessment without sugarcoating the real facts. Good consultants also provide useful documentation—diagrams and documents that show the existing as well as the desired systems and processes.

Selecting the right consultants takes time, energy, and homework. The manager should be prepared to spend appropriate time during this search.

MANAGEMENT WANTS TO OUTSOURCE THE DATA WAREHOUSE ACTIVITIES

A company is making some major changes. The executives have decided to outsource the operational systems to an application service provider (ASP) and are considering outsourcing some or all of the data warehouse activities. The new focus is on the company's customers, so the executives are planning significant customer relationship management (CRM) capability. The company has some minor data warehouse capability today, but with this major change in focus, should the executives start from scratch for their decision support systems? How can the executives be sure the outsourcing organization will deliver the needed functions and capabilities?

Sid Adelman

How can the executives be sure the outsourcing organization will deliver the needed functions and capabilities? The answer is they can't be sure. In an outsourced situation, contracts are very clear about what will and won't be included. The very nature of a data warehouse is that the users are never able to articulate all their requirements up front; that means each new request requires renegotiations and contract changes. By the time these details are worked out, the opportunity will be lost. The data warehouse should not be outsourced!

Joyce Bischoff

The company needs an overall information strategy that should be defined before the outsourcing plan is complete. An evaluation of the effectiveness of the current data warehouse should also be performed. One can never be certain that an outsourcing firm will deliver the functions and capabilities needed over the long term. Technology and business changes occur quickly in today's world, and there is no assurance that an outsourcing firm will respond as desired. The firm may also charge an excessive amount of money for complex changes because there is no competition. Since ideas that are unknown today may need to be implemented, it is difficult to include all the needed wording in a contract. With this information at hand, the executives can make a decision regarding the outsourcing of the warehouse.

Chuck Kelley

Outsourcing data to an ASP is dangerous not only for operational systems but also for data warehouses. Do the executives really want to trust one of their important corporate assets to live and breathe under someone else not in the executives' ultimate control? We already know that having data under our own control is not totally secure (ask the Internal Revenue Service), but having data under the control of someone else is likely to be even less secure. I would do some serious soul-searching before I would allow my corporate data to be outsourced.

As for this situation, in which the ASP seems like a done deal, I would look at the current data warehouse and ask, "Does it add any value to the company?" If it does, no matter how minor, I would keep it. During the time when we are building the CRM data warehouse, I would look at ways to align the current data warehouse with the new data warehouse produced for the CRM system. You know the old saying: "If it ain't broke, don't fix it."

When creating a contract with an outsourcing company, management needs to put in strong terms and conditions to ensure that the outsourcing company will deliver the functions and capabilities required. The contract should include penalties for late delivery or nondelivery. However, this means the executives will have to come up with a strong understanding of what they want and the time frame of delivery.

Larissa Moss

I do not believe that starting from scratch is a cost-justified approach, unless there is justifiable reason to do so. One such reason might be that nothing— no data, no database, no program, no tool, no technology component— can be salvaged from the existing data warehouse environment.

Current CRM capabilities are largely operational and collaborative in nature, not analytical. Any CRM analytical applications will most likely be customized data marts developed by data warehouse consultants and not CRM consultants. These data marts could be merged or added to any existing data warehouse capabilities, unless a completely unsalvageable situation exists as described above.

My main recommendation to this company is not to outsource the strategic and managerial components of data warehousing. One of the benefits of a data warehouse is to give a company some competitive advantage. That usually means that a company wants to learn about its own business performance in relationship to customers and business partners in order to maximize on that performance before the competition does. This maximization is a dynamic process, and the underlying analytical functionality of the data warehouse should be under the strategic direction and management of the company and not the outsourcing organization.

Clay Rehm

I do not recommend outsourcing the design and development of a data warehouse. The development of a data warehouse cannot be purchased off the shelf or done offsite. The true challenges of data warehousing lie in the difficulties of the data, the business process changes, and the changes to the resources' jobs. Simply put, data warehouse projects are systems integration, business process reengineering (BPR), and organizational change management (OCM) projects all rolled into one. How can anyone expect to outsource this?

More specifically, the data challenges include lack of data quality, difficulty in mapping the correct sources to targets, integration, business rules of transformations and derivations, aggregations, and reporting. How can anyone expect to capture all these requirements offsite?

Bottom line: To really develop a successful data warehouse, the company must consider all the aspects that include BPR, OCM, a true understanding of the data, and integration of many disparate systems.

CHAPTER SEVEN

Project Planning and Scheduling

The reason we don't have the time to fix it today is that we didn't take the time to do it right yesterday.

—H. James Harrington

OVERVIEW

Project Management

While project management is critical for operational projects, it is even more critical for a data warehouse project, especially since there is little expertise in this rapidly growing discipline. The project manager must embrace new tasks and deliverables, develop a different working relationship with the users, and work in an environment that is far less defined than that of traditional operational systems.

Some overlap in project management exists between a data warehouse project and an operational project, but many tasks are specific and unique to a data warehouse project. The data warehouse team must

- Define data warehouse objectives.
- Define a query library.
- Integrate meta data.
- Develop a refresh strategy.
- Define data warehouse product selection criteria.
- Prepare ETL specifications.
- Develop query usage monitoring.

Data warehouse project management deals with project plans, scope agreements, schedules, resources, change control, risk management, communication and project management, and a data warehouse methodology. The first three of these are discussed further below.

Project Plans

A good project plan lists the critical tasks that must be performed and when each task should be started and completed. It identifies who will perform the tasks, describes the deliverables to be created, and identifies milestones for measuring progress.

A project plan is essential to convince management that the project manager knows what he or she is doing. Management often demands an unrealistic delivery schedule, and a project plan can support the project manager's desire for a realistic schedule. A project plan can help track the project's progress and identify problem areas.

Scope Agreements

The scope agreement is the primary document of understanding between IT and the user. It specifies what functions and data will be delivered and excludes what will not be delivered. It lists dates, responsibilities (for both IT and the users), end-user tools and training to be provided, and who will be picking up the tab for the project. The scope agreement—or lack thereof—can be the primary reason for user dissatisfaction. Without a scope agreement, the user usually expects more than IT is planning to deliver. Without a scope agreement, there is no basis for determining whether the project was a success or a failure.

A wise project manager we knew counseled those team members new in the field to read the scope agreement every Friday afternoon. It may make sense to deliver some capability over and above what is specified in the document, but if you don't deliver what is written in the scope commitments, you have failed as a project manager. You should review the scope agreement periodically with the users to let them know you are working toward the specific deliverables itemized in the document. We often hear the lament that the users don't respond to requests to attend meetings and don't complete decision sign-offs in a timely manner. If you include user responsibilities in the scope agreement, it should be easier to get users' attention when you point out their commitments.

Schedules

It has been said that business managers might not know what they want but they know exactly when they want it delivered. Managers are often doubtful of the schedules created by their project managers. They want the efforts and the dates backed up by something more than a wild guess. Students at seminars on data warehouse project management have almost unanimously indicated they have been given a deadline by management, and these deadlines are almost always unrealistic. These deadlines are usually created out of whole cloth with little input from the project manager. A project plan would have given a more realistic date based on the tasks to be executed, the dependencies of the tasks, and estimates of the time required to complete the tasks. Highly optimistic estimates given by the vendors (to let you know how easy it is to install their tools) strongly bias management as management imposes short and unattainable deadlines. Every project manager faces scope creep. Rarely is extra time allocated for the additional functions requested as the scope of the project expands. The business is used to asking for everything in the initial phase of an operational system and is unfamiliar with the phasing that is a data warehouse best practice.

Schedules should be based on project plans that include all the tasks that need to be performed. Since the concept of a data warehouse is still new to many organizations, estimating tasks is very difficult; thus estimates are often grossly incorrect. Not much knowledge and experience are normally captured about previous data warehouse projects, and even when the information is captured, it rarely is disseminated within the organization. Even the few industry standards that exist for estimating are at a level too high to have much practical use.

In the remainder of this chapter, we'll explore five situations that deal with planning and scheduling.

MANAGEMENT REQUIRES SUBSTANTIATION OF ESTIMATES

Management does not understand why the data warehouse project will take so long. The executives are unimpressed with the project plan, which shows task durations and work efforts. Believing these estimates are inflated to protect the project manager and the team, the executives now demand substantiation of the estimates. If there are no standards the project manager can use to back up his estimates, he knows that management will impose standards. What should the project manager do?

Sid Adelman

Other organizations have been down this path before. The project manager should connect with people who have implemented analogous data warehouse projects, even if those projects are only somewhat similar to the one proposed. He should ask these folks for their project plans, especially if those plans have been updated to reflect the reality of how long the tasks actually took. The project manager should be sure to ask about the skill levels of those who performed the tasks. If his people are not as skilled, the data warehouse tasks will obviously take longer. Then the message to management is, "We aren't smarter or better organized than those folks who actually implemented other data warehouses; therefore, based on their experiences, we have a pretty good idea of how long it will take." Although the most believable people to talk with are project managers from organizations that implemented data warehouses, consultants can also provide input; however, they don't have the same level of credibility.

Joyce Bischoff

The project manager should ask an experienced data warehouse expert to review the project plan and its estimates. If the consultant agrees with the estimates, this would provide evidence regarding the accuracy of the project plan. If management insists on an earlier delivery date, it may be necessary to argue for a reduced project scope. The consultant could also assist with this.

Douglas Hackney

The project manager should leverage case studies and expert testimony of other data warehousing projects. There's a plethora of information available about data warehousing projects on the Web and from data warehouse associations.

Sean Ivoghli

The project manager should research other similar projects and use those numbers to justify his. He could also hire a well-known consultant to review the project plan and bless it (assuming it is good).

Larissa Moss

Substantiating estimates is not difficult if the project manager has been diligent in tracking time on previous projects. Task estimates should be calculated based on a variety of variables, not on guessing and padding. Assuming the project manager has calculated and tracked actual time for each of these variables in the past, he should present the actuals as empirical evidence to management to back up his current estimates. The variables he should use in his calculations are listed below.

- *Average effort:* Based on activities performed on previous projects, the project manager can calculate an average amount of time per task.
- *Skill level:* The documentation for the project management methodology or tool used should state the recommended adjustment percentage for skill level. The employees' past training record and performance evaluations should substantiate the skill level the project manager chose for them.
- *Additional (unscheduled) project-related activities:* In addition to assigned activities, many interruptions occur during a work day. Some of these "interruptions" are project-related, such as brainstorming sessions, review meetings, and unanticipated research.
- *Company-related activities:* Many other "interruptions" are not project-related but work-related, such as attending department meetings, troubleshooting another system, helping a coworker, and processing e-mails.
- *Personal activities:* During the duration of a project, team members frequently need some personal time: they get sick, go on vacation, tend to an ill parent or child, have a dental problem, or need to stay home for repair of a maintenance problem (for example, a broken water pipe).

The project manager's responsibility is to take all these variables into account when producing the final task estimates. It is also his responsibility to track actual time and compare those numbers against the estimates. If the project manager did not do his job right in the past, he may have nothing to back up his estimates except his gut feeling, which is (justifiably) being disputed.

Clay Rehm

In this case, an experienced consultant who is a good motivational speaker is needed to provide the required support. If the project manager has time, he could hire the consultant to do an independent evaluation to provide the substantiation. This consultant or a very small team of consultants must prepare an assessment within days. The project manager shouldn't hire someone who wants to take over the project—he just wants someone to back him up, someone who has years of experience and can substantiate the estimates.

When considering a consultant, the project manager should locate someone who has designed, implemented, and sustained multiple successful data warehouses. The project manager needs a credible consultant to bring to bear best practices, industry standards, and experiences to show the typical time required to develop a data warehouse.

The moral of the story: At times it is appropriate to call in the cavalry.

IT MANAGEMENT SETS UNREALISTIC DEADLINES

IT has missed deadline after deadline and has a reputation for never bringing in a project on time. This time the IT team members really don't want to miss the deadline. IT managers have already made commitments to their bosses for an unrealistic schedule, but they are counting on the project manager to come through and deliver on time. Management has made it clear to the project manager that her reputation and career within the company depend on meeting the schedule. What should the project manager do?

Sid Adelman

Assuming that the project manager has no intention to fail—some project managers have taken the lemming philosophy and accepted an unrealistic schedule, knowing they will not make the deadline and knowing that failure is imminent—the project manager has three options.

1. Have a heart-to-heart discussion with IT management and make the managers aware of what can realistically be accomplished, letting them know that the schedule will have to be extended. The discussion may go as follows: "Do you want to tell upper management the bad news now or later?"

2. Bring in selected contractors who have specific skills (for example, in the ETL or access and analysis tools) and can shorten some of the major activities. This option still makes meeting the unrealistic schedule unlikely.

3. Move some of the major functions, source files, or user groups to subsequent phases and deliver a subset of the originally agreed-upon functions. This is probably the best approach since management will be able to see a real and, hopefully, valuable deliverable in the originally agreed-upon time frame. If the project manager takes this approach, she should tell management early that the data warehouse will be delivered in phases, describing what will be included in the first phase and how the rest of the phases will be rolled out.

Douglas Hackney

The project manager should carefully examine the deadlines; if they are unrealistic, she should resign the position. There is no magic black box in the project plan labeled "a miracle happens." If anything, data warehouse projects are often, if not usually, late. If the project manager thinks the schedule is unrealistic at the beginning, the situation is only going to get worse.

There are only three variables in data warehousing: scope, resources, and time (quality is a prerequisite). Unless the project manager can significantly reduce the scope, it is likely the project will not meet the deadline. Adding additional resources fairly quickly results in diminishing returns.

Sean Ivoghli

Knowing that the schedule is unrealistic, the project manager should aggressively descope as much as she can from the deliverables until it becomes realistic to deliver something useful. She should start by cutting the most expensive, lowest profile requirements, making sure that the resulting product has some value (meets some requirements) and is usable. If meeting the deadline is that critical, chances are that the project manager will win some points for being on time and lose some points for not delivering everything management expected. That will leave the project manager in a neutral position, which is better than a negative one!

While working to meet the deadline, the project manager should make sure the team is working in parallel to deliver the descoped functionality as soon as possible after the deadline. The team could add functionality to the data warehouse while the users are still testing and getting used to the system, and they'll never even know it was missing. Of course, the project manager needs to plan very carefully for this and must have a very dependable team. If she plans it right, the team could deliver the descoped product on time and then work hard to add new functionality on a daily basis until caught up. If the project manager has to deal with unrealistic management, this is one (very stressful) approach she can take. The problem with this approach is that management will keep expecting her to come through this way.

Chuck Kelley

IT departments in a lot of companies never meet deadlines. Telling a person that her reputation and career is on the line does not reinforce good employee–employer relationships.

The project manager can handle this issue two ways.

1. She can work with the data warehouse team to define what the real deadline should be. The team members can estimate how close they can come to meeting the deadline. If close, perhaps adding one or two people to the team would help. If so, the project manager should go to IT management and ask for one or two more people immediately to meet the deadline. If management says "No," the project manager must work the team very diligently to meet the deadline. This is usually a no-win situation. However, if the team pulls it off, the team members are heroes. If not, no one expected to meet the deadline anyway. During this time, the project manager should keep in close contact with the project team to see if any "show stoppers" occur and let IT management know immediately if that happens. The project manager should keep a well-documented log of questions and answers. Human resources should be able to protect her from unreasonable management items. If not, then the final outcome will be the same as option 2.

2. The project manager could dust off the ol' résumé and search for a better employer. While working diligently to meet the deadline, she should start searching for another position either within or outside her current organization. Again, if the team meets the deadline, the

project manager and her project team will be heroes; otherwise, she will have learned a great deal she can use to help the next company that employs her.

David Marco

The project manager should update her résumé. When the initial schedule is unrealistic and career threats are being made, this is a formula for disaster. If I were in her position, I would try a couple methods I use to jump-start a project. I would implement weekly status meetings during which I would check with each team member to see if he or she is on schedule. I typically schedule these meetings for Monday morning at 8:00 A.M. This sets people's minds on their jobs, right at the beginning of the week. Also, I would order dinner at 5:30 P.M. for the people working late. This helps to motivate people to put in extra time.

Larissa Moss

The project manager should examine her reasons for working at a company that keeps putting their project managers into difficult no-win situations and doing so under threat. Assuming this company is "the only game in town" and the project manager needs to hang on to her job, she needs to negotiate the remaining four variables of a project plan. Since the fifth variable, time, is fixed, the variables left to negotiate are scope, quality, resources, and money. The most important of these four variables is *scope* because the size of the scope dictates the quality of the product. The larger the scope, the less time is left to spend on quality. Obviously the necessary resources and money must be available to support the desired scope and quality. If the project manager is given a nonnegotiable scope along with a nonnegotiable deadline, she should seriously consider quitting because she is in a no-win situation. Pushing her team to work around the clock will only demoralize the team members, if not anger them, and the project will probably still not get done in time. Then she will not only have her management against her but also may be ostracized by her own staff. Why put herself into that situation?

Clay Rehm

If the project manager is concerned about her reputation and career, she is thereby limited to the choices within her control. Three project components are available to her—time, resources, and scope. Since she cannot control the time, she can try to control the scope and resources. Considering there are diminishing returns as the number of resources grow, she must be careful to have the appropriate number of people on her team. Additionally, she cannot scale the scope down below the point of adding any business value.

When constructing the project plan, the project manager should focus more on capturing each and every task needed instead of putting in start and end dates. Since the date cannot move, she needs to focus on the tasks that need to get done. This is important—she cannot afford to slip up because she forgot to work on a task that was not accounted for in her plan.

She should engage contractors or other internal expertise even for a short time and consider hiring temporary administrative resources to work on writing documentation and technical notes, scheduling work sessions and meetings, taking meeting minutes, documenting decisions, and so on.

Finally, she must come to the realization that she may have to work extra hours. She needs to inform her team now that this project requires long days and seven-day work weeks to get through it. She should promise her staff extra vacation time or other gifts within her budget and control that she can give them after the delivery of the data warehouse (on time, by the way).

The moral of the story: Desperate times call for desperate measures.

THE SPONSOR CHANGES THE SCOPE BUT DOESN'T WANT TO CHANGE THE SCHEDULE

Based on a project agreement, a project manager developed a project plan, allowing an additional 20 percent time, effort, and budget for unanticipated contingencies. The sponsor and a few others in his department asked for some minor additional functions, which the project manager accepted. However, the sponsor has now made major requests for new data and told the project manager that he doesn't want her to change the schedule. What should the project manager do?

Sid Adelman

I hope that the sponsor participated in creating the project agreement or at least read and signed it. I also hope the sponsor was aware of the project plan and understands its basic components. It's time for the project manager to have a meeting with the sponsor to discuss the project agreement and the project plan and explain what can and cannot be accomplished.

There are a few things the project manager should not do.

- *Do not throw additional people on the project.* Frederick Brooks [1995] in *The Mythical Man-Month* indicated that putting more people on a project increases the schedule, not decreases it. In a few cases selected skilled people could be valuable, but generally this does not work.
- *Do not agree to the changes without other concessions.* If the project manager agrees without concessions, most likely she will fail. If by some miracle the project does come in on time, the project manager will forever be known as someone who pads the schedule, and management will no longer believe her estimates.
- *Do not say "No."* IT has a terrible reputation for being unresponsive to the user community.

It's time to negotiate on the following points:

- *Is the original schedule sacred?* Yes, the sponsor wants to keep the schedule the same, but maybe he is willing to accept an elongated schedule.
- *Can these new requests be deferred to a subsequent phase?* A data warehouse lends itself nicely to phasing. This would be the least disruptive approach.
- *Can some of the original functions be deferred to subsequent phases?* This may not be as good a solution, depending how far into the project the team members have delved—they may have already addressed, modeled, designed, and incorporated into the system some of the original functions, so those efforts could be wasted if the functions get deferred to a later phase.

Joyce Bischoff

The project manager should decide whether the extra 20 percent she built into the project schedule is enough to allow the team to meet the required date. If necessary, she should explain to the sponsor that the requests for new data and functionality will delay the project and suggest that the additional work be done in a second phase. If the sponsor does not accept that, the project manager should explain her concerns in writing to cover herself in case the project is late.

Douglas Hackney

If the project manager has a valid project agreement, there is no issue. A project agreement or detailed scope statement clearly defines exactly what will be delivered and within what general time frame. A good scope statement also clearly delineates the impact if changes are made in the scope; that is, an expanded scope leads to a later delivery date. This is why the project agreement or detailed scope statement is so important. It becomes the scope management device for the project. Once the agreement is signed by the steering committee or sponsor and by the project team, it becomes a binding agreement for both sides. This includes the project team's obligation to deliver the defined scope and the steering committee or sponsor's obligation to honor the defined scope. A project without a valid project agreement or detailed scope statement is simply a blown deadline waiting to happen.

Chuck Kelley

I congratulate the project manager on having the forethought to include additional time in the schedule. We in IT don't always project accurate schedules or build in contingencies. Scope creep is one of the biggest issues that every project manager has to deal with. When the sponsor requests additional functions, the project manager should make it clear that this change in scope adds time to the project and that she will accept the changes only if the sponsor agrees to add time to the schedule. The project manager should let the sponsor decide whether to slip the schedule to include the additional functions. The project manager should keep track of the additional functions requested. If the sponsor decides not to let the schedule slip, the team should build the project according to the original scope. Then if there is some extra time as the project ends (which I doubt), the team can add some or all of the additional functions into the project.

The sponsor has gotten used to being able to add new functions with no change in schedule. The project manager will need to sit down with the sponsor and make a good case explaining why this request for new data cannot be delivered within the schedule. She should request that the new data be put in release 1.1 of the data warehouse.

David Marco

I would explain to the sponsor the three Ss of project development: staff, scope, and schedule (Figure 7–1). Changing one requires changing them all, or else the quality of the project will be impacted.

Larissa Moss

The sponsor needs a quick lesson in Project Management 101. To educate the sponsor, the project manager should take the following steps.

1. Compile the actual time spent working on tasks already performed on the project.
2. Prepare a detailed impact analysis report for the major change just requested.
3. Find a project management book (for example, *Microsoft Project 2000 Bible* by Marmel [2000]) that details the adjustment variables involved in estimating: average base effort, skill level of resources, unscheduled project-related activities, company-related activities, and personal activities.
4. Gather the numbers for the actual time spent for all these variables on previous projects by the same staff members now on the data warehouse team. Compare those times to the estimates for these variables on the current project plan.
5. Slowly walk the sponsor through all this information, plus the original project plan, and show him how it is not possible to complete the requested major change in the same time period as the original project.

Figure 7–1: The three Ss of project development. From *Building and Managing the Meta Data Repository* by David Marco. Copyright ©2000 David Marco. All rights reserved. Reproduced here by permission of Wiley Publishing, Inc.

If the sponsor argues with the base estimates or the adjustment variables, the project manager should point to the empirical information she collected on previous projects and show him how they correlate to the actual time already spent on this project. If the sponsor still argues with the information, the project manager must face the fact that she is working with an unreasonable and uncooperative, if not downright irrational, sponsor who does not respect the project manager's professional expertise and opinion. In that case the project manager should find another project to work on.

Clay Rehm

First off, the golden rule is that nothing exists unless it's in writing. The project manager should write a formal change request statement and distribute it to the sponsor and other stakeholders.

The sponsor has a responsibility to manage and limit scope creep, to have a big picture (strategic) perspective, and to challenge the value of the data warehouse. He also needs to be told when he has unreasonable expectations.

A strong project manager does not allow scope creep. The project manager is part politician and must know what the business needs and how to provide value to the stakeholders while keeping everybody happy. This is not an easy job, especially for the average project manager.

The project manager should state that the original project plan works only for the original scope. She should provide an estimate for each new data source: how many mappings it will take and how long each mapping will take. She should determine, document, and communicate how much more time, money, and resources this scope change will cost the sponsor.

Bottom line: There is no free lunch.

THE USERS WANT THE FIRST DATA WAREHOUSE DELIVERY TO INCLUDE EVERYTHING

The users are afraid that if they don't ask for everything in the first release, they may never see the functions they want, so they are asking for all the functions they will eventually need and much more. This nullifies one of the benefits of a data warehouse implementation—the ability to phase deliveries. What approach should the project manager take to convince management that trying to put all the functions in the initial release is a sure formula for either failure or for a very long delivery schedule?

Sid Adelman

The project manager should start by educating management on the data warehouse best practice of phased delivery. The education should include examples of other implementations; they do not have to be in the same industry, although that does add credibility to the approach. The major emphasis should be on delivering something of value to the users in a reasonable period of time and continuing to deliver additional function in three- to four-month periods. The next emphasis should be on reducing risk. Large and long projects are much riskier, often resulting in slipped schedules, budget overruns, general failure to deliver, unhappy users, and unrealized benefits. The phased approach allows a better control of schedules and budgets and measurement of user satisfaction as well as measurement of benefits and comparisons to benefit expectations.

Joyce Bischoff

The Big Bang approach, which includes delivery of a very large data warehouse in a single project, has usually proven unsuccessful for the following reasons:

- Significant funding is required.
- If the organization does not have previous data warehouse experience, it is difficult to estimate the time required to accomplish each phase of the project. Historically, very large data warehouse projects have been late and over budget.
- The level of risk is higher if the project is very large.
- It is difficult to estimate the impact of a large ad hoc database on the performance of the system.
- Managers and users may not have a full understanding of the impact of the warehouse on the technical staff and the business users.
- Technical problems may be associated with the new databases.
- Organizational politics can cause problems as job responsibilities are modified to address the technical support, training, user support, and organizational impact.

- If databases are very large, expensive tools may be needed and they may have a long learning curve.
- A data warehouse should be based on a logical data model. The time needed to develop a larger data model may not be tolerated well by the organization.
- It is common for users to realize that they have many additional requirements after they see what can be done with the data. If the warehouse is opened to a large number of users on day one, it is likely that there will be an excessive number of requests for enhancements, which may be difficult to address from a political perspective.

It is more practical to deliver the warehouse in smaller phases for the following reasons:

- Funding will be more reasonable.
- A data warehouse staff that has done a successful job with a small project will do a better job of estimating the work to be done in future phases. If a three-month project takes four months, the schedule slippage is not as serious as a 24-month project that takes 32 months to deliver.
- Managers and users will have a better understanding of the impact on the organization because they have seen the impact of a small project.
- A corporate model may be built over time by merging the data models from each small phase in an iterative fashion.
- Standards and procedures will evolve in a more controlled manner.

The project manager should obtain management commitment to deliver the data warehouse in small phases about every three to six months. If the project plan covers several phases, it may be easier to sell it than if only the first phase is planned.

Chuck Kelley

This is quite commonplace. IT has generally failed in its ability to release version 2 of systems that meet the users needs.

The project manager needs to put together a plan to develop a data warehouse with everything scheduled in the first release. This will probably require about $5–7 million and will take about three to five years to deliver. Then the project manager can break the plan into small steps, which is essentially the same approach as using the iterative development process to build the data warehouse.

David Marco

An important component of the initial release of the data warehouse is to document the future, desired benefits and state of the decision support system. This should be done right in the project scope document. When the business users can see that the project scope includes their needs, the users will realize they won't be forgotten.

Larissa Moss

The users are probably thinking of the data warehouse as "just another system" and "just for them." The project manager must explain to them that a data warehouse is not just their system but a cross-organizational decision support environment that will eventually contain many "systems," that is, many shared databases, many applications, and many users. Since the data warehouse has to be able to grow, the underlying infrastructure components have to be able to change as well—technology is constantly changing and improving. A Big Bang approach would never present any opportunities for learning lessons and for refining and tuning the data warehouse. In addition, it would simply be too risky to build such an environment all at once because the enhancements, which are guaranteed to follow, would take too long to implement in a large environment. Bottom line, environments are not built—they *evolve*.

Clay Rehm

When interviewing the key business users, the project manager should document any and all requirements. He or she should instruct the users to prioritize each requirement as either mandatory or optional and to indicate whether they need the requirement fulfilled in release 1, release 2, or subsequent releases. The project manager should construct a desired-state document and diagram suitable for framing. Visual aids are a boon to nontechnical people and will help educate users about the final deliverable. The project manager will need to do this for each release.

Are the users educated on data warehousing? If not, the project manager should either create an internal presentation or outsource a presentation on the benefits of data warehousing.

The users must be held accountable for what they need and held responsible for proper, continuous, and timely communication with the project team. The users must be committed to the effort. Do the user representatives really understand the business and what they need? The organization may not be ready for a data warehouse; an assessment by a reputable consultant can help determine this.

The project manager must take a positive approach with the users. He or she must be strong enough to stand up to the users and tell them exactly what *can* get delivered in release 1. The project manager should focus on the positive, telling the users what they will be getting instead of focusing on what they won't be getting.

Easy-to-understand visual diagrams and documentation go a long way when educating users.

THE PROJECT MANAGER SEVERELY UNDERESTIMATES THE SCHEDULE

A project manager has decades of experience and is very competent in a number of computer languages and operating systems. He has extensive experience in his industry and knows whom to call and where to find whatever he needs. On top of this, he is an eternal optimist, believing everything will progress perfectly with no delays or false starts. He bases his team's work estimates on how long it would take him to perform the task. What should his manager do?

Sid Adelman

This is an opportunity for the project manager's manager to both complement him and explain that the other people on his team do not have the same skills and abilities to accomplish the tasks as quickly or as well. His manager should suggest asking those who will be doing the work to create their own estimates. A good approach is to ask the team members for three estimates: a best case, a worst case, and a most realistic case. The project manager should use the most realistic case but temper it with the reality of the organization, the project, and any other factors that should be included. Some successful project managers plan on six hours per day as actual work time, thus accounting for meetings, absences, systems that are down, and other events that distract from the work day.

Joyce Bischoff

The project manager should ask each team member to review the time estimates and make suggestions about the time allotted to him or her. At that point, the correct estimates should become clearer.

Chuck Kelley

Everyone in the computer field is an optimist until serving as a project leader on a project that is really late. Then he or she becomes realistic and tries to overcompensate. Early in my career, I severely underestimated the time my team needed to do a job. I had based my estimate on how long I thought I needed to complete the project (but in retrospect, I couldn't do it that quickly either!). Ten times the amount of time later, we completed the project. After that, I started using the following seat-of-the-pants estimating formula: my original estimated time multiplied by 15. I always came in within budget and on time (or early). Eventually I started drifting back toward basing my estimates on how much time I thought I needed to complete the project.

An excellent project manager is worth the expense. One way organizations go wrong today is by taking a good technologist and making him or her a project leader. Some people are great technologists but don't know how to deal with human nature.

This manager has a couple of options. First, the manager could hire an excellent project manager and put him or her in the project lead of the data warehouse, placing the current project manager in a technologist role. Yes, there may be some hurt feelings, but that needs to be balanced with meeting delivery schedules. The manager could place him in a "second lieutenant" role.

Another option would be for the manager to hire an advisor (an excellent project manager advisor) to review the task list and time frames and work as a mentor with the current project manager.

The key decision point will need to be made by the organization and the project manager. Most organizations do not have highly paid technology tracks. At some point, if people want to keep getting raises, they have to start doing more managerial tasks. This organization's leaders need to decide whether they will be the forward thinkers of tomorrow and build technology and managerial tracks or stay the course. The project manager will have to decide whether he wishes to remain a technologist and wants to start a managerial track. Then there needs to be a meeting of the minds with the project manager and the organization to put a plan in place to move the organization and/or the project manager into the future.

Larissa Moss

This project manager should immediately attend two seminars: a project management seminar followed by a data warehouse seminar.

1. In the project management seminar he will learn that estimates should be calculated by those who perform the work, not by those who manage the work. He will also learn how to apply the variables of skill level, additional unscheduled project-related activities, company-related activities, and personal activities to the base estimates. In addition, he will learn how to determine task dependencies and how to level resources.
2. In the data warehouse seminar he will learn about all the new activities that must be performed for the data warehouse, such as tool selection, cross-organizational data analysis, triage of data cleansing, integrated ETL staging areas, and so on. He will also learn about the parallel development tracks, shifted roles and responsibilities, and other key issues for managing data warehouse projects.

In other words, this project manager's seemingly impressive background is not serving him well in preparing the project plan for a data warehouse because he is basing his estimates on his own skill level and on developing traditional systems. He is not taking into account other staff members' skill levels, their learning curves, new data warehouse development tasks, technical and nontechnical infrastructure tasks, and cross-organizational tasks.

Clay Rehm

The manager should have the project manager lead a team of deadbeats on his next project—that will learn 'im! Seriously, though, it sounds like he has never led a complex project or a project staffed with underachievers. This project manager has been fortunate to operate in this manner. Until this project manager faces a complex project with people who are not as good as he is, he will fail to understand just how difficult it is to really accurately estimate a project using the resources provided to him.

His manager will need to spend time educating and coaching him on the finer points of managing people who are not as smart as he is or not as positive as he is. The manager should require the project manager to take formal management and project management training. The manager should be there to provide continuous support when this project manager is faced with less than ideal situations. The manager could remind the project manager of when he was starting out, was not as confident as he is now, and did not have the level of experience he has today.

In summary: Building a data warehouse is a team effort. A true leader knows how to use each member of the team, knows his or her strengths and limitations, and bases the project schedule on reality.

PART II

Impossible Technical Situations

CHAPTER EIGHT

Data Warehouse Standards

Without a standard there is no logical basis for making a decision or taking action.

—J. M. Juran

OVERVIEW

Many dog owners give their dogs what they consider to be commands but are really more like guidelines. ("Boscoe, come!" *Pause....* "Well, I guess Boscoe is busy with his chewy toy and doesn't want to come just now.") A number of organizations claim to have standards, but they are also just guidelines. People follow those "standards" if they feel like it and if they think it benefits them. A standard essentially says "Thou shall," while a guideline is a recommendation, more like "You should if your situation warrants." The list below includes some of the standards every organization should address.

- Data sourcing
- Meta data
- Service-level agreements
- Security
- Privacy
- Code standardization
- Project prioritization
- Data stewardship
- Ease of use for access and analysis

- Testing and quality assurance
- Data quality
- Methodology

Standards are traditionally ignored for the following reasons:

- "We don't have time to be bothered with all that bureaucratic nonsense."
- "Following the standards will just slow us down."
- "I didn't know we had any standards."
- "Why do I have to follow standards? No one else follows them."
- "Those standards might have been OK for mainframe dinosaurs, but in the data warehouse world we have to be flexible, so we have thrown off the shackles of those old restrictive standards."
- "Standards are legitimate for OLTP, but we certainly don't need them for the data warehouse."

Why do we have standards at all? By having standards, we minimize the efforts that each project manager must exert to create his or her own working materials. With standards, we greatly improve the chances for the project to be successful and the deliverables to be of high quality. With standards, management should have greater confidence in the ability of the project managers to deliver a high-quality product in a controlled environment and a repeatable manner.

In the remainder of this chapter, we'll explore five situations that involve data warehouse standards and present suggested solutions for each one.

THE ORGANIZATION HAS NO EXPERIENCE WITH METHODOLOGIES

The data warehouse will be built in a company where people have no previous experience with data warehouses and little inkling of methodology. The data warehouse manager knows that the use of a data warehouse methodology is a critical success factor. How should he sell the need for a data warehouse methodology in an environment that is new to data warehouses and to methodologies in general?

Sid Adelman

Some organizations have no experience with any methodology, let alone a methodology for a data warehouse. Getting such an organization to even consider a data warehouse methodology is a formidable task. In this case it is wise not to make a big issue of methodology. The data warehouse manager shouldn't try to sell it as a methodology; he should sell it as a set of methods or practices that have worked well for many organizations. The data warehouse manager needs to find a workable methodology that is not too complex and that fits into the company's culture.

Joyce Bischoff

The data warehouse manager should hire a consultant to develop a barebones methodology for use in the first project. The methodology must not be cumbersome and should allow tailoring to meet the management needs of a particular project. The data warehouse manager could keep an experienced data warehouse consultant as an advisor to every phase of the first project.

Chuck Kelley

There are plenty of discussions on why data warehousing fails, although the number of data warehouse failures widely reported does not reflect what my associates and I have seen. From a technology standpoint, having a methodology to guide the process, especially the first time, goes a long way toward not increasing the failure statistics. The data warehouse manager needs to talk with people who have been involved in both successful and unsuccessful data warehouse projects to develop a good understanding of what makes a project fail. Then he needs to build a cost/benefit analysis for the purchase of the data warehouse methodology, using some of the data points he received while learning about data warehouse successes and failures.

Larissa Moss

The data warehouse manager should start by explaining that there are several hundred tasks to be performed and most likely nobody in the organization knows what they are or how to do them. He should also explain that there are new tasks to be performed on data warehouse projects and that since this is their first project and no one at the organization has any prior data warehouse experience, it is much too risky to proceed by the seat of their pants. In addition to the tasks, there are three possible parallel development efforts: the ETL track, the data access and analysis application track, and the meta data repository track. It would be too difficult to organize and staff these tracks without the help of a methodology.

Clay Rehm

A methodology is a series of well-considered and well-defined steps that achieve and accomplish a common goal. Any project of any importance uses a methodology, and the project management office makes sure the team members follow the methodology. Most important is that the systems development methodology uses an iterative approach that includes parallel tasks so that systems development is accomplished more quickly and more efficiently.

The project plan must be an implementation of the methodology. And speaking of the project plan, the data warehouse manager must make sure it is in the hands of each team member at all times. The data warehouse manager should keep it updated and distribute it each week. He should conduct status meetings that review the plan and focus on the tasks due in the current week. But he shouldn't just stop there—he must also have a methodology for supporting the system after it has gone live.

I am a big fan of the Project Management Institute's Project Management Methodology (PMM) and the *Project Management Book of Knowledge* (PMBOK) (see *http://www.pmi.org*).

This is simply how it is done. A methodology is a given; it is a best practice. The data warehouse manager should not give the users the option to create a data warehouse without it.

DATABASE ADMINISTRATION STANDARDS ARE INAPPROPRIATE FOR THE DATA WAREHOUSE

A major bank has very strong database administration standards for its operational database environment. The DBAs insist that the new data warehouse be designed and managed in the same manner as the OLTP environment. They do not understand OLAP design and the need for iterative development. They also do not comprehend the need for dimensional structures in the OLAP environment or the need for aggregations. The DBA manager does not understand the situation. How can the DBA manager and his staff be convinced to obtain a background in data warehouse design and to recognize the need for changes to standards to accommodate the data warehouse environment before the staff fails to meet user needs through incorrect design and inappropriate data management?

Sid Adelman

The DBA manager and the most influential DBA should attend a data warehouse conference, one that specializes in data warehouse topics. At the conference, they will learn about OLAP, and they will learn the differences between OLTP and data warehouse designs and how they are managed. There are excellent books on data warehousing. If the DBAs like to read, the data warehouse manager should buy and give them one or two of these books. Alternatively, the data warehouse manager could subscribe the DBAs to journals that specialize in data warehousing and make them aware of the Web sites that have information on data warehousing. (The appendix contains a list of references and resources.)

Joyce Bischoff

The DBA group members need training to raise their skills to the level required by the data warehouse environment. I suggest the following classes:

- An introductory data warehouse class
- A data warehouse design class

The DBAs should attend user group meetings and talk to others who are working with data warehouses about standards and differences between operational data and analytical data.

Douglas Hackney

This is a wonderful example of how an OLTP-oriented DBA is about the worst possible resource for a data warehousing project. It is very challenging to convince OLTP DBAs to forget everything they have learned during their last 20 years of database management training. Unfortunately, data warehousing success often depends on just that. Politically sustainable data warehouse database design should be oriented toward ease of use rather than ease of administration. DBAs are often so far removed from business issues and business users that it is very challenging to gain their buy-in for a design that is anything less than theoretical purity. In this case, the project manager would be much better off to recruit a data warehouse–specific DBA for the team and bypass the OLTP DBA organization completely.

Chuck Kelley

It is great that the bank has strong DBA standards for its operational database environment, but a data warehouse environment requires a different set of standards. This is a common problem since most people went to school (including the school of hard knocks) to learn how to design operational databases. The data warehouse manager needs to work with the DBA manager to lay out the plan for developing the data warehouse and explaining why the data warehouse needs a different set of standards. The data warehouse manager can approach this by showing

- How the data warehouse requirements differ from operational requirements
- Why the need for aggregate (summary) tables is important to the data warehouse environment
- Why normalization, while certainly a valid approach, may not be the best approach for the data warehouse, and what reasons exist to prompt consideration of other design approaches
- How business rule changes can affect the design of the data warehouse, making the iterative approach important for this environment

If the data warehouse manager is unsuccessful in this attempt, then he or she needs to take this issue to the data warehouse champion or to the senior IT management. Perhaps the best outcome would be to move the DBA function from the DBA group to the data warehouse team.

Clay Rehm

I have been in this situation many times in my project life. It boils down to mainly one thing: the data warehouse DBA must have a different mind-set than the operational systems DBA. When it comes down to data warehouse database design, not every data warehouse design is the same. The same dimensional design does not work in a cookie-cutter approach. In most cases, some kind of hybrid between OLTP and dimensional design is implemented.

Operational DBAs have been taught the basics of relational theory, of the forms of normalization, data integrity, and standards. These are all great things and must be present in the DBA world. They must also be present in the data warehouse world; however, the idea of normalization bends the rules. Not that normalization is completely thrown away—data warehouse fact tables are highly normalized. It is when modeling dimensions and aggregations that denormalization comes into play. The focus is ease of use for the users, not for the folks who maintain the databases.

Convincing the DBAs to change their mind-sets will not happen overnight. If it does happen, it happens over time due to constantly educating the DBAs and highlighting the benefits of the denormalized and dimensional designs.

What are the options?

• Use brute force.
• Provide gentle guidance.
• Give up.

All these options are appropriate. I always start with gentle guidance, offering explanations, education, and a chance for the operational DBAs to provide their reasons to me why I should consider their designs and their opinions. Education includes sending the OLTP DBAs to data warehouse conferences and providing literature on the subject. The data warehouse manager could consider bringing a consultant into the workplace to speak about the benefits of denormalized/dimensional modeling.

The data warehouse manager could also use the brute force approach if he or she has hired expensive outside consultants. They were hired to provide leadership and expertise. The data warehouse manager should send them into battle.

A lot of times, people just want to be heard. They want to express their opinions, or they want people to know they are providing value. The data warehouse manager should give these DBAs a chance and allow them to express themselves. He or she should be open to their side of the story.

Bottom line: The database design for a data warehouse is different than that for operational systems. Database design is not a one-size-fits-all proposition.

THE EMPLOYEES MISUSE DATA WAREHOUSE TERMINOLOGY

The employees of a large insurance company have misused data warehouse terminology for the past five years. They use "data warehouse" to describe independent data marts. They call legacy operational systems "operational data stores." In addition, they are planning to integrate all their operational and informational systems into shared databases. The company has 2,000 users, most of whom are quite active. Cooler heads have been unsuccessful trying to explain why it is difficult if not impossible to run OLAP queries and OLTP transactions against the same large databases. How should the IT executives solve this impossible situation?

Sid Adelman

I would forget the misuse of terminology; it's not that important. As long as there is communication within the organization, it doesn't matter that much if the terminology differs from the rest of the civilized world. However, when outsiders come in, they need to be given the organization's glossary so they, in turn, will be able to communicate. If the organization has not already done so, it should develop a data warehouse glossary and publish it on the internal Web site.

The plans to integrate the operational and informational systems will be a serious problem. The company's architects need to hear from people who have gone down that road and failed. They failed because the operational systems should have different designs from those of the data warehouse. Data warehouse queries will sometimes require heavy use of computational and I/O functions and will kill the online performance of the operational systems. Finally, decision support is normally a point in time, for example, yesterday's closing figures. Analysts do not want a moving target. They want data that does not change during their analyses.

Sharing raises additional problems. The organization may have sensitive data, for example, employee payroll data and financial results, for which access should be restricted. The owners of the data should be consulted about what can be accessed, by whom, and when. Some data owners do not want anyone outside of their departments to see their data. The sensitive issue of sharing data must always be addressed.

Joyce Bischoff

I would obtain top management support for explaining the advantages of using standard industry terminology.

- Without standard terminology, there may be increased risk. For example, people read about operational data stores and assume that this means the legacy data.
- It is difficult to talk with professionals from other companies when you do not share the same language.

The following actions may help the organization:

- Educate the staff on centralized, distributed, and federated implementations of data warehouse environments.
- Publish a document comparing standard industry terminology with the local terminology.

I would consider establishing a data warehouse user group within the company to sponsor regular meetings (possibly monthly) about the current status of the data warehouse and to encourage communication between various business groups and IT. The group would emphasize standard terminology, best practices, and technology alternatives.

I would also educate the users about the potential impact of running analytical queries against operational data and how long-running queries may have a serious effect on the response time of the operational environment.

Douglas Hackney

Recent advances in database technology actually allow us to do some limited blending of OLTP and OLAP functionality within the same database. However, the scale of the implementation implied in this scenario is probably beyond the scope of the single-instance databases at this stage of their development. In addition, the technology is no silver bullet for this misuse and abuse of the semantic terms around data warehousing.

In this scenario, each project team must be very careful to limit the scope of each iteration. It may be possible to implement some narrowly focused iterations that can support both operational and analytical uses of a single database. The team members will also need to rebrand their efforts to a name other than "data warehousing" in order to avoid mixing their efforts with the amorphous cloud of systems currently labeled by that term.

Chuck Kelley

There are two parts to this question. The first deals with the use of terms that don't fit the way the industry typically uses them (although there is not full agreement on what some terms mean—"data warehousing" is a good example!). Here we see this large insurance company use the term "operational data stores" for the legacy operational systems. While "operational data stores" are operational systems, they are not *the* operational systems. They are fed *from* the operational systems. The company employees use "data warehouse" as a term to describe independent data marts. I don't believe in totally independent data marts. Without some "centralized" control over common dimensions the team ends up building what probably already exists—stovepipes or silos. Stovepipes or silos are systems that have no ability to share data between each other. Therefore, by breaking the concept of "centralized" controlled dimensions (Ralph Kimball [1996] calls these "conformed dimensions"), this large insurance company has gotten itself into trouble.

The second part of the question deals with proving that it is not practical to run OLAP queries and OLTP queries against the same large database. If the people cannot see that running the "query from hell" will kill the OLTP performance (thereby proving that it is not practical to run OLAP and OLTP queries against the same database), then the data warehouse manager will need proof to do so. Some of this proof could include asking the opposing groups some questions.

- How can we tune the operating system to do five reads and seven writes (typical of a transaction system) versus reading one million rows and aggregating at the same time (typical of a data warehouse)?
- How can we tune the database to do the same? For example, how would we set the page size? Small as for transaction systems or large as for data warehouses? The issues, in this case, center on how much data is read from disk when performing an I/O operation.

If the discussions do not provide the proof, then the data warehouse manager's staff can build the proof by creating a test OLTP environment, building some test scripts to do OLAP and OLTP workloads, and show-ing the results.

But the real problem that this large insurance company has is not that the employees are misusing the terms (although that is a symptom of the problem) but that they have not properly defined the requirements for the systems. There should have been an architected data environment.

Larissa Moss

There is a plethora of material available on data warehouse terminology, data warehouse architecture, very large databases (VLDBs), operational data stores, and other data warehouse–related topics. In addition, numer-ous conferences and Web sites on data warehousing provide information supporting the cooler heads' position to keep OLTP separate from OLAP. Presumably these cooler heads have used all the available sources of infor-mation to educate this insurance company about data warehousing—obviously without success. If all attempts of educating and reasoning with the company executives have failed, I suggest just letting them learn from their own mistakes. If the decision makers cannot be convinced through education, they must learn the hard way—through experience.

Clay Rehm

The data warehouse manager must be able to present the case of not run-ning OLAP and OLTP queries against the same database. He or she should start with a glossary of terms, explaining what the company really has—this may include a matrix that lists each current system, the current type of data structure, and the new name of the data structure.

Education is the key here. The data warehouse manager should con-duct internal seminars of the components and benefits of a data ware-house. He or she will get more buy-in if a respected external consultant presents these seminars. If the data warehouse manager can't bring in an external resource, instead of relying on brute force, he or she should focus on getting personnel to agree on terminology. This requires an unbiased third-party facilitator who will have nothing to gain from these exercises. This is important because the name game is usually a political game, and certain people on this earth have nothing else to contribute other than their opinions that they made the right decision.

The data warehouse manager should implement ongoing educational sessions for the organization. He or she could create a data warehouse users' group to share war stories, query tips, data tips, and so on. Another data warehouse user group for the different development teams around the organization could share use of tools, conformed dimensions, and so on.

The moral of the story: There is no replacement for education.

It's All Data Mining

A company's employees fell in love with the term "data mining" and use it to describe all types of decision support activities. Now that the company is seriously considering data mining in a real sense, trying to justify it to an organization that is convinced it already has data mining is becoming difficult. How should the data warehouse manager properly educate and sell the company on the use of data mining?

Sid Adelman

The data warehouse manager should call it something else, depending on the product chosen ("pattern analysis," "neural networks," "artificial intelligence") or the name of the application ("fraud analysis," "customer retention," "outcomes analysis"). He or she should sell the expected benefits that data mining will provide and avoid having to change the corporate mind-set of how they refer to data mining; it's a waste of time and effort.

Joyce Bischoff

The data warehouse manager should bring in an outside speaker who is an expert on real data mining for a three- to six-hour class on data-mining techniques. He or she should also consider sending people to a conference that emphasizes data-mining topics and has an exhibit hall with demos of real data-mining tools.

Jill Dyché

Show me a company where everyone uses the term "data mining" as a synonym for business intelligence and I'll show you a company that has swallowed the OLAP vendors' sales pitch. I once defined data mining at a conference presentation, only to have a data analyst who had been using a popular query tool storm out of the room. Later he vehemently tried to make the case that he'd been doing data mining. His whole job identity was wrapped around the term. He'd been slicing and dicing critical financial information—a valuable activity that had helped his company determine customer profitability. But he wasn't doing data mining.

Data mining is really about discovering hidden or unanticipated patterns in data. In order to succeed with data mining, an organization should already have a robust, detailed, and cross-functional data architecture. It should also already employ a group of senior-level analysts or statisticians who are intimate with this data. If the company is really ready for data mining, these power users will understand the potential for data mining and the fact that it's not yet being done.

In this case, trying to reeducate the business at large about the real meaning of the term "data mining" risks not only creating confusion but also changing people's entire idea about what they've been doing. The company might consider using another term. In my experience, most data mining deals with some sort of prediction, so one suggestion would be to substitute the term "predictive analysis" for "data mining."

However, since data mining will likely be confined to a group of experienced data analysts, the best approach would be to describe data mining in terms of its business use. So rather than naming the algorithm—the difference between "clustering" and "association" doesn't mean much to most business people—the company should define a data-mining activity around its actual application. Thus in practice, rather than calling a data-mining activity "affinity analysis," it would be called "market basket analysis." In this way, more people will understand the term and accept it for providing differentiated and necessary business value.

Chuck Kelley

I ask people not to get caught up with "naming" things. If someone calls an operational data store a "data warehouse," then I try to correct them by telling them what the term generally means in the industry. I don't linger very long trying to change the internal naming issue. I recommend that the project team wanting to develop the "real" data mining put together a presentation that sets out many types of data mining, including the ones that the company already does. The team members should add to that the more complex (read "real") data-mining techniques and say that this is where they want to go next.

Larissa Moss

Terminology really does matter. The data warehouse team should explain and demonstrate the functionality of data-mining tools—functionality that the company obviously does not have yet. Since data mining is completely different from other decision support activities such as reporting and querying, a demonstration of the data-mining capabilities should convince the company to augment its tool suite with a data-mining tool if it needs that type of capability. An excellent introductory book on data mining is *Discovering Data Mining from Concept to Implementation* [Cabena et al. 1997].

Clay Rehm

I would have the data warehouse team create a demo and take it on the road to display what we have and what we don't have. During the demos, I would explain to the audience the misuse of the "data mining" term. I would start using terms like "executive information system," "data warehouse," "data mart," "operational data store," "reporting," and so on. I would develop a semantics dictionary—a glossary that defines what terms to use as we proceed—and publish it so everyone has easy access to it!

Bottom line: The game all comes down to education and communication.

A MULTINATIONAL COMPANY NEEDS TO BUILD A BUSINESS INTELLIGENCE ENVIRONMENT

The executives of a multinational company are trying to create a comprehensive plan for a business intelligence environment. They know they need to deal with very diverse requirements, budgeting issues, language translations, diversity in national laws, different standards for security and privacy, distributed versus centralized databases, administration and controls, and much more. What should the data warehouse architect consider? Is such a plan even possible?

Sid Adelman

A business intelligence plan that will support a multinational company is possible—but not easy. Besides considering the points mentioned above (and they are all relevant and important), the company should appoint and give authority to a high-level manager who can make and enforce decisions. This manager must be well respected in most of the countries where the company has activities. If the manager doesn't have enough authority, the leaders of company divisions in different countries will want to do things their own different ways. This multinational czar will get input from the members of each group and listen to their opinions, but in the end, the czar will make the final determination. Otherwise, since it will be impossible to get concurrence from everyone, this multinational endeavor will fail. However, the czar should know when to bend the standards that are not as critical and should be aware of important cultural issues that could cause problems and may require specific dispensations.

Joyce Bischoff

The key points of a federated data warehouse architecture (Figure 8–1) include the following.

- Each feed is associated with an ETL process (not shown in the figure) that may range from a direct extract without transformations to a more complex transformation process.
- The company should try to create operational systems using globally standardized software. If it is necessary to deviate from this, the data warehouse architect should allow the divisions in different countries to tailor the operational software to their needs. Although each country's division may have its own operational systems, it would be most efficient to have the systems as close to standardized as possible.

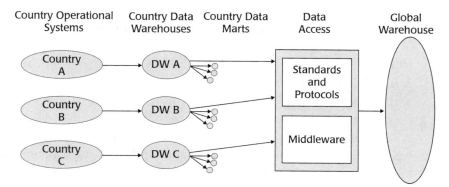

Figure 8–1: Global federated data warehouse architecture

- Each country's division could have its own data warehouse to feed its data marts. The feeds must follow standards and protocols.
- The company could develop a standard, shared, global data warehouse with core business information that will allow comparisons between the countries. Different privacy laws may prevent the sharing of detail data, and warehouse data may need to emphasize summarized data. The data should handle multiple currencies. Since there will be differences in the data coming from each country, it will be necessary to have standards and protocols in place that will be applied during an ETL process. If the differences are too great, it may be necessary to use purchased or custom software to achieve a federated environment.

Douglas Hackney

This plan is possible and achievable if the team and the business stakeholders adopt a pragmatic philosophy. In this scenario, as in all large organizations, the system will be based on a federated business intelligence (BI) architecture. The diversity of the underlying BI systems and the global scale of the organization require a federated approach.

Chuck Kelley

Putting together an architecture for this environment is intriguing, quite difficult, but not impossible. There needs to be a strong understanding of the issues involved in each of the different areas described above. Most data warehouses relegate meta data repositories to the "nice to have" category. A strong meta data repository will be critical to the success of this data warehouse. I would look at each of the different areas and then develop a plan to attack each one in small but attainable steps.

Clay Rehm

A multinational plan is possible but it will be very complex, challenging, and time consuming. Politics, communication, and language barriers will be constant problems but can be minimized if standards, rules, and guidelines are dealt with up front. The technology will be challenging as well, having to deal with protocols and standards from many different locations.

The data warehouse architect must answer the following questions before proceeding:

- What is the business problem?
- What will the multinational BI environment solve?
- Are the business users 100 percent committed to this effort?
- Are top, middle, and lower management singing from the same hymnal? That is, do all layers of management agree on the problem and its solution?
- What are the agreed-upon requirements, and what are the requirements disputes?
- Are there common goals and objectives?
- Are the requirements coming from one group or from all affected departments?
- Who has been chosen to interpret differences in language?
- Has a cost allocation scheme been developed, agreed to, and presented?
- Do standards and best practices exist? If not, how will they be created, agreed upon, distributed, and followed?
- Is there an agreed-upon data model that includes common data elements and data definitions? Does everyone agree on what is a customer, product, and so on?
- What security is required, and what security is just nice to have?
- Is a security specialist who has experience in data warehousing and government regulations assigned to the project?
- Can users access data from a centralized site, or must data reside on local computers in the native language?
- Who is overseeing the project? What authority do they or don't they have?
- Who is representing and validating international laws?

A multinational BI plan is accomplishable, but everyone involved must be realistic about the complexity, time, and effort involved.

CHAPTER NINE

Tools and Vendors

Praise from a salesman, in my humble opinion, is one of life's less convincing compliments

—Peter Mayle

OVERVIEW

Data warehouse tools have made the implementation of data warehouse projects much easier, but they are not (in spite of what the vendors tell you) the silver bullet that guarantees success. Projects are impacted when vendor support falters. Vendor support is usually considered one of the mandatory requirements for tool selection. The data warehouse software market has seen and will probably continue to see acquisitions, mergers, and buyouts of software firms that are in financial trouble. In some acquired companies, the development and support people either are laid off or leave on their own volition. In some instances, the acquiring company has no interest in providing good tool support.

We have all had positive and negative experience with various types of tools, with software itself, and with vendors. These experiences can cloud our decision-making powers and can cause us to make the wrong decisions. Existing mind-sets or standards can dictate tools that may be inappropriate. The choice of unsuitable tools can affect the success of the project.

Some tools require significant skills, and these skills, in turn, require significant training and a commensurate learning curve.

Performance is always a problem with very large databases (VLDBs), as is the ability of the tools to satisfy performance requirements. We are seeing more and more VLDBs as organizations capture more and more of their transactions and as they maintain extensive historical detailed data. Different tools have very different performance characteristics and capabilities. The ability to perform well is becoming one of the important criteria for tool selection.

Requests for proposals (RFPs) are a requirement for many organizations, particularly those in the public sector. A long and complicated RFP discourages vendors and will usually negatively impact the project's schedule.

Vendors have been known to embellish the capabilities of their products and to minimize the complexity of their use. These misrepresentations sometimes cause management to underestimate the effort involved in data warehouse projects. Vendors are notorious for bypassing IT and instead marketing directly to the end-users. In the vendors' defense, in situations where IT is apathetic and does not support the information requirements of the end-user, the vendors have no choice.

Many companies rely on their vendors for primary architecture and direction. Some vendors maintain a staff of people at their larger customer sites. Vendors can be very powerful and can influence software choices, architecture, direction, and even the client company's organization, including hiring and firing employees. We often hear about vendors who are out of control, for example, calling on key people when a decision is not in their favor and undermining an internal decision. Vendors often go over the heads of the people who have made a software decision.

This chapter discusses eight difficult situations that can arise regarding tools and vendors and suggests solutions for these situations.

WHAT ARE THE BEST PRACTICES FOR WRITING A REQUEST FOR PROPOSALS?

A nonprofit organization is considering a data warehouse to keep track of its membership and solicitation activities. Any project this large requires an RFP. Of course, the executives do not want the RFP process to significantly slow them down. What should the organization do?

Sid Adelman

The organization should keep the RFP process as well as the RFP document as simple and short as possible. A large, complex RFP document will result in vendors either not responding or responding just with boilerplate proposals that do not adequately answer the RFP. The more complex the RFP document, the longer it will take to adequately compare the different responses. The RFP should include only the points the organization will use to compare the vendors. This means including only "mandatory" and "highly desirable" features, not the "nice to have" ones and definitely not any "blue-sky" requirements.

Chuck Kelley

The RFP process will inherently slow down the development of the data warehouse. Then the question becomes how much time is the organization willing to allow for the RFP process? It might be possible to go through the whole process in four weeks, but that would be extremely difficult.

David Marco

The organization should keep the RFP clear and concise. A quality RFP can thoroughly cover a particular data warehousing initiative in less than 30 pages. RFPs that go on for 50 or more pages take a great deal of time to read, digest, and respond to. Also, the longer the RFP, the greater the likelihood that vendors will have questions.

As much as possible, the organization should limit the number of vendors bidding on the project. Each vendor will significantly expand the entire RFP process.

Someone in the organization should follow up with each of the vendors. This includes answering questions, distributing information, and following up on meetings.

Clay Rehm

It is possible to create an abbreviated RFP: very short, concise, and to the point. The traditional RFP process requires the identification of the proper vendors. This in itself can slow the process. The organization should narrow the field of RFP vendors to a very short list. How? The project manager could contact a consulting organization to provide the short list of vendors for the specific tool targeted in the RFP. The text of the RFP should state that the vendor must reply by a certain deadline to avoid being removed from the evaluation list.

Bottom line: The goal is to document every decision yet reduce the amount of time spent to evaluate every vendor.

THE USERS DON'T LIKE THE QUERY AND REPORTING TOOL

A company was dismayed to learn that only 5 percent of the users who went through training used the data warehouse regularly. On further investigation, the executives learned that those who did not use the data warehouse were uncomfortable with the query and reporting tool and reluctant to use it. What should the company do?

Sid Adelman

The training needs to be geared to the users' levels of interest and capability. The casual users are not going to learn to write SQL. The data warehouse team should give them predefined queries and reports and teach them how to launch those queries and reports. The training should also teach the users about the data and sell them on their newfound capabilities.

The data warehouse team should evaluate the effectiveness of the training with course evaluations both immediately after the class and two months after the class ends. The two-month evaluation should ask users what material presented in the class was useful and what was not, what should have been taught but was not, whether and how they are using the data warehouse today, and the manner in which they are using it if they are.

Joyce Bischoff

Was there a business reason for building the data warehouse? If so, the company should provide additional training and support on the query and reporting tool for the users. The support may consist of classes, one-to-one sessions with experts, an effective help desk, distribution of user manuals, sample queries and reports, and round-table discussions about problems and solutions for using the tool.

If there was no business reason for building the data warehouse, it has been an obvious failure. A full review should be conducted to determine whether there is anything worth salvaging from the current implementation.

Douglas Hackney

If this data warehouse system were providing life-saving relief to life-threatening business pain, it's unlikely that anyone would avoid using the data warehouse because of reluctance to use the query and reporting tool. Systems that are built to address specific, life-threatening business challenges have high utilization rates, even if the query and reporting tool is not the most intuitive. It is much more likely in this scenario that the tool is being blamed when, in actuality, the data warehouse is viewed as a "nice to have" rather than a "must have" system.

Sean Ivoghli

This situation is very common, and training alone will not do the job. First of all, the data warehouse team must make sure that reports are extremely easy to use. One option is to turn off most of the powerful analytical capabilities of the tool for the majority of the users. This makes it easier for them to use the tool and less likely that they will get lost in the tool. The team should make the reports extremely simple and make meta data easily available. Over time the team can start introducing more and more of the tool's capabilities as people start using the basic features of the tool and get more comfortable with the tool. Placed into each business unit, power users who are experts with the tool and know the business very well can help the business users with new reporting and analytical needs. If the business is not willing to pay for this staffing directly, the costs should come out of the data warehouse budget. The power users should take the "let me show you" approach for users when time permits. The adoption of business intelligence tools by most users will take time. Some users will always want to be spoon-fed, and that is becoming a reality for many data warehouses in just about every industry.

Chuck Kelley

It is time to set up small group training classes. These classes should have no more than five users each and should last no more than half a day. That allows the users to dedicate relatively small blocks of time to learn about new products. These half-day sessions should be offered at beginner, intermediate, and expert levels. Frequent sessions (at least for the beginner and intermediate levels) allow the users to bring questions they were uncomfortable with or unable to solve. Some sessions could address the problems encountered by the 5 percent of users who have been using the data warehouse.

David Marco

Several problems can cause this situation.

- The data warehouse does not meet the users' requirements.
- The data warehouse does not provide value.
- The query and reporting tool does not meet the users' requirements.
- Training was inadequate.
- Business meta data is not being integrated on the business queries and reports.
- Reporting performance is problematic.

I recommend meeting with the users to determine the issue(s). Once the problem has been identified, a proper course of action can be taken.

Clay Rehm

There are many possible problems, including those listed below.

- Training did not meet expectations.
- The query and reporting tool is difficult to use.
- Data quality problems occur when viewing data in the tool.
- Meta data is lacking.
- The report or query layouts are not intuitive.
- The data was not modeled or captured correctly.
- The data warehouse doesn't meet the business requirements.

Before spending time on finding ways to "fix" the query and reporting tool, the data warehouse team should investigate further on the other possible reasons for the problem by obtaining the services of a qualified data warehouse consultant or an internal experienced data warehouse expert who is an unbiased third party. He or she should perform a quick assessment on all the aspects of the data warehouse, including business processes, organizational change management, politics, technology, and the team.

If indeed it is only a problem with the tool, the team should find out why the users are uncomfortable with the tool. What would make it more user-friendly? What would it take for them to use it again? Often we either forget to ask or do not like to ask the obvious or tough questions. If there are other problems, such as a lack of good training or data quality, the team must spend the time, effort, and resources needed to resolve those items quickly.

Bottom line: Routine assessments of the data warehouse by outsiders can help prevent future problems.

OO Is the Answer (But What's the Question?)

A fairly young organization developed all its applications in an object-oriented (OO) environment. Since the implementations were successful, almost everyone in the organization believes that everything should be developed in an OO way, including the data warehouse. They expect the methodology and all the tools to be based on OO. Will this work for a data warehouse?

Sid Adelman

"To the man with a hammer, everything looks like a nail." The objective should not be to implement everything with a predefined technology. The objective is to give the business a strong strategic decision-making capability. The IT weenies pushing OO need to understand the objectives of the organization and the objectives of the data warehouse project. They also need to understand that there is a business justification, not a technical reason, for their salaries.

Sean Ivoghli

I've been asked to design OO data warehouses in the past. After attempting it a couple of times, doing a lot of research, and talking to others who have made similar attempts, I have decided against it. In the situation posed above, I am assuming that the team is being asked to design a relational database using an OO methodology.

Most OO methodologies define *data* objects as static (and *process* objects as dynamic). This means that the database will use object classes and inheritance but not many other OO concepts (which mainly apply to processes, events, user interface objects, and so on). In a relational implementation this translates to tables that define tables (data defines data), where the actual data (in rows) tells the users what a row of data is all about. The main benefit of this is reusability of tables: many kinds of data can be fit into very generic, data-defined tables. Doing this can significantly reduce the number of tables in the data warehouse but at the cost of creating very "deep" tables (too many rows), which impedes performance. Also, in order to use the data, the reports and the semantic layer need to have additional rules to interpret the data stored in the generic tables. This increases the size of the WHERE clauses on queries dramatically and results in the frequent requirement for multipass SQL, which has major performance disadvantages. Also, the users must know even more about the data in order to create a meaningful report or query. I could go on and on about this, but I think I've made my point.

Data warehouses are not the place for OO design. The closest the team could really get to incorporating OO technology is to purchase a graphical ETL tool for data acquisition that allows the reuse of objects. That still does not make an OO data warehouse, but it might satisfy some of the OO advocates. The team members should do themselves a favor: don't design a database with any OO methodologies.

Chuck Kelley

Sure, it will work, but at what added cost? And what is considered to be OO? Certainly, if the organization is using an ETL tool for development, most (not all) of those tools are somewhat OO. The team could certainly use OO methodologies to define the database of the data warehouse, although I would be extremely concerned about the performance of an OO design in a relational database. At this writing and in my opinion, OO databases are not quite ready to build extremely large data stores (such as the data warehouse). The end-user tools use the equivalent of class and objects to build the semantic layer on the data warehouse to provide an OO look and feel. Therefore, yes, I believe you can use the OO environment to build the data warehouse, but there will be some added cost associated with it.

David Marco

I would strongly discourage a company from building an OO data warehouse. The challenges of scalability and maintenance and the organic nature of the data warehouse makes this approach less than optimal. On the other hand, I could have easily said "yes" to this question. As the old saying goes, with infinite money, resources, and time, anything is possible.

IT HAS ALREADY CHOSEN THE TOOL

Even though a tool selection committee supposedly has the authority to chose data warehouse tools, some powerful people in the IT department already know what they want and will resist any recommendations that do not correspond to their choice. Some members of the tool selection committee are concerned that the chosen tools won't perform. What should the selection committee do?

Sid Adelman

The easiest political decision would be to acquiesce to the powers and accept the chosen tools. However, if those tools won't perform or are otherwise unacceptable, the selection committee cannot go along with IT's decisions. The selection committee must first determine whether or not the tools will perform well. This research should include seeing these tools in action at other installations. The committee should determine whether the tools are running the volume and complexity of the intended workload and whether they are running at the data volumes anticipated for the project. Note that this means what will actually be run, not what can be done theoretically.

Joyce Bischoff

The committee members should develop a list of criteria for tool selection. After the initial evaluations, they should select the top two or three tools, including the tools preferred by the powerful people and the ones that the committee prefers. The committee can bring the tools in-house and run them head-to-head to provide an objective evaluation of which tools best meet the criteria. This should show whether the committee's fears are well founded and will provide documented proof as to which tool is best. If a poor tool is selected because of management interference, the team's reputation should not be damaged.

Jill Dyché

The selection committee should just say no. Any tool chosen based on bias and not on deliberately drafted business requirements is an accident waiting to happen.

The eventual business users will be disaffected by having a tool pushed down their throats—and as we all know, a data warehouse is only as valuable as its degree of usage. They'll probably begin a skunkworks project of their own, or worse, simply cancel the effort altogether. Abandoning critical decision support capabilities could ultimately harm the company at large.

At the very least, the company could be wasting a large amount of money by investing in a toolset, only to deliberate on its value and replace it later.

Instead, the selection committee should undertake a requirements gathering activity, retaining an outside consultant to ensure the necessary objectivity and structure. The resulting requirements should then be translated into RFP selection metrics that are distributed to a handful of qualifying vendors—including the one IT favors. This should result in a balanced, metric-based, apples-to-apples product evaluation. The likely result is that there will be a higher degree of consensus around the right choice and fewer squabbles down the road.

Douglas Hackney

It is unfortunately fairly common for a team of technologists or business people to become enamored with a particular tool and then to build a system around it. These projects almost always fail. It is critical to start with the needs of the business and then apply appropriate technologies. All too often the technologies are selected first and the needs of the business are considered later. This is, by definition, an answer looking for a problem. In this scenario, both groups, the IT tool bigots and the concerned committee members, should leverage proofs-of-concept by the vendors to address their concerns. By demonstrating its product's capabilities in a proof-of-concept, each tool vendor can show the IT department that its tool is suitable, while simultaneously demonstrating performance and capability to the selection committee.

Chuck Kelley

This is quite a common problem, especially in the end-user tool area. At this point, I would allow the tool selection committee to continue moving with its charter. Then I would take the powerful people in the IT shop and the committee to form a pilot test for each of the desired areas where the tools will be used. I would want clear agreement that the pilot test is representative of what needs to be done, and the winner of the pilot test would be the final choice.

David Marco

It will be critical to document and publicize that the selection committee and its procedures are being bypassed in the data warehouse tool selection. On occasion this negative publicity can create pressure on the "powers that be" to change their direction.

At a minimum the committee members should evaluate the tools that IT is proposing and then document the specific concerns the committee members have. This document will be very valuable when the next group of powerful IT managers comes in and asks why the current data warehousing tools are not working and new tools need to be purchased.

Clay Rehm

As hard as this will be, the selection committee must provide the facts to the business that is spending the money. If some powerful IT person or group is favoring any tool, it is the responsibly of the selection committee to identify, document, and present the facts to the appropriate audience. The tool selection committee must document every decision made and every tool feature tested.

If I were a member of the tool selection committee, I would do a thorough examination of the tools. I would create an easy-to-read, detailed, and thorough document that included an executive summary and hand this document to the data warehouse stakeholders and interested parties. I would follow up the distribution of the document with a presentation and question-and-answer session with the stakeholders, inviting the powerful IT decision makers to attend as well. I would conduct this presentation in such a way that the best tool for the job is made clear, and I would give everyone a chance to speak his or her mind.

The moral of the story: Instead of giving up, bite the bullet and do the hard work that is necessary to research, identify, document, and present the facts.

WILL THE TOOLS PERFORM WELL?

A company's data warehouse manager expects to have a data warehouse with over 50 million records within two years. He would like to use an ETL tool, but he is concerned about the tool's ability to perform. He knows this tool is expensive, and he does not want to get started with a product that will have to be abandoned as the volumes increase. How can he be sure that the tools under consideration will perform up to their expectations?

Sid Adelman

The data warehouse manager should ask the vendors for references from their customers who have large volumes of data, preferably running volumes similar to those the executives anticipate for the new data warehouse. The evaluation team should ask the vendors' customers about their platforms (hardware, operating systems, and RDBMS), database designs, and monitoring tools. The team needs to find out what skills were employed for the initial implementation as well as for ongoing maintenance, what skills the references feel are necessary, what training they recommend, and what consulting services they used and what services they feel are necessary for a successful implementation.

Joyce Bischoff

The data warehouse team should obtain references from the vendors for companies with a comparable amount of data. Use of networking skills can help find technical people in the reference sites who may be willing to talk off the record. Professional meetings are a good place to meet users informally. This is the only way to obtain really accurate information. If an executive is asked if a particular tool is successful, the answer will almost always be a resounding "yes." It is not in an executive's interests to admit that a decision was less than ideal. Even if a tool is an abject failure, the executive will usually say it is successful.

Another alternative is to create a large test database, bring the tool in-house, and test it.

Douglas Hackney

The most common route is to rely on reference site testimonials and proof-of-concept testing. Of these two, proof-of-concept testing is the only truly reliable option. Reference site testimonials are provided by customers who can be trusted to say nothing but good things about the vendor and their products. In this scenario, the ETL tools will need to be stress-tested in a proof-of-concept that replicates the expected load volumes and frequency of update in the anticipated production environment.

Sean Ivoghli

Some very mature ETL tools in the market have been used successfully for many years in many large data warehouses. Successful use of these tools depends more on the proper use of them and the management of expectations. The two most common problems I have encountered with regard to ETL tool performance (for industrial-strength ETL tools) is in either the way the ETL process is designed or the amount of system resources allocated to the ETL processes. ETL tools typically are RAM and CPU hogs, so the company should be generous and make sure the systems administrator has set up the system resources so they are available and allocated to the ETL process efficiently. Also, the developers who are designing and developing the ETL processes with the tool must be experts in using the tool. Remember the old saying, "A fool with a tool is still a fool." The way the ETL processes are created makes a big difference in performance.

Chuck Kelley

The data warehouse team members need to understand what the ETL tool is supposed to do before they start to search for the best tool; otherwise problems will likely arise. Most of the time, generic RFPs are used to choose the tool. Tool choices must be made based on what is needed, not what is available. In my opinion, one of the big problem areas with ETL tools today is that they do not understand processing of large files.

For example, if the company will be feeding files from the operational system that provides year-to-date summaries of expenditures and the data warehouse stores monthly snapshots of expenses, there is a need to match and merge last month's file with this month's file to subtract the values and get the difference. This data will be stored in this month's measures. If there are only a few hundred rows, then loading last month's data into a table, reading this month's data, and looking up last month's data might be a good solution. However, if each month there are 10 million rows, then loading them into a relational table for lookups will not be efficient. If you do not know what the environment is, how can you expect to find the right tool? Choosing a tool takes time: understanding the requirements, asking the vendors to explain their solutions to the problem, and then selecting the right tool for the job based on a weighting of the important versus the "nice to have" requirements.

David Marco

First, I would obtain references from the vendors about their clients that are running large volumes of data on a platform (hardware, memory, disk space, and so on) similar to what the company is running. These references may not be easy to come by, and client references are not always 100 percent accurate. Second, if time allows, a well-designed stress test would have a great deal of value. I would create a testing environment that mimics 100 million records (I believe that doubling the record number would provide some needed room for the warehouse to grow), with the approximate record length that the company anticipates. Then I would bring the vendors in to see if their tools could handle the volumes of data.

Clay Rehm

The data warehouse team should identify the current ETL tool vendors by searching the Web and/or contacting their favorite data warehouse consultant. It is important to identify *all* vendors in this space, not just the couple of vendors that advertise in the favorite data warehouse magazine. The team also needs to consider other tools that deal with data movement, which do market themselves as "ETL" tools. The project may not need the full functionality of an ETL tool.

After creating the list of vendors, the team should create a very short RFP that states the requirements and makes very clear that the company expects to have over 50 million records in the database within two years. The RFP must detail the current environment (RDBMS, operating system, hardware, and so on) and also include any upgrade plans for the next two or more years. The RFP should make it clear that the company expects an evaluation of the product on the expected table sizes.

Once the RFP responses roll in, the data warehouse team will be able to create a matrix document to match the requirements to the vendors. The goal is to create a short list of vendors and tools to make the final comparison easier and less time consuming. The team can then conduct a bake-off contest, whereby the remaining vendors compete against each other in a real-world situation to show whether their products perform as promised.

The moral of the story: Don't rely on what you read or hear; kick the tires yourself.

THE VENDOR HAS UNDUE INFLUENCE

A data warehouse vendor has a suite of data warehouse products, some of which are excellent; however, some are far from best-of-breed. The vendor's representative is pushing the entire suite. In fact, he is making it clear that the only way to get top-level support is to buy the complete package. How should the organization respond?

Sid Adelman

Shame on him. The vendor's representative is using the shabby ruse of the threat of not getting adequate support as a lever to sell the whole suite. Top-level support should never be negotiable. If the vendor cannot guarantee top-level support for each product, the organization should go to a vendor that will—there are plenty out there.

Joyce Bischoff

The organization should first develop requirements for data warehouse products. IT should then compare requirements with the features of the products being offered. If only some of the products meet requirements, the company should refuse to buy the full suite. The organization's staff can make it clear that they expect good service even if they buy only a few of the products. The vendor should provide a service-level agreement with appropriate guarantees. If not, the organization should find another vendor.

Douglas Hackney

The organization should ask the vendor to provide the substandard products for free. This will effectively call the vendor representative's bluff and force him to recognize that there is no upside for the customer in adopting and implementing substandard products merely to ensure that the sales representative meets his quota. If the substandard products cost nothing, then the customer does not suffer financially when these products become shelfware. At the same time, the sales representative wins by meeting the vendor's goal of full-suite sales.

Sean Ivoghli

The organization shouldn't listen to the story the salesperson is telling. He just wants to get a larger commission check. The customer should take back control of the deal by introducing a competitor or two into the mix and not returning the salesperson's phone calls. Rather than letting a vendor push them around, the organization's data warehouse team members should buy only what they need. Most sales representatives for vendors have nothing to do with the support level provided after the sale. The data warehouse team members should pay for the support level they want, and that's what they'll get. If they don't get the support they paid for, chances are that they wouldn't have gotten it anyway. That depends on the quality of the vendor's support organization.

Chuck Kelley

The data warehouse team needs to decide whether the top-level support is worth the problems that the "far from best-of-breed" products could cause. Some analysis needs to be made on just where the products fit in and how much time, effort, and cost it would take to work around the problem areas. If the vendor's tools come close to meeting the organization's requirements, the data warehouse team can try to negotiate with the vendor service levels for each product. If the vendor doesn't agree, the team can move to another vendor. The vendor needs to accept some of the risk.

If the vendor does not wish to sell individual parts of the product suite and provide the best support, then I think the vendor may not be the best choice for this organization.

David Marco

If cost is an issue and the vendor is offering significant discounts for buying the suite, then I would consider the purchase. If not, I would send the vendor packing and buy the tools the corporation really needs from another vendor.

Clay Rehm

"No thanks!" It is easy to be swayed by smiling, friendly, talented, smart, and good-looking sales representatives. The sales representatives know this and use it to their advantage.

What should the organization do? Bring in an unbiased vendor-neutral consultant who can assess the current products and determine which tools meet the organization's needs, not the vendor's needs. The consultant should demand and obtain the vendor's list of clients that use the product suite. He or she could then visit these client sites and view how they are using the products. The consultant should interview the clients on the vendor's list and ask tough questions. The consultant should also locate consultants and other companies that have used the suite. He or she should compile and document the information gathered and be prepared to present this information to anyone at anytime.

Bottom line: Know what you want, document that, and be prepared to support your decisions.

THE REJECTED VENDOR DOESN'T UNDERSTAND "NO"

An organization went through the software evaluation process and made a well-considered choice of a vendor and tool. The losing vendor does not know how to take "no" for an answer. The vendor has appealed to higher management for reconsideration of the proposal. What should the evaluation team do?

Sid Adelman

The evaluation team should have created an understanding with the vendors before making the tool selection, asking the vendors to sign an agreement that after the decision was made, they would not appeal. Assuming no previous understanding was in place, the evaluation team needs to contact the vendor and indicate that there will be no reconsideration; if the vendor pursues its course of action, the vendor will be blackballed from any further marketing at this company. The evaluation team should meet with management and explain the evaluation process, explain why the decision was made, point out that any reconsideration undermines the evaluation team and delays the data warehouse implementation, and ask management to direct all future communication from the vendor back to the evaluation team.

Joyce Bischoff

The evaluation team should inform higher management regarding the reasons for their selection. If there has not been an onsite test of both products, it may be necessary to conduct it to prove the team's case.

Douglas Hackney

The evaluation team should make clear to the losing vendor that if any further attempt is made to contact a member of the selection committee or upper management, the vendor will be barred from further product or service sales indefinitely. This message should be communicated to the manager of the offending sales representatives and the relevant vice president of sales from the vendor company.

Sean Ivoghli

Hopefully the higher-level managers trust their evaluation team enough to not reopen the evaluation. If that is not the case, a good way to deter them is to threaten to miss deadlines as a result. Hopefully the evaluation process included influential business people who would become good allies in this process as well. The evaluation team should use them.

Chuck Kelley

This is always a problem. It needs to be made clear at the outset, with management buy-in, that the software evaluation process is the method used to choose the software. When the vendor goes over the heads of the evaluation team (and the vendor will), the team needs to ask management what part of the evaluation was faulty. If that does not appease management, the team should ask for additional money to do the evaluation over again. The team should remind management that everyone had to follow the same procedure.

David Marco

The evaluation team should inform management of the results of the evaluation process and that the vendor is attempting to circumvent the company's evaluation process.

Clay Rehm

The evaluation team should make it clear to the losing vendor and higher management that the vendor's appeal to management violates the terms of the evaluation and that this vendor has ignored the evaluation terms. If the team members don't nip this appeal in the bud immediately, their inaction will send a message to the losing vendor that it is okay to go behind their backs, and it will only continue to get worse in the future. This situation should happen only once. The evaluation team should not tolerate this behavior.

In summary: When communicating with vendors, be very clear about the terms and expectations. Nothing exists unless it is in writing.

THE VENDOR'S ACQUIRING COMPANY PROVIDES POOR SUPPORT

An organization was happy with the query tool it was using, but the vendor was in financial straits and sold out. The acquiring company fired most of the developers and the support staff. Needless to say, support is now terrible, and based on the reputation of the acquiring vendor, support is not expected to improve. What should the company do?

Sid Adelman

If the company stays with the existing tool, the company will have ongoing problems, some of which may never be resolved. As time goes by and as the query tool gets behind in support of the associated products (products that interface with this tool) and their new releases, it will hamper conversions to current products. The company should evaluate how difficult it will be to convert to another query tool; this will depend on the number of users who need to be trained and the extent of the query library. The company should create a plan for the conversion and sell the need to convert to IT management and to user management. Then the company should convert as quickly as it makes sense to do so. The longer the company waits, the more difficult the conversion will be.

Joyce Bischoff

This is a common problem in our industry. Certain vendors are known to acquire products only to milk the maintenance fees while failing to improve or support their products. The organization should keep informed about other products in case it needs to change vendors. The company should also make sure there is a cap on maintenance fees in the original contract.

Jill Dyché

The first question here is whether the application supported by the query tool has current and future business value. The development team should revisit the original business drivers in the requirements document to see if this is the case. Regardless, the next step is to sit down with the end-users.

The development team should then explain the trade-offs. If the users want to keep the query tool, then the developers may be unable to fix software bugs as they come up, and the given application should be the last one developed using this tool. In other words, the users will need to be willing to live with what they have. Maybe the application is robust and enduring enough to warrant this as an acceptable solution.

On the other hand, the users might see the potential of their application and decide it's best to cut their losses and migrate to a new tool. The big issue here is the impact to current business activities. (If it's August and the company is a retailer, for instance, all new development activities will be suspended from September through the holidays, so it doesn't make sense to migrate to a new tool during this time.) The other issue is, of course, finding a new query tool that can cover the functionality of the existing application and its desired enhancements.

The key is not to overreact to the product's acquisition. If the tool is working now and business users are productive, a transition plan should be drafted and a gradual migration should take place that serves the dual purpose of keeping the end-users happy while serving the business for the long term.

Douglas Hackney

Unfortunately, this scenario is a common fact of life in technology acquisition, implementation, and sustenance. This company has learned the hard lesson that the investment you make in a query tool is not in the cost of the software itself but in the cost of the development of reports, analysis, and processes around that tool. In this scenario, the company should face the fact that things are not going to improve. It should begin the process of evaluating and selecting another query and reporting tool.

Chuck Kelley

Too bad the financial shape of the vendor was not known during the selection process. Every selection process needs to consider this area and put together a plan to deal with the issue. One way to deal with it is to have the software put in escrow in case something like this happens; then the company can take over the code and modify. If that was not done, then the company's upper management needs to meet with the vendor to come to agreement on what each party's role in this situation is and what the vendor's plans are (including how concrete the plans truly are). If this proves an unacceptable situation, the company needs to start looking for a new query tool.

David Marco

It sounds like it's time to purchase a new tool. The company should keep in mind that every small software vendor is looking to create an initial public offering of stock or, more likely, to sell out to a larger vendor.

Clay Rehm

The company needs to follow two courses of action.

1. *What to do now:* The company data warehouse team should contact the vendor's acquiring company and determine what the company's rights are. The executives should involve the legal department and, if they have not already done so, establish a contract. They should identify and investigate vendors who provide training on the tool and consider outsourcing the tool support to a third-party vendor. The team could also consider getting hold of the source code and maintaining the tool in-house.
2. *What to do for the future:* Any contracts the executives sign with vendors should allow the company an "out" if the vendor is purchased by another vendor. Any existing contracts should be revised to allow for such a clause. Before purchasing anything from anybody or signing any contracts, the team should establish a contingency plan for the possibility that the vendor or consultant may go out of business.

CHAPTER TEN

Security

Distrust and caution are the parents of security.
—*Benjamin Franklin*

OVERVIEW

We have the misguided notion that since data should be a corporate asset, everyone in the organization should have access to all the data. It doesn't take long to realize that this Pollyanna vision of the world is inappropriate when we consider sensitive payroll data, health claim information, and financial data that would affect the price of a stock with all its implications for insider trading.

Many department heads are concerned about anyone looking at their data. We have seen these managers be less than forthcoming with information about how their division is performing. This reticence may be a function of the division managers' desire to digest their performance numbers before anyone else sees them (to be able to make effective excuses), to put a spin on the numbers, or to adjust the numbers to reflect how these division managers see the reality of the results. Spin provides a slant on the measurements that can make the results more attractive—not cooking the books but just warming them up a bit.

If division managers have the authority to restrict access, the security officer must set up the procedures to implement the restriction and to make the division managers feel comfortable that they have retained control on the access. This type of control is especially important when data has been classified as private even within the company. Examples are personnel records, sensitive client data, and patient data in the health care industry.

Security is becoming more important all the time. Some organizations are allowing Web access of their data warehouses by suppliers and large customers. Some manufacturing companies give access in an effort to improve the suppliers' ability to supply quality parts in a timely manner. Commercial customers are being given access to tie them as closely as possible to the organization's products and services. Security is especially important for Internet access since data warehouses may contain information about the suppliers' or customers' competitors. With access allowed outside the organization, security must be exact and uncompromising.

Data can be secured at different levels of granularity. For example, data may be made available at the summary level but not at the atomic or detailed level.

Security officers should work closely with the people who administer security (Web administrator, DBAs, query tool administrators, repository administrators, data modeling tool administrators, and ETL tool administrators) to understand the capabilities of the products and determine the optimal approach to establishing security. This would include exposures, difficulties in administration—we don't want to make this a bureaucratic nightmare—and the productivity of administration.

The primary role of a security officer is the identification of exposures with recommendations and actions to plug security holes. Another important responsibility of the security officer is to understand the interaction of security features between the tools and the RDBMS. In some reported cases, the security feature of one tool negated that of another.

In the remainder of this chapter, we explore three situations that arise in the realm of security and present suggested solutions for each one.

THE DATA WAREHOUSE HAS NO SECURITY PLAN

A data warehouse that tracks departmental and product-related profitability was developed for a large mortgage lender. Revenue and expense information is captured from the company's general ledger system, employee and organizational information is obtained from the payroll systems, and product definition and sales information is extracted from various loan application and servicing systems. Development proceeded normally, and the data warehouse was implemented with both OLAP and ODS reporting mechanisms. Shortly after implementation, the project manager was summoned to the CFO's office and asked to explain why a lowly financial analyst was able to extract from the data warehouse detailed payroll records that belong to a vice president of the company (a serious violation of company policy). The data warehouse has no security plan and no provisions for encryption and/or tokenizing of sensitive information. How can the company rectify this situation?

Sid Adelman

The company should convene a committee chaired by the company's chief of security. The goal of this security committee should be to establish policies and procedures for granting access to the data. The committee should also establish policies and procedures for making any changes to the data, including updates and deletions. Other members of the committee should be the data warehouse manager, the DBA manager, and the respective owners of the data for the general ledger, employee data (including payroll), and customer service and loan systems. The data owners need not all be present at all the meetings but could attend only those meetings when their data is being discussed.

Joyce Bischoff

The company should shut off access to all known data that poses security risks, such as payroll and general ledger data, allowing access on an "as needed" basis only for the time being. The company should gather and implement security requirements as soon as possible. Company policies form the starting point for these requirements. Since proper security should be implemented at the operating system level, DBMS level, database level, table level, and column level, much work will be required. Network security and firewalls must also be addressed. In a warehouse environment, the flow of data through a network is often one of the weakest security points.

Chuck Kelley

The quick fix would be to deny all access to the base tables. Next, the DBA should create views that each of the users will use to access the data. Then he or she should grant users the right to use these views. This will allow users to see *all* the data within a particular column but will not solve the whole problem.

For the secondary part of the quick fix, the DBA can create summary tables that provide a higher level of granularity with a higher degree of security. Then he or she can grant the users the rights to see those summary tables. The lowly financial analysts will be able to read only the summary tables, which might be defined to have payroll records without name or payroll rolled up by department (or whatever the correct rollup summary is).

After the quick fix, I would develop the correct security policy and start to enforce it. The security policy can be implemented in many different ways, depending on the full policy.

One word of caution: Sometimes the security defined can hurt the business intelligence that the data warehouse is trying to accomplish. The project manager should make sure that the security being requested is really needed. For example, a manufacturing company may have multiple plants that produce similar products. The plant managers may not want other plant managers to see their production statistics. However, looking at other managers' production statistics may help a manager increase the production output. Most of us would not like to share our statistics unless we believed (or knew) that ours were not the worse. Individually motivated security considerations should not override the overall good of the company, and so the project manager must make sure that the security requested does not hurt the overall data warehouse project.

David Marco

Obviously the data warehouse needed a security plan from the onset. I recommend a couple of methods for handling this specific problem with payroll information while a more encompassing security plan is developed and implemented. Technique number one is to summarize the payroll information in the data warehouse. This prevents the analyst from seeing the salaries of specific individuals. If employee-level payroll granularity is necessary, then the employee name, social security number, employee address, and employee number can be hidden at the database level or at the presentation level. Personally, I favor technique number two, masking at the database level, because most companies have too many employees who have read-level access to the organization's data warehouses.

Clay Rehm

If the original requirements did not state how secure the data warehouse should be, then I bet the team did not plan to address security issues or assumed that the security in place would be enough. That's okay! The project manager should tell the users that he or she will rectify the situation immediately.

It is not too late to incorporate a security design and to implement it. This requires a team to identify the design. User representatives need to be identified and interviewed about the requirements. A model needs to be developed. For example, the data administrator should identify the components of the security design:

- Department
- Product
- Role

Does the data warehouse need to have security by department, by product, by role, or all of the above? These are things to be discussed and decided by the user representatives and the IT staff.

Bottom line: It is better late than never to add new functionality to the data warehouse.

RESPONSIBILITY FOR SECURITY MUST BE ESTABLISHED

A data warehouse consultant told an organization that it must consider security and assign the role to one of its staff. The organization has multiple servers with more than one operating system (UNIX, NT, OS/390) and different RDBMSs (Oracle, DB2, and SQL/Server). The person assigned to the job, the new IT security administrator, is not clear what her role should be. She has no idea how big the job is, what security exposures and what problems she will face. What procedures should she follow?

Sid Adelman

Software vendors whose products offer security features (access and analysis, RDBMS, and so on) have people in their organizations responsible for implementing these features. The IT security administrator should seek them out and talk with them. She should network with other companies that have mature data warehouses and find out what they are doing to deal with security. This would include learning about their issues, exposures, and solutions. The IT security administrator should also connect with people in her organization's security office and get their input on what they believe to be important. Finally, she should talk with the technical people who have the tools for implementing security and elicit their thoughts and ideas.

David Marco

First, the IT security administrator should study as much about IT security as she can. Operational systems, RDBMSs, servers, software, and so on all require a security strategy. Second, she should work with her manager and the data warehouse consultant to define specifically what her role should be. Third, the security administrator must understand the security needs of her company. The IT security needs of a furniture manufacturer are not the same as those of a government air force base.

Clay Rehm

It is the project manager's job to know each employee's roles and responsibilities. Since the organization has hired and paid for a consultant to make recommendations, it is appropriate for the consultant to provide a job description for each role being assessed. If this consultant has really worked on data warehouse projects before, the consultant could easily provide a template or example of an IT security administrator job description.

Going forward, the project manager and the new IT security administrator must agree about the expectations and deliverables of the role. These expectations and deliverables should be in writing and should be signed by each party. The project manager must make sure the new IT security administrator is clear on what is expected from this new role. This means the two will create a training plan together: they will identify the training needed, when it will occur, and actually make sure the new IT security administrator not only attends the training but graduates as well.

The project manager and the new IT security administrator can get a quick education on security by viewing the details of the Systems Administration, Networking and Security Institute (*http://www.sans.org*). In addition to the great information at that site and the links there, they both should spend time in the local library reading any books that cover security issues. Finally, the project manager should create a plan of goals for the new IT security administrator to reach by specific times.

The moral of the story: Document and get agreement on expectations and deliverables before work begins.

WHERE SHOULD A NEW SECURITY ADMINISTRATOR START?

A company has recognized the need for enhanced security for the data warehouse. The position was posted and filled. The person who got the job had been a data analyst with little background in security matters. How should the new security administrator get started? What should her role and authority be on the data warehouse team?

Sid Adelman

The security administrator needs to connect with the company's security officer and learn what policies and procedures are already in place. She needs to meet with IT people responsible for tools that have security capabilities. For example, the RDBMS has the ability to limit access as well as restrict update and delete capability. The access and analysis tools have the ability to limit query and report access to the data warehouse. The security administrator needs to review the requirements document to uncover requirements related to security. She needs to be clever to determine which security capabilities are appropriate, which ones close security gaps, and which ones are administratively friendly.

Joyce Bischoff

The security administrator should consider the following options:

- Take available classes to become familiar with various levels of security.
- Attend security conferences.

- Read publications about auditing and security.
- Talk to the in-house staff in the data administrator group, database administrator group, network group, audit group, and so on to gather information on the current status of security.
- If necessary, bring in a security consultant to evaluate the situation and make recommendations.

Chuck Kelley

First, the security administrator needs to learn about security and put into place a security policy that fits the needs of the data in the data warehouse. These policies will have to be implemented and kept in place by the DBAs and end-user tool administrators. Her role should be that of defining and checking to make sure that the policies are implemented.

Larissa Moss

Security is a very big topic, and it will take some time for the security administrator to come up to speed. She should immediately immerse herself in an educational program on security by pursuing the following actions:

- Sign up for security seminars like the ones offered by MIS Training Institute (*http://www.misti.com*).
- Subscribe to one or more security trade magazines like the *Information Systems Control Journal*, which is an international journal published bimonthly by the Information Systems Audit and Control Association (*http://www.isaca.org*).
- Research the Internet for additional security Web sites.

Clay Rehm

I recommend that the new security administrator get familiar with the Systems Administration, Networking and Security Institute (*http://www.sans.org*), Meta Group (*http://www.metagroup.com*), and the not-for-profit International Information Systems Security Certification Consortium (*http://www.isc2.org/*). In addition to the great information at those sites and the links provided, the security administrator should spend time in the local library (remember that place where books are free?) reading any books she can find on security.

Also, as of this writing, the National Research Council published a report called "Cybersecurity Today and Tomorrow: Pay Now or Pay Later." This great report provides very useful advice on closing security gaps. It can be found at *http://www.nap.edu/html/cybersecurity/*.

I also recommend certification such as the Certified Information Systems Security Professional (CISSP) and the System Security Certified Practitioner (SSCP).

CHAPTER ELEVEN

Data Quality

There is no manual that deals with the real business of motorcycle maintenance, the most important aspect of all. Caring about what you're doing is considered either unimportant or taken for granted.

—Robert Pirsig

OVERVIEW

Data quality encompasses many characteristics of the data, including compliance with business rules, conformance to valid values, completeness—especially for mandatory fields—timeliness, and referential integrity. Data should be understandable, nonconflicting, and nonredundant. Most organizations have some level of redundant data, and it's always difficult to address how to handle redundant data and to understand the impact of redundant data on the success of the data warehouse.

"Dirty data" is a pervasive problem in every company and in every industry. We have lived with dirty data for decades, so why is it such a problem now? It's a problem because we promised to deliver data warehouses with "clean, integrated, historical data in a short time frame for low cost"; yet we are unable to deal with the preponderance of dirty data within the framework of this promise. Some data warehouses are failing because the promised "clean, integrated, historical data" could not be delivered "in a short time frame for low cost."

The responsibility for data quality is unclear for operational systems but even more so for the data warehouse. As bad data is detected, the responsibility for evaluating the problems associated with the bad data and the responsibility for cleaning the data are typically not assigned. The sorry state of the data and its degraded quality did not occur overnight. We struggle with inherited legacy systems that contain suspect data accumulated over the years. Data elements that were clean when first generated have degraded into fuzzy, undefined content that we must now attempt to reconcile and understand.

The users often do not understand their data, or to put it more accurately, they do know their data but are sometimes unsure of the real business definition for each data element and of the actual content stored in the database. If you ask users how clean they want their data to be, they will tell you that they want it 100 percent clean. Some are so obsessed with data quality that they will accept nothing less than 100 percent accurate, complete, and nonredundant data.

Users are often frustrated by inconsistent reports. This frustration extends all the way up to boards of directors. Reports that should have the same numbers often do not. Reconciliation of inconsistent reports exhausts many hours that could be spent on more productive activities. The inconsistencies often result from discrepancies in the timing of the source data. Most organizations are familiar with the problem of "end of month." Is it the last business day of the month or is it the last calendar day of the month? In most situations, we have seen both definitions being used within the same organization. Different coding schemes as well as different business rules for rejecting a transaction may also contribute to the inconsistencies. Finally, the assigned definitions may be a problem; two columns with the same name are computed differently and have a different business meaning.

Because of these inconsistencies and because of the data quality problems, users often don't trust their reports and don't trust the underlying data that produced the reports. This lack of trust forces the users to verify the results, often at great expense and with a time delay. The lack of trust may result in a decision not made or the halfhearted implementation of a decision. When users realize the data does not meet an acceptable level of quality, they often choose to no longer access the data warehouse, or the actions they take on the results are so timid they make the data warehouse all but worthless.

Organizations always have a difficult time understanding their existing level of data quality; then they have difficulty determining just how clean the data needs to be. This lack of understanding about the existing data quality (or lack thereof) is endemic among management. It is almost axiomatic that when management claims the data is clean ("After all, we just went through an expensive conversion process, and in that conversion we must have cleaned up the data"), the data quality usually is the absolute worst. Organizations always overestimate the cleanliness of their data and are often clueless about just how dirty their data is. The organizations that do have a clue make valiant efforts to evaluate the quality of their data. If organizations have very large databases (greater than 1 terabyte), the machine resources needed to perform the evaluation could be prohibitive, so some organizations resort to sampling. Sampling can be tricky, and improper sampling leads to erroneous results.

Organizations have had a very difficult time determining how clean data needs to be. The quality that is adequate for operational systems is rarely acceptable for decision support. Organizations have also struggled with understanding the costs of cleansing and determining the value of such cleansing. It has been very difficult to develop a plan to deal with dirty source data. Organizations would like the data to be as clean as possible when the data goes into the ETL process, but data warehouse teams often lack the leverage to demand a fix of the operational processes that generate dirty data. Since management often does not recognize the value of data quality, organizations are therefore unwilling to provide the resources to fix the problems.

In the remainder of this chapter, we discuss solutions for seven data quality situations that confront data warehouse projects.

HOW SHOULD SAMPLING BE APPLIED TO DATA QUALITY?

A data quality analyst is trying to determine how clean the data in the data warehouse needs to be. The company is in the process of loading a data warehouse from a mainframe source. Some of the files contain millions of records. Instead of checking all the records for accuracy, the data quality analyst is considering sampling the data, but she does not know how much data to sample and how to proceed with the sampling. She also does not know how to represent to the users that the data is accurate with, for example, a 95 percent or 99 percent confidence level for sampling. How should the data quality analyst proceed?

Sid Adelman

Many statistics books present formulas for calculating the sample size needed based on the requirements for the level of confidence of the data. However, sampling is still not a trivial exercise, and the results of a sampling analysis may still be in question even if the sampling is done properly. Data quality analysis can be run during off hours, and there is rarely a drop-dead date and time by which the analysis must be run, so the data quality analyst may be able to analyze all the data rather than just sampling it. By analyzing all the data, there will be no need to address the confidence level of the sampling.

Joyce Bischoff

The data quality analyst should consider a data analysis and cleansing tool that will perform a data analysis on a column-by-column basis. To prove the value of their products, vendors of data quality tools are often willing to take sample records offsite and analyze them to determine the type of data, distinct values, frequency of data values, and any problems with formatting of names, phone numbers, addresses, and so on. This should provide some information about data quality and possibly provide a justification for buying this type of tool.

Chuck Kelley

When dealing with data quality, you need to determine the trade-off for data that is not the highest quality. For example, let's say you are building a customer data warehouse. You can spend a lot of money trying to clean all the name and address data (and still end up with duplicates), or you can do some "poor man's cleaning" and accept the possibility of multiple customer records that are identical or have slightly different data. What is the cost of both solutions? Is the organization willing to accept the "poor man's" quality?

I recommend taking a sample of data, maybe 10 percent, and checking the accuracy of the sample. The data quality analyst could take some rows from each of the years (or months), not just the beginning or end of the table or file. Testing this sample will indicate an estimate of the data quality. It may be that the data quality of the earlier data is not as good as the later data, and that should be factored into the equation. From this a cost model should be created for and approved by the business group(s). This will give a true indication of the level of data quality that the data quality analyst should achieve. The ETL tasks should reflect this acceptability and then be built. She then needs to run tests to make sure the data quality is achieved. There will always be times when the sample used does not accurately reflect the data quality. At that time, a new cost model needs to be created and approved by the business group(s).

Regardless of what the data quality analyst chooses to do, the meta data needs to have a confidence level indicator to let the users understand what level of confidence she has in the data.

David Marco

Let's first discuss thorough data sampling. If it is available, the best approach is to build a process (a series of programs) that will automatically check and record the quality of the data. If the company doesn't have a true system of record for the key data or does not have meta data that specifically defines the data's domain values, then this may not be an option.

If the data quality analyst has to resort to manual data quality checking, I recommend that she choose a sample size of 200 randomly selected records from each of the large mainframe files, always including the first record and the last record of a file. In my experience the sampling results will be statistically very similar from 200 to 1,000 to 10,000 records. If the data quality analyst is pressed for time, she can reduce the sample size from 200 records to 100; however, I have seen some occasions where the statistics can become skewed in such a circumstance.

For smaller data files I recommend sampling 5 percent of the records, with the rule that the 5 percent chosen can be no less than 50 records (unless the file doesn't contain 50 records) and no more than 200 records.

Sometimes the number of files, the size of the files, and the urgency of the need for data quality statistics prevent the data quality analyst from being able to sample all the data files. In these situations the data quality analyst should select a key block of data (for example, customer, product, supplier, invoice, and so on) and go through the data-sampling methodology that I just described. Once the data sampling is complete, she will be able to present to the business users her level of confidence in the data.

Larissa Moss

Most data-cleansing tools can help with a wide range of domain analysis (the assessment of the data content in the source files). Sampling the data is a hit-and-miss proposition. Depending on what records the data quality analyst pulls, she may or may not expose all types of data violations in the files. Sampling the data will also not give her reliable statistics of how widespread the problem is. If the organization does not have a data-cleansing tool, the analyst can write her own domain analysis reports. A domain analysis report is a count of records that violate edit rules, business rules, dependency rules, or integrity rules. Examples of such domain analysis reports are the following:

- Count the number of records for all data elements that have default values, for example, 0, 9, blank, FF, 00, or another default.
- Count the number of records for all data elements that have no value at all, that is, null or blank records.
- Count the number of records for all data elements that fall outside a mathematical data domain (the allowable range of values).
- Count the number of records for all data elements that fall outside the business data domain (the business rules governing the data element).
- Count the number of records for all data elements that have inaccurate values in their dependency, for example, if the property type is a single-family residence, the number of rental units must be 0.
- Count the number of records for all data elements that do not have a value in a dependent (parent) file.

The data quality analyst must use more sophisticated analysis reports to find other data violations (such as using a data element for multiple purposes or redefining a field in a file). Michael Brackett [2000, 1996] has written several books on the topic of data analysis, including domain analysis.

Clay Rehm

The first mistake is trying to predict the goal without understanding the source data first and without a solid understanding of the users' requirements. This is a wrong approach—why is the data quality analyst trying to determine how clean the data should be? Who cares if it is 95 or 96 or 99 percent accurate? If I were the user, I would want the data to be as clean as possible without having to run complex algorithms to tell me how clean or dirty it is.

All data must be loaded, clean *and* dirty. It is the job of the data quality analyst to design systems, applications, and business processes that identify the records in error and specify what the errors are and how to fix them. The biggest hurdle is not identifying the errors but getting somebody to care about them so the source systems are fixed. To make sure the data stays clean, source system edits need to be put in place. At the same time, the data quality analyst should get someone to care about the quality of the data in the source systems. Until this happens, both she and the users will never be able to rely on the quality of that data.

If the source systems team will not build in the necessary edits, then the data warehouse team members face a decision point. They could find a new source or accept the data from the nonedited source and make the edits themselves. If the data warehouse team has to build the edits, the project manager should communicate this additional work to all stakeholders and add the tasks to the plan. This will extend the time line and increase the cost of the project.

The data quality analyst must immediately perform the following action items. If a project plan does not exist, she should build one; if it does, she should add these tasks to it.

1. Meet with the users or user representatives and gather data quality and data validation requirements. Each requirement must be understandable, testable, and accomplishable.
2. Analyze, understand, and document the current source data.
3. Analyze, understand, and document the current source applications and systems.
4. Analyze, understand, and document the current data validation processes, procedures, and applications.

5. Present the findings to the sponsor and stakeholders.
6. Get a "go/no go" decision from the sponsor.
7. Design the data validation management application.

An application (no matter what it is) must, at a minimum, always meet the needs of the business users.

REDUNDANT DATA NEEDS TO BE ELIMINATED

A telecommunications company has a data warehouse that contains 14 terabytes of data. It has been estimated that more than 10 terabytes is probably redundant. The company has no naming conventions, and only 20 percent of the data has associated meta data. How can the company identify and eliminate unneeded redundant data?

Sid Adelman

The first step is to capture the meta data that will help to identify the redundant data. The estimate of 10 terabytes of redundant data will probably change as the real situation unfolds.

There must be a cost justification for eliminating redundant data. The company should determine the cost of creating, storing, and maintaining redundant data. The cost is probably quite high, but the cost of eliminating or at least controlling the redundant data is also quite high. No company has ever eliminated all its redundant data, so a triage approach is appropriate for determining which redundant data to eliminate and which to leave alone.

Joyce Bischoff

The company should take the following steps:

1. Develop a standard naming convention to use for all future development. A standard should be created that will forbid the movement of data from source systems without definitions. This will help prevent the problem of redundant data in the future.
2. Identify tables that appear to have identical format and determine whether they contain the same information or different subsets of the total information of that type. This process could be automated to use information from the database management system's catalog.

3. Track the sources of all warehouse data on a table-by-table basis through analysis of ETL jobs. The frequency of data loading should be considered because a monthly download of summarized account information contains different data than a more detailed daily load even though it has the same source. After the sources are identified, the data warehouse team should determine which tables are based on the same source. This should provide the initial information on which to determine redundancy.

The job of identifying redundant data is challenging and time-consuming. It is important to understand that names of identical data elements may be different. This approach is only a starting point in the analysis and identification of redundant data.

Douglas Hackney

First the company must identify the specific business problems the data warehouse is targeted to address. Then, only the data required to address those problems needs to be analyzed. This scenario sounds suspiciously like a system in which a "put all the data in, surely someone will use it" approach was adopted.

Chuck Kelley

There are three costs to look at.

1. How much does it cost to continue to keep the redundant data (assuming that the business users are performing all their analyses correctly)?
2. How much would it cost to identify and eliminate the redundant data?
3. How much it will cost in the future to continue keeping the redundant data?

Once a determination is made that it will indeed benefit the company to eliminate the redundant data, a task needs to be defined to analyze the data warehouse as if it were a source system to feed to a new data warehouse. At this point, the data warehouse team will need to start the process of building the data warehouse with a new methodology (since the first one didn't work). The methodology needs to take into account the requirement of creating a data dictionary with naming conventions and meta data.

David Marco

The telecommunications company needs to capture meta data on the remaining 80 percent of its data. To begin this process, I recommend creating standardized nomenclature for the business terms, and preferably for the physical data names as well. In going through this task the company will identify the redundant data in the immediate term and will be able to avoid the problem in the future.

Clay Rehm

Where are the data models? Are the descriptions captured? The data warehouse team has really fallen down on the job by not creating a thorough meta data repository. This team needs to create an inventory of every single table in the data warehouse. From that list, the team members must describe each table by the technical name, the easy-to-understand business name, the source of the table, the description of the table, and the users of the table.

Table 11–1 presents an example of collecting meta data at table level first.

Table 11–1: Meta Data

Technical Name of the Data Warehouse Table	Business Name of the Data Warehouse Table	Source Table(s) and/or File(s)	Brief Description of Table (in Easy-to-Understand Language)	ETL Program Name	User(s) or Group(s) That Have Access to the Table
DW_CUST	Customer	CUSTMST and so on	A customer is a person or organization that has purchased products from our organization.	DW001	AB001, CX004, and so on

The team members will need to fill in each column of the grid. They can then sort on different columns to see where duplicates show up. Obviously, if they cannot fill in certain columns, the team members need to question whether the table is in use. Once done with collecting the tables, it is time to collect the same information at the column/attribute level. This will not be a fun or easy exercise. However, since the needed documentation was not done at the time the tables and columns were built, it needs to be done now to understand what data is in the data warehouse, what is adding value, and what is not.

Bottom line: Document early and often. Creating documentation is very difficult after the fact.

MANAGEMENT UNDERESTIMATED THE AMOUNT OF DIRTY DATA

Management has never recognized just how dirty the data is in the operational systems. The executives are unaware of the degree of redundancy, the incompleteness of many of the records, the use of inappropriate defaults, the data that does not conform to the valid values, the lack of referential integrity, and the data that is just inaccurate. As the data warehouse has been piloted, feedback from the project team and from the users has made it clear that the quality of the data is not acceptable enough to allow the project to proceed. Cleaning up the data will take significant time, and that time has not been allocated in the project schedule. What should the project manager do?

Sid Adelman

The project manager should get a report card on the data quality and provide that report card to management—recognizing that the executives will not like what they see. The report card should indicate the following items by field:

- Data elements that do not correspond to the valid values
- Missing values in mandatory fields
- Other missing values
- Nonunique values in fields where the values should be unique
- Violations of business rules (for example, a negative number of dependents, year of birth greater than the current date)

- Invalid data types (for example, a "character" type that should be "packed decimal")

Tools can provide this report card, but the project manager should be aware that someone needs to provide the input for the tool to do its job.

The owner of the data should be able to determine which data should be cleansed and which can be left as is, and the owner should help determine the order in which the data should be cleansed. The data warehouse team should estimate the time and money needed to cleanse each data component and incorporate these estimates in the project plan, which then must be discussed and approved by management.

Joyce Bischoff

The data warehouse team should perform a sample analysis of data quality as I described in a previous scenario. He or she should try to estimate the cost of poor data quality, present the results to the executives, and hope they will agree to a cleanup before the project begins. The alternative is to complete the project and wait for the users to complain about poor data quality.

Douglas Hackney

The project manager should immediately present the findings from the pilot to the data warehouse project steering committee. The steering committee, made up of senior business stakeholders, will then make the determination on how to either adjust the scope or adjust the delivery date of the system. The incomplete and inaccurate data contained in the operational systems requires process changes in the business to correct the data. Project teams should never make business process changes a prerequisite for their success. Instead, business process changes must be owned by the steering committee, by the change management group, and ultimately, by the business itself.

Chuck Kelley

It is always amazing to me how organizations can function as well as they do with such dirty data. It must be because they worked that way before the computer systems were implemented and they continue to work around the current implementations.

The project manager needs to put together a cost/benefit analysis that describes the issues of data quality and presents the analysis to the business users. He or she needs to create a plan that offers some alternatives. These alternatives can range from simple data-cleansing routines (what I call "poor man's cleaning") all the way to making the data "perfect." The project manager needs to meet with the business users and outline the case for each alternative, including cost and time. Then agreement needs to be made with the business users and a new project schedule created.

David Marco

The project manager should gather the data quality statistics and direct quotes from the key business users and present these to management. In this presentation the project manager will need to ask for the additional time to clean the data, preferably at its source.

Unfortunately, quite often companies do not want to spend the money or the time to uncover, evaluate, and resolve their data quality issues. Several years ago I had one such client, a very large international company where we had multiple business intelligence projects going on simultaneously. In my initial work proposal I allocated time and resources to conduct a data quality study to gauge the quality of the source system's data during the feasibility phase of the data warehousing initiative. However, the client did not want to spend the time or the money on an activity the executives felt had minimum value; despite my urgings, the company would not conduct the evaluation. In the executives' minds the company had no data quality issues, so why spend valuable time and money evaluating the data? As the project continued, we were well down the design path of one of the data marts when our development team discovered that the quality of the data in the source system was so poor that the reports the business needed would not have accurate computations. Moreover, the data in this system was so bad that it did not have the information necessary to clean it. To make a bad situation even worse, our project sponsor did not have the authority to go back to the IT team members maintaining the system and ask them to change it. As a result, I was left with a task that every consultant dreads. I recommended to senior management that development on the one data mart be stopped. Because of the severity of the data quality problem, senior management supported my recommendation. The other components of our data warehousing initiatives were very successful; however, this client lost approximately $225,000, above and beyond what it would have cost to evaluate its data up front in the development process.

Larissa Moss

It is clear that the users will not use a data warehouse loaded with dirty data. The project manager has no choice but to halt the current development work until the dirty data is addressed.

While the development work is suspended, the project manager should assemble a team of business analysts and systems analysts to perform a data quality assessment. By running domain analysis reports and comparing the actual data content to the business rules, code translation tables, and data policies, the data warehouse team should be able to get an understanding of the types of data quality problems that exist and how widespread the problem is.

The next step for this team would be to triage the cleansing process. The team members need to categorize all data elements by business significance or criticality in order to prioritize what data elements must be cleansed at once, what can be postponed, and what can remain dirty. Being a business initiative, not an IT initiative, it is imperative that business users drive this assessment project.

Once the cleansing requirements have been triaged, the project manager and the users have to revise the project plan. They must agree either to extend the schedule to include the cleansing tasks or to reduce the original scope of the deliverable (data as well as functionality) so that the additional cleansing tasks can be completed within the schedule.

Clay Rehm

There is no point in allowing the project to proceed. A data warehouse is meant to provide value to the business community. If the users do not trust the data, they will not use it—period. It is time to raise the red flag and halt the data warehouse project. It is prudent to identify problems as they are discovered and deal with them in a proactive way instead of finishing the data warehouse and spending many hours and dollars creating something that will not be used.

If the project manager does not feel he or she has the skill set to address this issue with the source systems' owners and the data warehouse stakeholders, he or she must talk to his or her manager and decide on a course of action. The correct approach may be to retain an experienced individual or group who can facilitate working sessions with the interested parties.

It would be a downright waste of time and money to keep moving forward—the data warehouse project must be temporally halted. A project definition and plan must be created and resources allocated to fix the data quality problems in the source systems. The project manager should shift the resources from the data warehouse team to this SWAT team effort.

The moral of the story: It is wise to surface issues early.

MANAGEMENT DOESN'T RECOGNIZE THE VALUE OF DATA QUALITY

No one is sure just how dirty the data is, but it's pretty clear that the level of quality will not be acceptable for the data warehouse. It is also clear that the cleansing process will be costly and will require dedicated staff. Management is not even aware of the data quality problems—the data seems to be working just fine for the operational systems. Furthermore, management is not inclined to spend money or resources fixing the very dirty data. What should the data warehouse team do to convince management of the need to clean the data?

Sid Adelman

It's like when you go the doctor, but you don't want to hear that your cholesterol is 295 and your blood pressure is 190/110. However, once you do know the reality, it may encourage you to start exercising and to give up your daily half gallon of Ben and Jerry's Chunky Monkey ice cream. Management must also hear the bad news. The executives must be informed about the cost of poor quality data with explicit examples of how keeping the data at its existing level is costly to the organization.

Unfortunately, the managers responsible for the operational systems are often not motivated to do anything to clean up their data. Their responses are often that the data is clean enough for their purposes, and please close the door on the way out.

Joyce Bischoff

The data warehouse team should work with a vendor of a data-cleansing tool to perform a sample analysis. If the results are poor, the data warehouse team should present them to management with a cleanup proposal. The team should be sure to identify the business impact of the bad data with examples.

Douglas Hackney

Business management will not pay to clean the data until such time as cleaning the data will make a difference in their lives. Unless the business needs to perform analysis, trending, or reimbursement calculations based on dirty data, the company will not be inclined to invest in cleaning up the data. The message here is that the data warehouse team cannot take up a general cause like "cleaning up the data." From a business perspective, that is akin to trying to solve world hunger. The team must tie data-cleansing efforts and funding to specific business challenges. For instance, cleaning up the data required to calculate bonuses for key executives will easily be funded.

Chuck Kelley

There needs to be a clear-cut case on how dirty the data truly is and an explanation about why the problem doesn't seem to affect the production systems. Some examples of what data would not be acceptable in a data warehouse environment would be extremely appropriate. There must be a cost/benefit analysis on different alternatives for cleaning the data, from not cleaning the data at all to cleaning the data 100 percent. The data warehouse team needs to meet with the management team and discuss the cost/benefit analysis and get agreement on what the business users wish to do. There is no reason why the data cannot be cleaned better in following years.

Larissa Moss

Most likely this management does not understand the enormous costs of dirty data because the costs are not directly apparent. Many of the costs related to dirty data are hidden as "overhead" both in IT and on the business side. This "overhead" must be itemized, and the cost for each item must be calculated. The cost can run into the millions of dollars per year.

Loss of revenue due to bad business decisions can also run into the millions of dollars per year. The data warehouse manager must calculate the amount of damage already being done to the organization's bottom line by its dirty data and bring this problem to management's attention. The presentation should include specific examples of the financial impact dirty data is having on the organization right now.

Several excellent books on the market provide examples and formulas for calculating the financial impact of dirty data. Three such books are *Improving Data Warehouse and Business Intelligence Quality* by English [1999], *Quality Information and Knowledge Management* by Huang et al. [1998], and *The Data Warehouse Challenge: Taming Data Chaos* by Brackett [1996]. Other sources for education are any materials on the Capability Maturity Model (CMM) and total quality management (TQM). CMM describes the five levels of business maturity of organizations, what to do to progress from one level to another, and how to get CMM certification. TQM describes a holistic approach of 14 steps to achieving total quality of products (in data warehousing, the product is *information*) from inception (data entry) to distribution (data access and analysis). Reading CMM and TQM literature may be the most effective eye-opener for the management in this organization.

Clay Rehm

The data warehouse team members could build a prototype that displays data in an easy-to-use and easy-to-understand format. Additionally, they could use real data from the intended source systems. They then could demonstrate this prototype to many people around the organization to show how neat and cool the new data warehouse will be. The problem with this approach is that the data warehouse team will make enemies with the data source owners. Why? Without approaching the data source owners first and identifying and resolving any data quality problems, the data warehouse team will identify problems with the source systems that will most certainly embarrass the data source owners.

The project manager must first meet with all the intended data source owners and explain the recommended course of action. He or she should explain that exposing their data as it is could be most damaging to their reputations and careers. The project manager should explain in the most diplomatic and tactful way how the data warehouse team and the data source teams must work together. Once the teams agree to work together, they should assess the quality of the data by creating the prototype but should show the prototype with the real source data only to the support team members of the data source, so they can fix the quality problems. The data source support team members can resolve their data quality problems over time as the data warehouse team builds the data warehouse. These can be concurrent efforts with the goal that the source team members will resolve a majority of their problems first.

In summary: Work to resolve your issues without unnecessarily exposing weaknesses and creating embarrassment.

THE DATA WAREHOUSE ARCHITECT IS OBSESSED WITH DATA QUALITY

An inexperienced data warehouse architect insists that only data that is 100 percent clean can go into the data warehouse. He requires the development of a complex suspense mechanism to store, review, correct, and reprocess errant source data. Eventually, the data warehouse goes "live," and the suspense data store soon grows to a monumental size. Because so much data is being rejected (mostly for minor errors), the metrics generated by the data warehouse can't be reconciled to those published by the operational systems. User confidence in the data warehouse is waning fast. What should the project manager do?

Sid Adelman

The inexperienced data warehouse architect needs to get his head out of the clouds. He needs to recognize that his "all or nothing" approach is unworkable and will never deliver anything to the business. If the project manager cannot convince him of this, the situation should be escalated and the data warehouse architect's approach overridden. Experience from other data warehouse implementations should be able to show that almost perfect data is better than none at all.

Joyce Bischoff

The business users must determine how clean the data must be. It is not always necessary for every field to be 100 percent populated and correct. The project manager should revise the integrity checks to reflect the business need for timely, accurate data without holding an excessive number of records in the suspense file.

Sean Ivoghli

This is classic! Data warehouses are no place for perfectionists. Users will most likely reject a data warehouse that is incomplete before they reject a data warehouse that has some errant data in it. That's why suspense mechanisms don't work. My approach is to build a data warehouse that accepts the data that comes from source systems and to have either the ETL process or a post-load process identify data that is errant and publish it and its location to a group of error capture tables. The information in the error capture tables is provided to users as meta data (data about the quality of data) and is used by data quality analysts to resolve the problems.

Chuck Kelley

The goal of the data warehouse should always be 100 percent clean data. However, there is always a cost associated with getting data to that point. An analysis needs to be made on the cost of having data totally cleansed versus not having it totally cleansed. The project manager needs to speak with the business users to get agreement on a set of more relaxed cleansing algorithms. Next the ETL developer will need to write an ETL process that takes the errant source data and processes it using the new rules. This should take care of some of the minor integrity problems. Then the project manager needs to fix the current ETL processes to implement the newer, more relaxed cleansing algorithms.

David Marco

I believe it is important to trap and record data integrity problems; however, when building a data warehouse, the data warehouse architect must work with the business users to find out their requirements. In many instances minor problems with the data will not impact their analyses.

Larissa Moss

There is rarely business justification to cleanse every single data element. However, data that is determined to be critically important to the business should always be cleansed. Although the percentage of critically important data varies among organizations, it rarely exceeds 20 percent. Some of the data can remain dirty indefinitely because it is not taken into consideration when making strategic decisions. Most of the data falls somewhere in between because most of the users will tolerate a certain amount of incorrect values in most data elements. For example, the data element Customer Type Code could be 20 percent wrong and still acceptable to the users, while the acceptable dirty data tolerance for the data element Daily Loan Balance could be 1 percent. What should be cleansed and to what degree is not a decision for the data warehouse architect to make. This decision should be made by the users who will be using the data—*all* the users who will be using the data, not just the user directly involved in the data warehouse project. The data warehouse is not a customized application for just one user; therefore a balance must be struck among all users.

A completely different problem is the inability to reconcile metrics between the data warehouse and the operational systems. The metrics generated by the data warehouse ETL process should always be reconcilable to the operational system regardless how many records are rejected. Reconciliation does not mean that the dollars in the data warehouse match the dollars in the operational source files but that every dollar, accepted or rejected, is accounted for. If the metrics cannot be reconciled, this failure points to algorithm errors in the ETL programs.

Clay Rehm

Data warehouses must have all data loaded, whether clean or dirty. The project manager must insist on this belief and have buy-in from the project sponsors, management, and the data warehouse team. In this situation, the project manager must use his or her authority and override the inexperienced data warehouse architect's decision. This must be done privately and in person before this design decision is announced to the rest of the team. If this does not work, the project manager must replace the architect with an experienced data warehouse architect. As in most team situations, the data warehouse team members will have their own opinions on design and architecture decisions. However, it is up to the project manager to manage expectations and to get every team member to buy into the design they select and ultimately will support.

As a side note, the large amount of rejections could be in part due to referential integrity (RI). Data warehouse best practices dictate leaving the RI turned off at the relational database management system (RDBMS) level. RI is a feature of an RDBMS that ensures that implied relationships in the database are enforced and protects users from accidentally or intentionally creating discrepancies in the database. The point is that turning off the RI (if it was turned on) can be an easy fix and may remedy many of the rejections.

Simply put, all data must be allowed to be loaded into the data warehouse.

THE ETL PROCESS PARTIALLY FAILS

A data warehouse for an annuity company was carefully designed to cleanse incoming source data to the desired quality level. It handles all manner of integrity errors including missing data, data type errors, domain errors, synchronization errors, correlation errors, and so on. Detailed test scripts were developed, and the system was thoroughly tested using large batches of real production data. The data warehouse was implemented with high expectations, but after only a few months the metrics produced by the data warehouse are diverging from those published by the operational systems. Developers diagnose the problem: File Transfer Program (FTP) scripts that send data extracts from the source systems fail midstream and do so randomly. ETL processes in the data warehouse cannot determine that they are processing only partial data sets, so no alerts are generated, and the problem goes undetected. Now the data warehouse is seriously not synchronized with the source systems, with no way of identifying which data feeds were compromised. How can this data warehouse get back on track?

Sid Adelman

The company must first develop a process to validate that the FTP processes completed successfully. Validation of the number of records transmitted is mandatory. The company also needs to assign responsibility for the validation and assurance that both the FTP process and the ETL process completed successfully.

Joyce Bischoff

The ETL architecture and design needs a thorough review. Checkpoints and restartability should be established in the processes. Alerts should be generated when needed. Audit and control processes must be in place to ensure that the warehouse is synchronized with the source systems. The company should consider the use of a control table to track job status and ensure that failed jobs are not rerun without procedures to guarantee that the same updates will not run twice.

Sean Ivoghli

The company needs to implement check totals and record counts to the staging area or before the ETL process begins and after the FTP ends for each file. Check totals balance the totals of key (additive) metrics (such as `sales_amt`) in the files received to the totals from the file sent from the source system. Record counts just count the number of records to ensure the same number of records sent was also received. Together, these steps ensure that the ETL process received what was sent. As far as getting back on track: since the company has no history of the files sent and received, the most accurate way to get back on track is to truncate all the data from the point when the data began getting out of synch and to reload it going forward. This solution is ugly, but it will work.

Chuck Kelley

In data warehouses, there should always be some mechanism to roll back bad runs. I use the concept of a job run number. This ties all the data to a single run to indicate when and how the data was loaded. A sample job run table might look like this:

```
create table job_run_table
(job_run_number number,
source_file varchar2(100),
target_file varchar2(100),
source_rows number,
target_rows number,
reject_rows number,
source_amount number(15,2),
target_amount number(15,2),
rejected_amount number(15,2),
target_table varchar2(100)
);
```

With the job run table, the ETL developer can track which records were loaded to which tables, do a quick validation on source versus target amounts, and determine whether the rejected amount is higher than usual.

So, what happens if there was not the foresight to build a table similar to the job run table? Three options for the next course of action come to mind.

1. Start the ETL process all over again with the correct data feeds from the source system. Obviously, this option will take the data warehouse down for some time while the data is truncated and reloaded. The ETL developer must put into place a way to capture how much data the source system should have and what the source system should send. It may be appropriate to add a record indicating the dollar amount expected from the operational system.

2. Capture the correct data and build a process that can search the data warehouse to determine whether or not a particular row is correct or not. This may entail the reading and capturing of all the data in the data warehouse, but it would be a way to try to fix the problem.

3. Keep the data the way it is and when business users find the problems, go back and fix them. Mark in the meta data that the confidence level of the data during this time frame is extremely low.

If there is truly no way to implement option 2 and option 3 is not a real option in the system, then rebuilding the data warehouse is about all the project team can do.

David Marco

The points of failure in the FTP scripts need to be resolved. This can easily be done with the use of header and trailer records, passed parameters, and so on. In addition, I would check the ETL's entire error-checking process because, most likely, additional points of failure exist. All the error statistics need to be stored in the meta data repository.

Cleaning the existing data warehouse is another problem altogether. I would see if we could drop the entire warehouse and just do a complete reload. Depending on how the data warehouse was built and depending on the business users' requirements, this may not be an option. If it isn't an option, the users may have to live with the bad records or have them purged.

Larissa Moss

The first thing to determine is the tolerance level for missing data (records) and whether the data warehouse database in its current state exceeds that tolerance level. If it does, the database should be restored to its last reconciled month (or the last month it still "looked OK"), and each subsequent load should be reprocessed.

However, before embarking on this costly and timely process, the entire ETL process should be revamped. All programs and scripts preparing the data for transmission, transmitting the data, and manipulating the data after transmission should be enhanced to produce reconciliation totals and input and output record counts. If the input and output numbers don't match, the process should be halted.

Bottom line: Producing reconciliation totals on key data elements is part of ETL best practices. Producing input and output record counts is common sense!

SOURCE DATA ERRORS CAUSE MASSIVE UPDATES

A data warehouse for a large financial services company extracts data from several source systems based on "last update" time stamps in the source records. After running very efficiently and error-free for many months, the data warehouse's ETL scripts begin seriously overrunning their batch window. Users are complaining about system availability. The problem is traced to one of the source systems where a developer is periodically applying "mass changes" to the source database to correct an ongoing problem that has yet to be rectified in the application code. Every time a "mass update" is applied, a database trigger resets the "last update" time stamp on the affected rows, and the data warehouse is forced to reprocess massive amounts of source data in a single night. What's the solution to this problem?

Joyce Bischoff

The project team members should analyze the use of "last update" time stamps and the mass changes that have caused problems. They should correct the errors in the operational procedures and application code.

Sean Ivoghli

For this answer, I am assuming that the company does not want to reprocess this data and that "reprocess massive amounts of data" means reloading data. The project team might also want to investigate whether the data warehouse now contains duplicate data as a result of this problem (for data that is loaded incrementally), unless the project team is completely reloading the data warehouse every night (which would at least partially explain the batch window problems). This is a common problem. When extracting data incrementally from source systems, the project team needs to use some time key. System time stamps are convenient but prone to the problem described above. If this is causing the team members to reload the fact tables, then they need to find a business time stamp (and not a system time stamp) for the source of the fact. That should be easy since facts are usually related to events, which depend on time (for example, `order_time`, `sales_time`, and so on). If the project team is reloading dimension tables, and the source does not have an "effective date" for the different versions of the data, then the team members may have no choice but to do a net change comparison based on attributes of the dimension that they want to track. The good news here is that most dimensions (and their source system counterparts) are small tables; otherwise net change comparisons could be very expensive.

Chuck Kelley

The solution depends on the data to which the developer is applying "mass changes." I think that in this situation the facts are likely to be off (double counted, for example), which will cause great grief in the business community, especially if the project team is keeping a historical picture of the dimensions. If these changes are a requirement for the data in the data warehouse, then the team can either tune the ETL process to do more in parallel or buy more hardware to speed up the process.

An analysis needs to be performed on why these "mass changes" are occurring. If real business issues need to be addressed, then the users need to understand that it will take a long time to process the solution. Maybe the "mass changes" could be scheduled just before the weekend of processing the data warehouse; therefore the ETL process would have the weekend to process the extra data.

CHAPTER TWELVE

Integration

. . . [F]ew things are less productive than duplication of effort and the resulting need for reconciliation of inconsistent data.
—*Repository Data Model Strategy Paper*

OVERVIEW

Large and medium-size organizations have multiple operational systems that run the business. This is especially true when other companies have been acquired. Often the acquired companies are allowed to run their systems and not convert to those of the acquiring company. These systems usually contain redundant and terribly inconsistent data. It's no wonder that these organizations have so much difficulty consolidating systems and integrating data in an attempt to understand their overall business performance. It becomes even more difficult when they try to merge systems and merge the inconsistent codes, processes, and business rules contained within each system.

In mergers and acquisitions many of the knowledgeable people in IT have fled or were laid off. The business rules embedded in the code are difficult to understand, and the application knowledge in the heads of those leaving the business disappears as they walk out the door.

Some organizations have attempted to integrate multiple operational databases with a concurrent requirement to understand and clean the data. The data warehouse has often been tasked with accomplishing the integration and providing a common view of the customer, the supplier, the products, and an overall image of how the company is doing. This integration requires a commonality of codes and keys from the source systems, and the job of finding this commonality has come to rest on the shoulders of the data warehouse team.

While true cleansing should be the responsibility of the source systems team, data should be cleansed whenever it's possible and practical to do so also in the ETL process. In addition, in the ETL process data should be consistently transformed to a common format. This means that the data in the data warehouse will be different than the data in the operational systems, and the reports coming from the operational systems will have results that differ from those of the data warehouse reports. The data warehouse has sometimes been faulted for its results not matching those of the operational systems. In fact, management has assumed that if the numbers in the data warehouse deviate from the operational reports, the data warehouse must be incorrect.

In the remainder of this chapter, we discuss solutions for seven integration situations that confront data warehouse projects.

MULTIPLE SOURCE SYSTEMS REQUIRE MAJOR DATA INTEGRATION

An automobile manufacturer with over 650 dealers designed the operational databases to include 22 transaction-oriented files from three separate dealer management systems. How should this installation collect, cleanse, and integrate this data?

Joyce Bischoff

An operational data store could be used to integrate, cleanse, and standardize the format and content of the data. The users must create and review business rules to ensure that data from each system is transformed consistently and correctly.

Chuck Kelley

Hopefully, the three dealer management systems are close in terms of what they collect. My first recommendation is to make sure that the reference data (or dimensions) is consistent throughout all the 650 dealers. For example, is the information about the cars consistently stored (horsepower, color, cylinders, brand, model, and so on)?

To collect the data, there will need to be an upload of the data from each of the dealers to the staging hardware. The network administrators will need to make sure there is sufficient bandwidth in the network (or from the ASP) to do this.

A set of ETL routines will need to be written (most likely three sets of routines, one for each dealer management system) that will process the uploaded files and produce the output to be loaded into the data warehouse. There must be a common set of rules that defines the dimensions and how they are to be populated. For instance, if storing information about the purchaser, the rule set must ensure this can be done consistently across all the dealer management systems. If one system does not collect the same amount of data, then a decision needs to be made about whether to keep the information not collected by all the systems and what to store (if anything) in the columns where the source system does not collect the data.

Integration of the data is done through the values in the dimensions. All the different information about the cars is stored in one dimension, about the purchasers in another dimension, about the dealers in another dimension, and so on. If a user wants to see how many "hot pink" cars were sold, then choosing the color "hot pink" and the sum of the amount of dollars in the fact table will produce the requested results from the integrated view of all the dealerships. A basic (very, very basic) star schema is shown in Figure 12–1. The following SQL code determines how many hot pink cars of each brand and model all the dealers sold and the dollar amount the cars sold for.

```
select automobile.brand, automobile.model,
    sum(sold_amount), count(*)
from automobile, fact
where automobile.id = fact.autoid
and automobile.color = 'HOT PINK'
group by automobile.brand, automobile.model ;
```

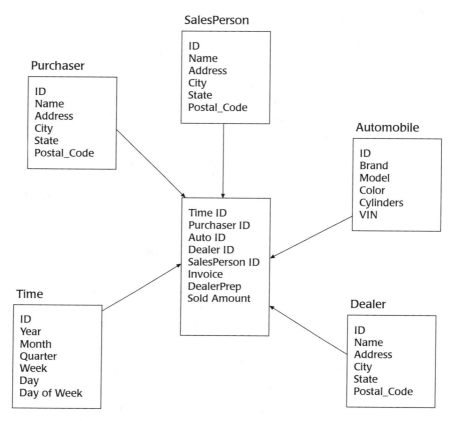

Figure 12–1: Star schema

David Marco

Once the data warehouse data model has been defined, it will be critical to decide on the valid values for each of the attributes. When the ETL process is built (tool or custom), integration will have to be done in accordance with the domain values.

Larissa Moss

The most effective technique for data analysis and data integration is still the old and proven Entity-Relationship (E-R) modeling technique with its normalization rules. Since its invention, E-R modeling has always been used first and foremost for business data analysis and only second for relational database design. Therefore, regardless of whether the data warehouse will be based on a traditional relational database design schema or a multidimensional schema, the E-R modeling technique should be used for data integration and cleansing purposes.

The company should start a business data analysis and logical data modeling initiative, performing the following three steps:

1. Identify the true unique business objects once and only once as they apply to all 650 dealers, independent of current or future process or access needs. The company should standardize the names and definitions for all its unique business objects and all the object's legitimate subtypes (if any).

2. Use normalization rules to assign all the data elements once and only once to their appropriate entities. In order to know how to assign each data element from the 22 source files to its owning business object, the company must perform a thorough domain analysis on all the data elements. Domain analysis refers to analyzing the data content to find and remove any embedded process logic, find and separate data elements that are used for multiple purposes, and find and correct data elements that violate business rules. (See Chapter 11 on data quality in *Data Warehouse Project Management* [Adelman and Moss 2000b].)

3. Connect the business objects through relationships and cardinality (the degree of a relationship) in the same way they are connected in the real word. This step validates the standardized names and definitions of the business objects.

Performing these three steps produces a completely integrated view of the business data. Unfortunately E-R modeling has been rejected by many data warehouse practitioners for the sole reason that it is often not the appropriate database design schema. What the practitioners fail to understand is that integrating and standardizing data is not a database design issue. E-R modeling is still the most appropriate—and the only scientific—technique for business data analysis because it focuses on data integration and data purity as it reflects the business view of data, as opposed to on design issues for the database view of data. Once the logical data model (E-R diagram and business meta data) is validated, the normalized and standardized entities are automatically the conforming dimensions sought after in database design.

Clay Rehm

First things first. Before jumping into the solution, it is wise to do the proper amount of requirements gathering, analysis, and design. Resist the urge to code! However, spending too much time analyzing leads to analysis paralysis.

I highly recommend that the data warehouse team follow a systems development methodology and a project management methodology. The systems development methodology must use an iterative approach, and it should use prototyping in the analysis stages. A full treatment of the subject of analysis and design goes beyond the scope of this book. See Whitten et al. [2000] and Moss and Atre [2003] for a detailed discussion. However, I will highlight some important aspects of the ETL process.

The business customers, data architects, and business analysts must work together to first form a conceptual data model, and from that a logical data model. The conceptual data model must be very easy for a non-technical person to understand. It is usually a diagram with squares (entities) and lines connecting the squares (relationships). In this case, the conceptual model may contain such entities as `Dealer`, `Automobile`, and `Date/Time`, with lines drawn connecting them with statements such as a `Dealer sells Automobiles`. The actual movement of data needs to be designed.

The data model will go through many iterations of design and validation, even after the ETL coding has begun. Enough key players must provide input and review the model. Once the data model is complete and approved, then ETL specialists, technical architects, and systems analysts must be involved to design how the data will be moved and how many staging areas are required, if any. The data administrator should keep in mind that he or she will not think of every question to ask, nor will he or she be able to appropriately answer all questions. The goal is to understand the current environment and the desired state environment as much as possible to make informed decisions and designs.

During design and development, the data administrator should keep reviewing the scope document. The collection process needs to be designed to support the requirements. The data administrator should ask the clients and the data warehouse team: Does the data need to be collected every week, every day, or every second? When designing the data model, the data administrator should make sure it supports the proper time period.

When considering the cleansing process, the ETL developer should validate that either all data is loaded or only clean data is loaded. This is important because if dirty data is not loaded, the data warehouse may end up missing a lot of data! Also, the project manager should verify which systems and users need to be included for data verification purposes. Does the project plan include enough time for manual verification of data?

Other questions to ask: Which data elements need to be captured and which do not? Where will the lookup tables reside? Do they exist? Does the team need to build an application to maintain lookup table data? Is the data replaced or updated? How often will the ETL process run? What disaster recovery, backup, and restore and rollback procedures are to be implemented?

The moral of the story: Gather and document the requirements, follow a methodology, and stick to it!

THE ENTERPRISE MODEL IS DELAYING PROGRESS

A data administration manager has been given the job of creating a consolidated business model for the entire enterprise. It is well known that without such a model each business unit is likely to create a model followed by a data mart that cannot be integrated with any other in the organization. This would nullify two of the major objectives of the data warehouse: (1) to provide a single version of the truth, and (2) to allow integration of data across the different lines of business. Unfortunately, two projects are ready to get started and the individual project managers are unwilling to wait for the enterprise model to be built. What should the CIO do?

Joyce Bischoff

The CIO should allow the projects to continue with some constraints. If each project team models the data needed for its specific project, each model may be regarded as a step toward the development of an enterprise model. The data administration staff can integrate the models, and a single model can be provided for the use of the two projects. Eventually, like the pieces of a puzzle, a complete corporate model could be developed. It is not advisable to postpone a data warehouse project until a corporate model is available. It could take years to complete the corporate model, and the model may still be inadequate to support each detailed data warehouse project.

Jill Dyché

In the 1980s and early 1990s, the enterprise data model changed from a corporate strategy that promised to ensure continuity of data and its definitions to the excuse for why everything was taking so long. As well intended as enterprise data modeling was, it wasn't a trivial exercise. It took a while—too long for many business people awaiting key functionality. As a result, enterprise data modeling got a bad rap.

Fast forward to the twenty-first century. Enterprise data modeling still exists, but it's incremental. Many data administration managers faced with this dilemma might still insist on delaying the projects until a complete enterprise model is built, but most are circumspect enough to understand the trade-offs. Insisting on the completion of an enterprise model could cost a manager his or her credibility and even department.

I say let the projects get started. Make sure that the projects' data modelers are chartered with developing project data models that will be validated against—and perhaps even contribute to—the enterprise model. Meanwhile, the enterprise data modelers should realign their activities to address the subject areas that the individual projects will need in order to get started. The enterprise data modelers should partner with the project data modelers to ensure that the enterprise and project models conform and that:

- The project data models map to the enterprise data model.
- The enterprise data model encompasses the data subject areas that are key to the projects.

The project models should in fact serve as units of validation for the enterprise model and—in cases where the enterprise model contains objects that pertain to the projects—vice versa.

Allowing the enterprise data model to impede the progress of IT projects can backfire both technically and politically. Just as a perfect data warehouse architecture with no business value can render a data warehouse worthless, a perfect enterprise data model with no applicability to actual projects is merely an intellectual exercise. Don't go into the light!

Douglas Hackney

The CIO would be wise to not be a speed-to-market barrier for the business. One of the greatest political challenges we have in data warehousing is being viewed as a detriment to speed by the business. For long-term political sustainability, it is essential for data warehousing organizations to be viewed as facilitators of speed rather than distributors of delay.

In this scenario the CIO should adopt well-known and proven methodologies to build incremental architected data marts for the two projects that are ready to start. This will ensure that their data mart systems will be capable of being integrated into the overall business intelligence architecture of the organization. At the same time, the enterprise data architecture project can move forward in parallel.

It is important to not tie the success of data warehousing initiatives to that of enterprise data model projects. Countless enterprise data model projects have been killed after nondelivery and lengthy time lines. Don't let your data warehouse project suffer guilt by association or death by proximity.

Sean Ivoghli

The CIO doesn't need to wait until the enterprise model is complete. The enterprise model should represent the true business model, while the data warehouse model will represent the requirements of any reporting, analytics, data mining, or other application that uses the data warehouse. The two data warehouse projects that are ready to start need to work together to ensure the consistency of dimensions and definition of metrics. They must ensure that the same objects are not created twice. The fact tables of the data warehouse will be related to event or transaction entities in the enterprise model, and the dimension tables will be related to master, code, and other entities in the enterprise model. The relationships in the data warehouse will represent reporting requirements, while the relationships in the enterprise model will represent the business rules. Although many of the relationships will be similar, some will not be. As the data warehouse model is developed, the CIO can provide feedback to the enterprise data modeling effort in order to account for the entities, attributes, and relationships, but he or she shouldn't expect a perfect match. The enterprise model may have entities and relationships that are not needed in the data warehouse because they are not needed for any analytical/reporting requirements.

In conclusion, the key to achieving the objectives of consistent data integration is for the multiple project teams to work together on the data models and also on data acquisition rules. It may help to have an enterprise data model, but it does not guarantee that different projects will produce consistent results. Most of the successful data warehousing projects I have witnessed did not use an enterprise data model.

Chuck Kelley

Most failures and black eyes of data warehousing in the early days was this exact problem—namely, trying to define the whole enchilada (data model) before starting anything. We need to realize that businesses will change, and therefore the data model is a fluid environment. The CIO needs to put into place a group that defines the dimensions that will be shared across any two data marts. This allows the sharing of data across the different lines of business. Let's say that we're defining two data marts for the insurance industry—expenses and income. Without a control over the dimensions, it is possible that we would never be able to compare the income from policies with the expenses from claims. This is because the granularity may not be equivalent, and the summarization might not be possible between the two data marts to share, and therefore compare, the data other than by a few dimensions. Those dimensions (like time) would be so highly summarized that reasonable analysis might not be possible.

Without control of the dimensions, the CIO will end up with what the organization has always had—no enterprise view of the corporate data.

Larissa Moss

There is no reason for any project to wait for an enterprise data model to be built. The practice of building the entire normalized enterprise data model top-down was abandoned in the late 1980s. Enterprise data models can just as easily be built a little at a time within the scope of every project. Over time, these project-specific, normalized logical data models are "merged" by the data administration staff into the larger enterprise data model.

The CIO must get the users as well as his or her data warehouse IT staff to understand that they are building an integrated decision support environment, not silo applications, and that these project-specific logical data models will help in that effort. The CIO and the data administration (DA) manager should explain to the data warehouse teams that a data modeler will be assigned to each core team. The data modeler's job is to concentrate on data integration and data content quality for the data elements that are in the scope of each project. The DA manager should further explain that each logical data model produced during a project must be reviewed and sanctioned (approved) not only by the data owners but also by other downstream users of that data. If any discrepancies or illegitimate use of the data are discovered during the review sessions, the business community will address them since the discovered problems may be the root causes for the current data problems. Should any discrepancies surface during the merging of the project models into an enterprise view (done by the data modelers "behind the scenes" while the projects are progressing), those will be brought to the attention of the project teams for resolution. If the project teams cannot resolve the problems due to a disagreement between users, the discrepancies will again be brought to the attention of the business community for resolution.

The final message the CIO should deliver to the data warehouse teams is that any tasks deemed necessary for developing a data warehouse, including cross-organizational data analysis and data modeling tasks, must be given adequate time to be performed in order to ensure a quality product. However, the scope of all tasks, including the data modeling tasks, must be restricted to the scope of the project.

Caution: Having all the important users of the data assembled in one room often leads to the temptation to turn data model review sessions into full-blown enterprise data modeling sessions. That should not be allowed. The review sessions should be used only to validate the accuracy of what is being modeled for the project; they should not be used to model the entire enterprise. Therefore, taking time to expand the data model to include all the different views of the other users (views that are not part of the project scope) should be considered scope creep and should be avoided.

Clay Rehm

An enterprise data model is very important to any organization. The challenges of creating (and maintaining) one are many, and the costs seem to outweigh the benefits, especially in the view of the business. The business managers usually view any enterprise data model or infrastructure work as something for which they do not see tangible benefits and thus will not spend the time or money to build. An enterprise solution can be accomplished, but this usually depends heavily on having the right staff involved. It is not the technology that will be the challenge—it will be the communication and political skills of the team that will be put to the test.

A rapid application development (RAD) approach is in order. The data administration manager must scope out a high-level enterprise model that can be done in two to three weeks. He or she will need a highly talented team that should involve external consultants who are willing and able to work long hours in this time frame and have the personalities that can cross business divisions. The data administration manager should hire an internal or external consultant to facilitate this team who has experience in facilitating groups and has knowledge of the industry.

Before starting this approach, the data administration manager should communicate the plan to all stakeholders and identify the required resources. He or she should be direct and honest about the challenges as well as the benefits. Here is the recommended course of action. The data administration manager and the representatives from the two start-up projects must work on the following tasks concurrently:

- Define and document the subject areas in their domains. This includes diagrams, descriptions, the entity names in each subject area, and relationships.
- Define and document the common (or conformed) dimensions identified so far across the enterprise or domains.
- Define and document the facts that have been identified so far across the enterprise.

Once complete, the data administration manager and the managers from the two start-up projects will work to share what is needed in the data model. Each team's project plans must include the time and the involvement required. An enterprise mind-set must be applied even when time does not permit.

Should a Company Decentralize?

A company has data integrity issues that appear to be caused by the lack of a good master data maintenance strategy. The company basically has no change control process for master data. Now there are some plans afoot to decentralize a number of the databases. The CTO is looking for some best practices and ideas involving centralization and decentralization and ideas for a data maintenance strategy. What recommendations would you give him?

Sid Adelman

Since this company had serious problems while in a centralized environment, the IT staff will be totally and hopelessly out of control if they decentralize. Decentralization is at least three to four times more difficult and complex than a centralized architecture. This company needs to master the basics before it embarks on a complex architecture that would include decentralization. The CTO needs to develop a good data strategy that includes a master maintenance strategy. After this strategy has been in place for a few years, they may then be in a position to consider decentralization. A data strategy would also include

- Meta data
- Standards (data naming, RDBMS, operating systems)
- Business intelligence
- Data quality
- Security
- Categorization of data
- Organization (database administrators, data owners, data stewards, and so on)
- Application package databases
- Data integration
- Data modeling

Joyce Bischoff

The CTO should ask an expert to review the audit and control processes in the current movement of data from the source systems into the warehouse. Whether the system is centralized or decentralized, appropriate audit and control processes must be in place to guard data integrity. The architecture and design of the ETL processes must have controls in place during each step in the process to ensure data quality and accuracy. This can include record counts, control totals, statistical sampling, and, possibly, control files to manage the start and completion of various jobs. In addition, it can help manage backout procedures.

Chuck Kelley

For strategic reference data (master data), I would put a team into place that deals with the addition of new reference data. I wouldn't necessarily want to slow down the transaction systems, but I wouldn't want bad data entered either. Therefore, maybe the CTO could define that all data added to the reference data must be marked as "new" and all "new" rows should be checked for duplicates or better choices. Once a decision on those "new" rows is complete, the rows will be folded in and propagated to the transaction systems.

A lot of organizations fail in the whole reference data area. I believe that organizations need to implement reference servers: application servers that just deal with reference data and that are used by the operational systems. The benefit to this scheme is that there is a single representation of the reference data (and it is not stored in the data warehouse until the normal ETL process completes). The biggest negative to this environment is relational databases. Relational databases, as of yet, have trouble creating referential integrity across physical databases (or instances). Once this negative is solved (and I don't expect it for a while), the concept of reference servers should start to be used.

David Marco

It will be important for the company to not give up on its centralized activities since decentralization is much more complex and costly to maintain. The company needs to develop a good strategy for master data maintenance and to implement a change control process for the master data.

Clay Rehm

There is never a right answer to the question of whether to centralize or decentralize. Both options make sense and both are appropriate. The answer depends on the specific situation. Having said that, since the company is already having problems with centralized data, decentralizing it will only make matters worse.

I recommend that the data administration group implement data model change control. This is an easy solution that requires formal and documented change requests to any data elements.

This would also be a great time to introduce data stewardship. This implies that there is a real owner (a business person) for each entity in the database. Once there is ownership (real ownership, not just lip service), the CTO will be in a better position to control the data environment. Data strategies must involve the users. The users should choose to involve themselves as data stewards.

THE BUSINESS SPONSOR WANTS REAL-TIME CUSTOMER UPDATES

The business sponsor of a customer data warehouse wants real-time updates. Should real-time updates be allowed? Are there any good alternatives?

Sid Adelman

The requirement for real-time updates brings into question the vision for the data warehouse. The conventional view is that the data warehouse is aimed at tactical and strategic decisions, not at operational decisions. A real-time update requirement sounds like an operational decision. Not that there's anything wrong with operational decisions; it's just that they compromise the data warehouse. Any operational decision system should be put on its own track. Users want a point-in-time set of data they can count on. If they run two identical queries ten minutes apart and get different results, it makes them crazy. They then usually ask IT to explain why the results are different. The end result is unhappy users and much wasted time and effort.

Joyce Bischoff

The design must be evaluated with an understanding of the frequency and quantity of data involved in updating. With this understanding, the data warehouse manager can then decide whether updates should be run in real time, with a trickle feed, or in batch updates.

Jill Dyché

When I hear about the need for real-time data—and I've heard about it a lot lately when creating CRM business plans for clients—my first question is,

"Is the real-time data necessary for a particular department, or is the need enterprise wide?" Careful research should be done to determine what "real-time updates" really are. Should they occur within a given time window? How often will they happen? What data will be touched and how critical is it? What is the logging scheme?

Whatever the scenario, the client should focus on the business actions that will be taken on the data. What does the business require in terms of data timeliness to address the business actions, and are real-time updates necessary to meet this requirement?

The answer to how to enable real-time updates depends on how large the environment is, how much data there is, and the existing system's capacity. The most effective manner of handling real-time updates differs with the existing platform (symmetrical multiprocessing? massively parallel processing?), whether the real-time details are enterprise-oriented or department-specific (which tables will the real-time updates affect?), and the impact to user concurrency for existing analysis activities.

So, the solution to real-time updates might not be a data warehouse solution but a new operational application. If this is indeed the case, it should be architected as such. There is often an assumption that if the necessary data comes from a data warehouse, the requested functionality should be a data warehouse application. In truth, sometimes a data warehouse can be a very effective source system, availing centralized and cleansed data to a separate operational environment that may pull data from other systems as well.

After all, end-users don't ask for the data warehouse to be updated in real time; they ask for current data. Users focus on the timeliness of the data needed to solve their business problems. There are many different ways to update data, and updates to the data warehouse may not be the most practical or cost-effective. I know of some Enterprise Application Integration (EAI) vendors that will put their record-at-a-time update performance rates—complete with built-in process logic—up against a real-time data warehouse any day. I mean, I love data warehousing. I cut my teeth on it. It's just not always the right answer.

So, depending on the existing systems and usage constraints, the best answer here might not be to enable real-time updates on a data warehouse but instead to provide an operational platform that focuses solely on individual data attributes sourced from the data warehouse—and other key systems—for very specific availability needs.

Chuck Kelley

In the total data warehouse environment, one that includes operational data stores (ODSs), I would accept real-time updates assuming the business units really do require real-time updates. The business units need to understand what they are asking (and should be paying) for. They are asking for the current operational systems to be slower. Some recoding of the applications to offer a two-phase commit protocol is the only way to guarantee true real-time updates. There needs to be a valid business case before moving to the real-time update environment. The business case needs to define the added cost in hardware, network bandwidth, software, and personnel. Those costs will need to be balanced against the benefits. I would question the need for a real-time update for doing strategic analysis (the purpose of the data warehouse). Therefore, I would look to the ODS to provide the environment for the real-time updates.

Some alternatives would be to provide two- or four-hour updates. This is a lot easier. Database replication, hot standby databases, or a store-and-forward mechanism could easily support this situation. The architecture should define this with an ODS. The ODS will then load the data warehouse.

David Marco

Real-time updates should be occurring in the ODS. The data warehouse can then be fed from the ODS, which prevents the data warehouse from having to go back to the source systems again for data.

Larissa Moss

Real-time updates are typically operational requirements rather than strategic requirements. A data warehouse is meant to satisfy strategic decision-making requirements, not operational ones. Because a data warehouse stores large volumes of historical data, it is often a very large database (VLDB), and it is critical to tune it optimally. It is not possible to tune a VLDB (or any database) optimally for data updates as well as for data access. Besides, the types of operational or tactical requirements that may require real-time updates usually do not require years of historical data. And strategic trend analysis requirements that require years of historical data usually do not require real-time updates. Therefore, the two types of opposite requirements should be separated and satisfied from two different databases. For example, an ODS with real-time updates may satisfy the operational and tactical requirements, and a collection of summarized data marts may satisfy the strategic requirements.

Clay Rehm

Real-time updates are certainly achievable and appropriate as long as they are needed. The cost to create and maintain this kind of architecture is usually high and discourages many.

Before answering whether real-time updates can be done in this situation, solid business requirements need to be identified, documented, discussed, and approved. Having real-time updates is a great idea, but what is the real business reason? Does the sponsor fully understand how much more difficult it will be to maintain and how much it will cost? Once the sponsor understands each alternative and the cost of each alternative, he or she may choose not to follow this path. What about making updates once an hour, or twice a day, or once a day? The technology is usually achievable, but at what price?

THE COMPANY DOESN'T WANT STOVEPIPE SYSTEMS

After surveying other data warehouse implementations and paying particular attention to failures, a company is determined not to build stovepipe systems. However, there is a strong push from three of the divisions to deliver a data warehouse for their divisions and to do so as quickly as possible. How should the company avoid building stovepipe systems?

Sid Adelman

A stovepipe system is one that cannot integrate with any other system. This means a stovepipe does not have common keys that would allow joining of data across these stovepipes. It could also mean multiple versions of the same data exist, violating the idea of a single version of the truth.

In this situation, I would expect the divisions to want to build data marts to solve their own specific problems. Building data marts should still be allowed to proceed, but this does not mean the company cannot have common keys, common data definitions (this may be more difficult), and meta data that identifies the data elements in each of the data marts. For this to happen, someone in a position of authority must oversee all these data marts (not stovepipes) to assure the commonality that will allow joining across the data marts as well as a unified vision of the corporate approach to data marts and to a federated data warehouse.

Joyce Bischoff

To accomplish this, efficient processes must be developed that will ensure compliance with standards but not cause a bottleneck to the fast development of needed data marts. In addition, the following areas must be addressed:

- A data warehouse group to establish standards and coordinate the development of the overall data warehouse environment, including data warehouses, operational data stores, data marts, and so on.
- User-friendly naming conventions that must be used uniformly throughout the warehouse environment.
- Data definitions for all data.
- Logical data models encompassing the scope of data for the specific project. The models for specific applications can eventually be merged into a growing corporate-wide model.
- Design reviews at critical points in the development of each data mart to ensure that it fits into the overall architecture.

The following sections provide additional details on each bullet point.

Data Warehouse Coordination Group. This group could include persons representing data administration, database administration, the business community, security, networking, and so on. Many shops have found it effective to use matrix management, in which a member of the group reports directly to data administration, database administration, security, and so on but has a dotted-line reporting status to the data warehouse group. This improves communication and promotes cooperation. Another alternative is to have members report directly to the data warehouse manager to optimize database design, minimize data redundancy, and ensure the data assets of the corporation are used effectively.

Naming Conventions. The company should develop a user-friendly data-naming convention and require that everyone use it. It is important that the physical naming convention be as intuitive as possible from the perspective of the users. Users should be involved in the development of the naming convention to ensure their satisfaction with the final database design. An efficient process for the creation and approval of names is critical and cannot be allowed to become a bottleneck to designers and developers.

Data Definitions. Data definitions are a vital part of the data warehouse foundation and should be available for every data element at the time the data warehouse environment is implemented.

Data Models. Data models are a prerequisite to effective physical design. If a corporate data model is available, it should be used as a basis for design. Although most organizations do not have usable corporate data models, a data model encompassing the scope of the project should be required. If each project provides its model, they may be integrated into a larger model and, over time, a corporate model should emerge.

Design Reviews. When the data model for the specific project is completed, the data administration group and/or the data warehouse group and the users should review it for accuracy and completeness. The purpose of a data model is to convey the business knowledge of the data modeler in a format that can be understood by the users. Esoteric data-modeling techniques that cannot be easily understood by others should be avoided.

Douglas Hackney

In this scenario, it is likely that the three divisions will initiate, develop, and implement their own data warehouse systems. To avoid creating three stovepipes, the organization needs to adopt a strategy that will be conducive to implementing architected or integratable systems. The best route to achieve these goals is to implement methodologies based on either incremental architected data marts or a federated BI architecture. Either of these approaches will yield three systems that can share key metrics, measures, and dimensions. The federated approach will accommodate the three systems regardless of their individual approach (that is, top down, bottom up, hybrid, and so on) and is the most flexible and pragmatic approach when faced with heterogeneous, decentralized environments.

Chuck Kelley

The absolute first thing that needs to be done is to establish a group of people who will define the dimensions (or reference data) for the whole data warehouse environment. This group will need to keep a common definition of all the dimension data and will have authority over all the data mart development groups with respect to the dimensional data. Then the data mart groups can develop their systems based on those dimensional systems.

David Marco

Companies that build stovepipe systems have to eventually rebuild them. This fact needs to be explained to the divisions to avoid taking the stovepipe option.

Larissa Moss

Depending on the data warehouse strategy of this company, either the three divisions are not following the strategic direction or there is no strategic direction. Either case needs to be addressed. If there is no strategic direction, the data warehouse manager should meet with executives of the business community and the CIO to develop one. If there is a strategy and the divisions are not following the governance process, the data warehouse manager must review and discuss the company's data warehouse strategy with them to come to a common understanding or take the issue to the executives in the business community for resolution.

On the tactical side, the data warehouse manager must ensure that he or she has the staff and the infrastructure to accommodate multiple parallel development efforts, which must be coordinated, integrated, and reconciled in order to avoid building stovepipe systems. Taking the three steps below will accomplish that. The data warehouse manager will need a trained staff that has prior experience with cross-organizational development efforts. If the staff is untrained and has no experience with cross-organizational development, the project manager will need to allocate additional time for coordination, synchronization, training, and learning curve.

1. The first step in the process is to integrate the data from the three divisions into one business view. The most appropriate technique to do that is a normalized entity-relationship model. The entities of this model will become conforming dimensions later in the database design.

2. The second step is to agree on common data definitions and data content. The most appropriate technique for this step is developing business meta data. It involves the data owners, who are most likely not the same individuals as the users in the three divisions. If the company does not have data ownership, the project manager should expect significant delays in completing this step because all data disputes will have to be elevated to the business executives for resolution. This can result in unpleasant political repercussions.

3. The third step is to design and implement one central staging area for all three divisions—and for all subsequent divisions. This step will ensure that all data elements will be extracted from their source files only once, regardless of what data mart they will feed. It will also ensure that the extracted data elements will be cleansed and transformed in a consistent way, as opposed to each data mart cleansing and transforming the data its own way. During this step, tie-out (reconciliation) totals will be produced to ensure that all data marts reconcile to each other and to their source files.

The data warehouse manager, the three division managers, the users, the CIO, and the business executives must all understand that building an integrated and reconciled common data warehouse environment will take longer than building stovepipe systems. If the data warehouse manager continues to get pressured by the users of the three divisions to ignore the steps of cross-organizational integration, this organization is obviously not committed to anything other than stovepipe system development. In that atmosphere, there will be little else the data warehouse manager can do to avoid stovepipes.

Clay Rehm

The company needs to form an enterprise SWAT team that does not get into the "theoretical" design and development approach; this is a team of quick hitters who can design an enterprise data architecture. The team members must be able to identify, document, and get approval on conformed dimensions quickly. They must be able to design the high-level common meta data repository.

Bottom line: A talented team of individuals is needed to quickly build a central data warehouse using a virtual central data warehouse approach.

REPORTS FROM THE DATA WAREHOUSE AND OPERATIONAL SYSTEMS DON'T MATCH

The data warehouse manager is responsible for all the data warehouse initiatives in the company. He recognizes that he will have credibility problems if the reports and queries that come from the data warehouse do not correspond to those of the operational systems. He also knows that much of the operational data is dirty and must be cleansed to satisfy the needs of the analysts who will be the primary users of the data warehouse. He knows that if he transforms and cleans up the data as he brings it into the data warehouse, the report results will not correspond to those of the operational systems, and the validity of the data warehouse will be questioned. What should the data warehouse manager do?

Sid Adelman

The data warehouse manager must begin a major education effort for the entire organization that will be receiving reports. The education should include information about the current state of the operational data; that there will need to be an analysis of this data, the need for cleansing, and information about the cleansing process to create the data warehouse databases. The education must help the users understand that there will be differences between the operational reports and those coming from the data warehouse. Specific examples will help make clear how they will differ and that those differences are acceptable.

Joyce Bischoff

The data warehouse can be no better than the data that feeds it. Control totals and audit processes are needed to ensure consistency. The data warehouse manager should work with the operational staff to improve data quality. Numerous tools on the market can be used to identify dirty data. If data is dirty and cannot be cleaned up, a business decision must be made as to its inclusion in the warehouse.

Douglas Hackney

The data warehouse manager must document and publicize all deltas to existing reports prior to production release of the data warehouse system. The business users will almost always believe their existing numbers rather than the data warehouse, sometimes even after they're shown that their old numbers are wrong. The data warehouse manager must not underestimate the change management challenge associated with the correction of bad numbers in existing systems.

Sean Ivoghli

The only thing the data warehouse manager can do is to be prepared to demonstrate and explain (in detail) why the data is different and why the data from the data warehouse is better. He must win the support of those users with more clout. The rest will follow. The data warehouse manager will have to keep proving himself for some time before the users get comfortable with the new numbers.

Chuck Kelley

First, the requirements of the data warehouse should be to house the most correct data within the organization. If the data in the operational systems is dirty and lacks credibility, then it should be cleansed and stored in the data warehouse. One option would be to store both the dirty and cleansed data in the data warehouse so that the users can see both sets. Then the meta data repository can explain why the report results are different. There must be lots of user communication during this period so that everyone understands why the results are different and that, in fact, the data warehouse contains the best data in the organization.

Larissa Moss

The data warehouse manager and project managers must spend more time educating the users by having them participate more actively on the data warehouse project. The idea that the reports generated from the data warehouse must match to the penny the reports generated from the operational systems is false and must be dispelled for the following reasons:

- "Matching to the penny" is never a strategic requirement but an operational one, and the users should not be using the data warehouse for operational reporting.
- If the data is dirty in the operational systems, that makes the operational reports wrong, not the data warehouse reports.
- If the users actively participated on the data warehouse project, they would not question the credibility of the data warehouse reports and queries because they would be the ones discovering, correcting, and reconciling the dirty data.

Users should be full-time members of the data warehouse team working with the IT analysts and lead developers on the project specifications and on testing all program modules, including those that produce the reconciliation totals for dropped or modified dirty data.

This data warehouse manager has misdiagnosed his problem. His problem is not losing credibility because of different report results; his problem is that the users are not steering the boat—they're not even on the boat (the data warehouse project).

Clay Rehm

The project managers should work out a course of action on a case-by-case basis for each data source and each owner of that data source. Very important—they *must* take this information to the source data owners first. There is no reason to publicize the dirty data in public (don't air dirty laundry) if the managers can resolve it. The data warehouse manager and the project managers should work together with the data source owners since they will be "partners" for a very long time!

The project managers should be prepared to produce reports that show exactly what transformations the team conducted and how the data looked before and after the load.

The moral of the story: Do not bite the hand that feeds you!

SHOULD THE DATA WAREHOUSE TEAM FIX AN INADEQUATE OPERATIONAL SYSTEM?

It has become clear that the operational systems that feed the data warehouse are inadequate, and management believes that part of the job of building the data warehouse project is to fix the operational systems. Should the data warehouse team attempt this?

Sid Adelman

The data warehouse team cannot take on the responsibility of fixing the operational systems. If there are problems with the operational systems, it's someone else's job. Implementing the data warehouse is tough enough, and there are reasons these operational systems have not been easily fixed in the past—maybe because it's too difficult.

Joyce Bischoff

Since the quality of data in a data warehouse can be no better than the quality of the data that feeds it, every effort should be made to clean up the operational environment. It should be noted, however, that the level of cleanliness required in the warehouse might not be the same as that required in the operational environment. Although fields like names, addresses, and dollar values should be as accurate as possible, this may not be necessary if data such as hobbies and favorite magazines are tracked in the data warehouse.

Sean Ivoghli

No, the data warehouse team should not try to fix the operational systems. The owners and maintainers of the operational systems are responsible for performing such work.

Chuck Kelley

No, although one of the many roles of the data warehouse team is to provide feedback on how to fix the operational systems. The team members need to keep in contact with the operational staff to make sure that when the operational systems get fixed, the data warehouse can accept the new data feeds with the new business rules.

David Marco

I'm going to give the classic consulting answer: "It depends." If it will be fairly simple to fix the operational system in the data warehouse, then maybe the data warehouse team should do it. On the other hand, a good rule of thumb is that operational problems should be fixed as close to their source as possible. Anything else is just a bandage.

Larissa Moss

No. The data warehouse team has no responsibility over the operational systems. The team is not chartered to maintain the operational systems, it is not funded to modify the operational systems, and it is not staffed to support the operational systems. A data warehouse team builds and maintains data warehouses—not operational systems. However, it is the responsibility of the data warehouse team to bring mistakes and inadequacies of the operational systems to the attention of the users and the business sponsor as well as to the attention of the business owners of those operational systems and the IT units that support them. The data warehouse team is also responsible for assessing which operational problems would jeopardize the success of the data warehouse if left uncorrected. With the users and sponsor the data warehouse team must triage and correct as many problems as are critical to achieving the expected benefits from the data warehouse.

Clay Rehm

First, management needs to be educated that it is not the data warehouse team's responsibility to fix or replace any source system. A data warehouse is meant to capture and integrate disparate data into one place that is easy to access and use. Now, while data warehouses are very different than operational systems, they do have their similarities. The differences create the most challenges for any data warehouse design team. A data warehouse team must deal with a different set of requirements, users, and environment. It most often takes a different mind-set. However, having said all that, the data warehouse team stands in a better position to influence how the source system should be redesigned. The data warehouse team has a better understanding of the source and target data. In any case, the development of an operational system is a separate project. It has its own challenges, with separate time lines, resources, and issues; and it must be treated in this way.

Bottom line: The development of an operational system and the development of a data warehouse are two separate projects.

CHAPTER THIRTEEN

Data Warehouse Architecture

. . . [T]o keep the business from disintegrating, the concept of information systems architecture is becoming less an option and more a necessity for establishing some order and control in the investment of information system resources.

—John Zachman

OVERVIEW

In 1628, a ship's architect and master shipwright from the Netherlands was commissioned to build a warship for the Swedish Navy. This ship, the *Wasa*, was to be the largest and most powerful such vessel ever built. The ship was magnificent, measuring 145 feet long with 64 guns. The architect, who had built many smaller Dutch warships, built the *Wasa* using the same proportions that had won him fame and fortune in his native country. With the normal amount of ballast, the ship rode too low in the water, so ballast was removed. As the *Wasa* sailed into the Stockholm Harbor for its maiden voyage, a gust of wind caught the sails, the ship capsized (remember the ballast), water poured into the gun ports, and to the horror of all who watched, the ship sank. The *Wasa* has since been raised and now provides a fascinating museum showing the life of men aboard ship.

The tale of the *Wasa* is a warning to anyone who would assume that the architecture appropriate for 100 gigabytes with 20 users will also work for 10 terabytes and 500 users.

The ship's architect was reported to have caught the first stage out of Stockholm, choosing not to wait for his final payment. A data warehouse architect who fails to develop an architecture that will scale will also have to beat a hasty retreat when his or her designs are unable to perform as data volume and the number of users dramatically increases. Successful data warehouses will almost always grow in both the size of the database and in the number of users. An architecture built for a small data warehouse may not be able to support any type of significant growth. Many data warehouse environments have grown with little consideration to what is an appropriate architecture. Some organizations have been deluded to accept that the choice of a vendor tool or set of tools means they have defined an adequate architecture. A major source of data for the data warehouse is click-stream data. High-volume click-stream data presents significant challenges to the database design.

Historical data and how it should be treated is an important consideration for trend analysis, which is one of the major reasons for building a data warehouse. The number of time periods maintained and the ability to analyze trends on data (whose codes have undoubtedly changed) is a fundamental consideration, especially as code changes affect the effort to reconcile the codes. Historical data is usually associated with the need to analyze time variance. This becomes more complicated as the analysis calls for an OLAP capability. The standard for most data warehouses requires that no changes should be made to the data. However, some operational systems backdate data, and the problem is how to reflect the backdated data in the data warehouse.

Meta data is always cited as one of the critical success factors for data warehouses. The architecture of how meta data will flow from one tool to another, meta data standards, and how the meta data will be used are key components of the data warehouse architecture. The architecture for meta data remains a difficult problem as vendors have not followed standards, which makes interfacing of the vendor tools difficult.

A data warehouse architecture also encompasses the source data, that is, how the source data will be extracted, transformed, and then loaded.

Since the ETL process is such a labor-intensive and important part of the data warehouse, the manner in which ETL takes place, including the data-cleansing component, must be a fundamental part of the architecture.

Some organizations are considering using data warehouses for operational reporting. This has become a hotly debated topic. Some have taken the position that the firewall between operational and decision support should never be breached. The opposing side points to the availability of meta data, the relatively cleaner data, the advantages of using data that has already been aggregated, better reporting tools, and the desire to reconcile with operational reports as major reasons to produce operational reports from the data warehouse.

In the remainder of this chapter, we discuss solutions for nine situations that address problems related to architecture.

THE DATA WAREHOUSE ARCHITECTURE IS INADEQUATE

The data warehouse has grown from 50 gigabytes to 1 terabyte. It started with 20 users, and there are now 300. Response time is terrible, the users are complaining, and the DBAs are having great difficulty expanding the data warehouse and keeping performance acceptable. All new requests have been put on hold. The culprit seems to be an architecture that was designed for 50 gigabytes and 20 users. Any change in the architecture will undoubtedly be expensive and disruptive. What should the data warehouse architect do?

Sid Adelman

The data warehouse architect must determine whether the architecture is expandable and can be salvaged. In some cases, tuning and changes in design can keep the system performing well. Another consideration is the plan for future expansion. While the existing architecture may be salvageable, it may not allow any future scaling for additional users and more data.

If the existing architecture cannot be salvaged, the architect must find an architecture that can scale far beyond the existing workload, number of users, and size of the database. Data warehouses grow. The architect must decide whether it's best to maintain two architectures and leave some of the existing systems as they are, recognizing the difficulty of supporting two environments and the difficulty of integrating data from more than one platform. The alternative would be to migrate the existing data warehouse to the new architecture, keeping in mind the cost and disruption of any migration.

Joyce Bischoff

The answer may be in the database design, the hardware, the database management system, the operating system, the front-end tools, the network, or the basic architecture. The data warehouse architect should start with a database design and performance review to determine the weak points. He or she should correct the weak points and test the results. The results of the review should indicate whether there is a need to expand hardware or change the software environment.

Douglas Hackney

The architect should present a summary of the situation and the anticipated costs to the data warehouse steering committee. If the data warehouse is solving mission-critical problems, the business will find the funding to fix it. If no funding is forthcoming, this is a clear indication of where the data warehouse falls in the pecking order of systems in the business.

Sean Ivoghli

I would ask the data warehouse architect the following questions:

- Have you looked into partitioning DBMS tables, using bitmapped indexes, caching reports, optimizing the DBMS frequently, and other non-architecture-related performance enhancers?
- Are your primary keys simple and of integer/numeric data types?

If the data warehouse schema is of a snowflaked nature, the architect should consider creating consolidated, conforming dimensions to reduce the number of joins required per query. This means that he or she should consolidate multiple tables that make up dimensional hierarchies into a group of consolidated dimension tables that each represent a specific level in a dimensional hierarchy and have hierarchy columns that define the higher levels of that hierarchy. The fact tables should be joined to the appropriate dimension tables based on the aggregate level of the fact. An example would be to take a snowflaked Organization dimension with multiple hierarchy tables (Dealer, Branch, and Region, where Dealer reports to Branch, Branch reports to Region) and create the following tables: (1) a consolidated Dealer table with Dealer, Branch, and Region attributes, (2) a consolidated Branch table with Branch and Region attributes, and (3) a Region table with its own attributes. This approach results in a lot of denormalization of data, which increases the maintenance requirements for keeping the redundant data in sync. Therefore, this option should be used only when the snowflaked dimension tables have a high volume of records, resulting in expensive joins between large dimension tables. (The architect should also evaluate the query patterns). This approach is not pretty, but data warehousing is no beauty contest; it's all about performance and scalability.

The architect may also want to look at the number of concurrent users and the load that puts on the network, database servers, and business intelligence/OLAP servers. The company may need more hardware.

Another option is to create data marts for user groups that are heavy users of the data warehouse. These data marts should be limited to the subset of the data needed by their users and should have their own servers. The architect will need to evaluate whether the benefits of this approach will justify its costs.

Chuck Kelley

With few exceptions, every data warehouse grows rapidly beyond the estimates. The architect needs to rethink the architecture to take into account rapid growth. Once the new architecture is in place, there needs to be a new set of ETL processes put into place either to recast the old structures to the new structures or to start loading the data from scratch. This can be done, given sufficient disk space, while the users continue to use the old structures. Then when the new structures are ready, they can become the "live" data warehouse. This would not be significantly disruptive, except when it goes "live." Some time may be needed by the business users to deal with the new structures. Over the lifetime of a data warehouse, it should be the expectation that as the business changes, so will the need for structural changes. Putting in place those changes will cause some disruption, but they can be scheduled during off-hours. We all know that DBAs' weekends and holidays are always filled with the joys of work. The data warehouse architect's schedule should be no different.

David Marco

A company cannot run a 50-gigabyte/20-user data warehouse for the same price as a 1-terabyte/300-user system. This type of massive scope increase dictates a significant and costly change in the system's architecture (hardware, software, and so on). The only other choice is to reduce the amount of data in the warehouse (faster purge/archive dates) and reduce the number of users. When that option is presented to the users, the purse strings should open up.

Clay Rehm

The data warehouse architect needs to review the original data warehouse project scope and requirements. He or she should look for the sections that cover the desired state architecture. This will be useful when selling additional hardware purchases to management.

The architect should review the available options.

- Redesign the database.
- Evaluate the existing data delivery tool(s).
- Upgrade the network.
- Buy new hardware.
- Buy additional hardware.

Before spending money on new hardware, the architect should consider the database design. Any database design that has a high degree of normalization will usually require many table joins, which in turn hurts query performance. And not only that—users who write queries have to really know the data to join many tables together and to know which tables to join in the first place!

If the database design already includes fact tables, dimension tables, and aggregation tables, then the architect should consider creating fact tables that have dimension values in them. There are no rules that the database has to be in third normal form or that it has to be truly dimensional. Every company has its own needs, and most typically a hybrid approach is in order.

For example, the database may have hundreds of tables. If in a specific case a user runs a query that requires 12 tables to be joined and read to get the answer needed, the query response time will depend on how fast those joins can be made. If the architect eliminated some of the joins by denormalizing some of those tables, the query would run faster.

The architect must consider whether the data delivery technology is appropriate. Is it Web based or client/server based? Is it difficult for the users to use or get to? Were the users involved with selecting the tool that meets their needs?

If all else fails, the existing hardware may truly be the problem and may need to be upgraded or replaced. Is there a chance the existing network infrastructure needs upgrading or replacement, instead of the database or Web servers? This is a situation in which getting expert advice from an external consultant can prove very beneficial. Before replacing the hardware, consider looking at other design options.

STOVEPIPES ARE IMPEDING INTEGRATION

A large financial firm has 12 "data warehouses" that are really independent data marts. The company is adamantly opposed to a central data warehouse. Each of the 12 data warehouse owners wants to maintain control and independence. In addition, there are no naming conventions, even within individual warehouses. Meta data is lacking for more than half of the existing data. Available definitions are vague at best and contain no domain information. How can this company integrate and clean up its environment?

Sid Adelman

I don't think it can integrate. If the company is opposed to a central data warehouse and each owner wants to hold onto his or her own data mart, there is no way these data marts will ever be integrated.

It may be possible to clean up and improve what they have by creating a centralized meta data repository that would contain, among other meta data, common definitions and domains (valid values). The data warehouse manager should consider having the data owners define their own domains and data definitions. However, no one should be overly confident. It sounds like the level of independence will hamper efforts for any commonality.

Joyce Bischoff

This will require a culture change that can come only from the highest levels of management. Management needs to emphasize the need for cooperation and sharing of data and should reward managers on the basis of their willingness to work with other groups toward a federated data warehouse environment that will allow each area to maintain its autonomy while allowing the sharing of well-defined data.

A federated database system (FDS) is the best solution to the problem. An FDS is a collection of independently managed, heterogeneous database systems that allow partial and controlled sharing of data without affecting existing applications. An FDS presents an enterprise view of data. The architecture for a federated data warehouse is shown in Figure 13–1.

The four key points of the architecture appear below.

1. All data will pass through a single ETL process to ensure consistency of the transformations. Since the company is opposed to a central data warehouse, a shared data staging area may be developed with a central group managing the ETL processes from the source systems to

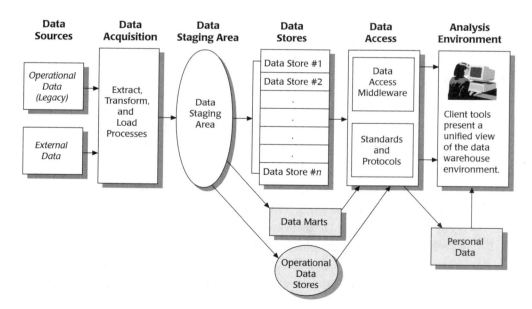

Figure 13–1: Data flow in a federated data warehouse environment

the staging area. Data in the staging area should carry standard names and full definitions. The 12 "data warehouses" should not be allowed to obtain data directly from the source systems.

2. Data in the warehouse environment, which includes data marts, operational data stores, and so on, should be available across the organization within the limits of security.

3. Existing stovepipe data marts will still have autonomy but must use the staging area as their only source.

4. Middleware may be used to transform data names and formats and provide a single warehouse image across the corporation.

Douglas Hackney

The first requirement is a fundamental business driver that would make it worthwhile to take on this task. Assuming there is a strategic reason that requires the integration of the 12 data warehouse systems, the business managers must adopt a pragmatic approach if they ever hope to achieve any amount of architecture and integration. A federated BI architecture accommodates fiefdom warehouses such as these and allows organizations to achieve the maximum amount of architecture and integration possible in their implementation and political realities.

It is important for the business managers to recognize that political realities will never allow them to achieve full integration of these data resources. They must focus on the critical metrics, measures, and dimensions that will provide the maximum added value to the business once they are integrated.

Chuck Kelley

It sounds to me that this financial organization does not quite understand the purpose of the conceptual data warehouse—the ability to do cross-organization analysis. This is exactly what brought us to the concept of the data warehouse to begin with—namely, each part of the organization doing exactly what it wants. This is the old information center idea taken to the next step of absurdity.

Senior management needs to decide whether cross-organization analysis is important to the company. If so, then the funds and authority need to be provided to integrate and control the stovepipe data warehouses. If the managers don't think such analysis is necessary, then it will take a long sales process to convince the management of the current data owners of the benefit of having cross-organization analysis capability. This does not mean there needs to be a monolithic data warehouse, but the dimensions must be common (or as Ralph Kimball [1996] wrote, "conformed") so that joins across the dimensions can bring in the appropriate measures to analyze.

David Marco

Let's discuss why independent data marts are not a sound architectural approach. Independent data marts are characterized by several traits. First, each data mart is sourced directly from the operational systems without the structure of a data warehouse to supply the architecture necessary to sustain and grow the data marts. Second, these data marts are typically built independently from one another by autonomous teams. These teams will usually use varying tools, software, hardware, and processes.

Possibly the most visually descriptive trait of a company that has constructed independent data marts is that the schema of the decision support systems (DSSs) resembles that of a "spaghetti" chart (see Figure 13–2). What is most disturbing is the number of companies that have expressed that this chart resembles their current DSS architecture.

This architecture is not an architecture at all. Instead it is a series of "stovepipe" data warehousing systems. This architecture greatly differs from that of an architected data warehouse (see Figure 13–3).

Several problems with independent data marts are outlined below.

Redundant Data. As the number of independent data marts grows, the amount of redundant data begins to grow uncontrollably across the enterprise. This redundancy occurs because each of the independent data marts requires its own, typically duplicated copy of the detailed corporate data. Often a great deal of this detailed data is not required in the data marts, which typically provide summarized views.

It would be enlightening to conduct a study to calculate the costs of maintaining nonnecessary redundant data for Global 2000 companies. The end total would be in the billions of dollars in expenses and lost opportunities.

Reporting Environment

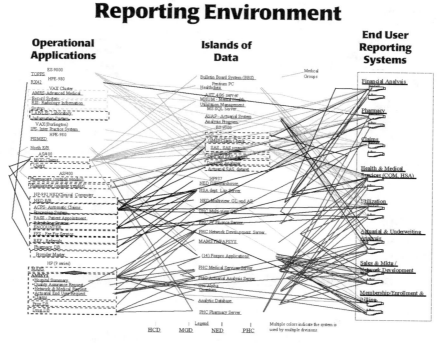

Figure 13–2: Spaghetti architecture of a decision support system that contains independently constructed data marts. From *Building and Managing the Meta Data Repository* by David Marco. Copyright ©2000 David Marco. All rights reserved. Reproduced here by permission of Wiley Publishing, Inc.

Redundant Processing. A data warehouse provides the architecture to centralize integration and cleansing activities common to all the data marts of a company. Without the data warehouse, all these integration and cleansing processes need to be duplicated for all the independent data marts. This greatly increases the number of support staff required to maintain the DSS, which, in turn, creates very costly systems to maintain.

Separate teams typically build each of the independent data marts in isolation from one another. As a result, these teams do not leverage the other's standards, processes, knowledge, and lessons learned. This results in a great deal of rework and reanalysis.

These autonomous teams commonly select different tools, software, and hardware. This forces the enterprise to retain skilled employees to support each of these technologies. In addition, a great deal of financial savings

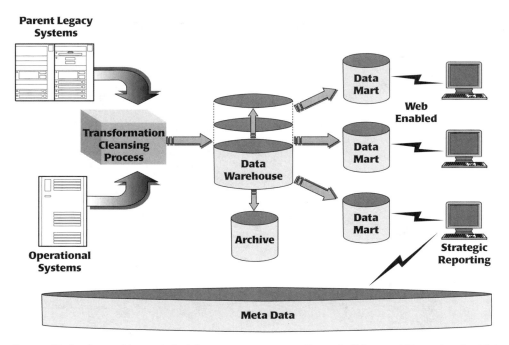

Figure 13–3: An architected decision support system. From *Building and Managing the Meta Data Repository* by David Marco. Copyright ©2000 David Marco. All rights reserved. Reproduced here by permission of Wiley Publishing, Inc.

is lost as standardization on these tools doesn't occur. Often a software, hardware, or tool contract can be negotiated to provide considerable discounts for enterprise licenses, which can be phased into effect. These economies of scale can provide tremendous cost savings to the organization.

Limited Scalability. Independent data marts directly read operational system files and/or tables, which greatly limits the DSS's ability to scale. For example, if a company has five independent data marts, it is likely that each data mart requires customer information. Therefore, there would be five separate extracts being pulled off the same customer tables in the operational system of record. Most operational systems have limited batch windows and cannot support this number of extracts. With a data warehouse only one extract is required in the operational system of record.

Nonintegration. As previously discussed, each independent data mart is built by autonomous teams, typically working for separate departments.

As a result, these data marts are not integrated, and none of them contain an enterprise view of the corporation. Therefore, if the CEO asks the IT department to provide him or her with a "listing of our most profitable customers," each data mart will offer a different answer. Having worked with companies that have experienced this exact situation, I can attest that the CIO is rarely pleased to have to explain why his or her department cannot answer this seemingly simple question.

One of the chief phenomena facing corporations today is the current merger and acquisition craze. Interestingly enough, one of the key factors fueling this movement is the desire of these companies to reduce their IT spending. In light of this situation the costs associated with independent data marts becomes even more magnified as companies continue to focus on controlling their ever-growing IT costs.

It is important to note that many companies that have built independent data marts are currently in the process of migrating away from them. Needless to say, the cost in dollars and time is not trivial.

For our situation, optimally it would be best to create a central data warehouse or at least a central data staging area (a federated approach); however, it appears as if the company does not want to interfere with the way each line of business operates. When the large financial firm realizes that it is spending over $100 million per year on data warehousing, I suspect the company will change direction.

Larissa Moss

If the users did not allow an integrated environment to be built, there is little chance they will be able to integrate it now. Having 12 separate data marts is not the problem—developing them independently from one another is.

To solve their problem they would have to feed all data marts from a central staging area (at least one per periodicity, that is, monthly versus daily). The extract and transformation specifications for all data marts have to be consolidated so that source data is extracted only once and transformation, including cleansing, is performed uniformly only once. In their situation this will mean redesigning the ETL process.

Integration by definition means standardization—you cannot integrate pieces that don't match or relate. In order to determine which pieces should match and relate in which ways, the data administrators can use the technique of logical data modeling (not to be confused with logical database design). This technique will also help them discover data domain and data integrity problems in the source files and databases.

This organization would have to be much more diligent in collecting and maintaining meta data. Each unique entity and each unique data element should have only one approved name and only one unambiguous definition (subtype entities would have their own definitions). Domains (valid values), business rules (process rules and data rules), data type and length, owner, source, and target are just some of the common meta data components that should be captured.

A data-cleansing team should be assembled and charged with a data quality inspection of the 12 data marts. The team members should use the logical data model and the meta data to determine the business rules for the data. Then they should analyze the source data to determine violations to the business rules. Finally they should inspect the 12 individual ETL processes to determine what type of cleansing is being performed. These processes will have to be combined and possibly enhanced for the central staging area.

Bottom line: If this organization continues to insist on developing nonintegrated silo data marts and not allowing any cross-organizational activities like the ones mentioned above, chances for getting to an integrated environment are slim—because the company doesn't want one.

Clay Rehm

There is no reason to build a central data warehouse, and even if the company wanted to, the politics would prevent it. The company can build a central data warehouse using a federated/virtual central data warehouse approach. The key to success is a central meta data repository. The central meta data repository has the responsibility for standardizing naming conventions, data definitions, data stewards, change control, and so on. The challenges are extracting the meta data from the existing data warehouses and getting the different departments to agree on common terms such as *customer* and *product*.

The federated/virtual central data warehouse would be fed from the existing data warehouses, not the operational systems. This central data warehouse would be useful for management and users who need a global or cross-departmental view of the data.

An enterprise team of talented individuals must be created using a RAD and SWAT approach. Their mission is to integrate definitions across the enterprise. This includes conformed dimensions, business rules, technical and business definitions, and data models.

As seen in Figure 13–4, each operational area or department has its own set of data used to support its day-to-day business. In turn, this data is fed into an individual data warehouse, which is really a "departmental data mart"! Each one of these departmental data marts can be sources for the federated/virtual data warehouse. Meta data will be supplied from each department's data marts and/or operational systems into the central meta data repository.

The enterprise team should leverage the work that has been done and communicate to the stakeholders the benefits and challenges ahead.

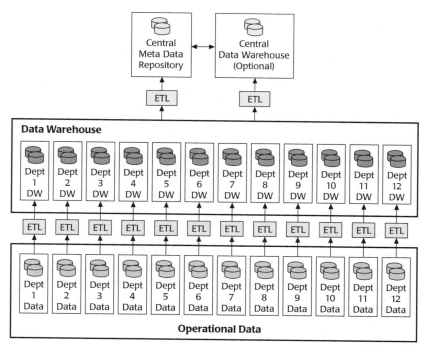

Figure 13–4: Data flow from operational systems to the data warehouses

SHOULD BACKDATED TRANSACTIONS CHANGE VALUES IN THE DATA WAREHOUSE?

Due to poor operating practices, a company sometimes has to backdate transactions. These transactions are entered a month or more after they actually occurred. The people in accounting argue that the "historic" information should not change. The standard in the data warehouse transformation process is this: if a transaction has a date that is 40 days old, the data warehouse data for that day will change. Should a backdated transaction not change the "historic" information in a data warehouse?

Chuck Kelley

I am a firm believer in not changing the data within the data warehouse but instead updating the data with deltas of the changes. Therefore in this example, when the transaction comes in with data that is 40 days old, I would then find the original data and determine the difference between this version and the previous version. I would store the difference in my data warehouse.

Larissa Moss

The first thing the data warehouse team must determine is whether the requirement not to change the data is a purely operational requirement or a strategic reporting requirement. The second thing to determine is whether the data warehouse was designed and built for operational or strategic purposes. It is quite likely that accounting is stating a valid operational requirement, seeing that the department's primary function is operational.

- If the data warehouse was built for strategic reporting and the business analysts (users) of the data warehouse need the data to be changed in order to produce the desired reporting results, then the data should be changed. "Changing data" in the data warehouse means deleting the old row and inserting the new row that reflects the change.
- If the accounting department uses the data warehouse mainly for operational purposes, then the requirement not to change the data must be honored.
- If there is a conflict between operational and strategic requirements, and both requirements must be reflected in the data warehouse, then the requirements should be separated and satisfied from separate databases. These databases could be an operational data store or operational

reporting marts for the accounting staff and an enterprise data warehouse or data marts for strategic business analysts. If these databases are developed under an integrated architecture and if they are reconciled to each other, it should be possible to satisfy both requirements.

Clay Rehm

The data warehouse transformation process must show exactly what happened for each transformation process. In industries that require solid documentation, if the data warehouse is ever audited, it must be able to recreate exactly what happened on a given date. The data warehouse must have a complete audit trail process so data can be reconstructed at any time.

A CLICK-STREAM DATA WAREHOUSE WILL BE HUGE

A retailer with a growing e-business is in the process of designing a click-stream data warehouse. The application is customer relationship management (CRM). The company managers expect to have billions of rows in this database, including Web traffic and call center information. They are looking for advice in designing this very large data warehouse. Should they be thinking about parallelism and partitioning? Should they consider any particular features of the RDBMS?

Chuck Kelley

I think three items are requirements for a very large click-stream data warehouse database.

1. *True parallelism.* I once spoke to a vendor who defined "parallel load" as being able to load two or more dimensions in parallel. This is not my definition. I would like to load the fact table in parallel.
2. *Horizontal partitioning by data value.* Horizontal partitioning is defining where a whole data row will be stored. For example, you could define the horizontal partition to be on time. Then all the rows for a specific time would be stored in a tablespace (or storage area) as defined, and many of them could be stored in parallel. The poor man's horizontal partitioning does not allow partitioning by data value. Having the partition by data value allows the designer to put the data on many different disk drives, thus decreasing the load times significantly by having parallel loads to different drives.

3. *Parallel index rebuild.* When loading massive amounts of data, analysis needs to be performed to determine whether or not there is a requirement to delete (or disable) indexes and then quickly build (or rebuild) the indexes. Being able to build an index in parallel decreases the time it takes to build all the indexes. Being able to create multiple indexes at the same time decreases load times as well.

There has been some work (though nothing implemented in general purpose database products) on collecting the large additions to the indexes and just inserting those. This might decrease the load time.

TIME-VARIANT ANALYSIS REQUIRES SPECIAL DESIGNS

A company has a requirement for time-variant analysis. The DBAs do not want to duplicate all their financial measures in the fact table to hold previous year and current year data because they have a lot of financial measures. The OLAP tool they use builds SQL statements, and they have found there is no good way to handle time variance in SQL. What should the DBAs do?

Joyce Bischoff

Although the OLAP tool builds SQL, the user does not see the complexity of the SQL. This should not prevent the user from doing time-variant analysis. If there is no good way to do time-variant analysis with the chosen OLAP tool, the tool should be replaced with one that can handle it.

Chuck Kelley

Time variance is one of the strong points of a data warehouse. There are many ways to solve time-variant issues. If the company doesn't want to change the database to a temporal database, then most of the time variance can be solved in the OLAP tool's semantic layer. Here are some solutions.

1. Create a fact table that holds only a single year's worth of financial measures (regardless of the granularity of the time dimension). Then in the semantic layer of the OLAP tool, the OLAP tool jockey can create an object that will automatically return the requested and previous years' data. Most of the top OLAP tools can do this quite easily.
2. Create multiple relationships to the fact table that define the current and previous time keys. Then the semantic layer can be defined to

join the two sets of data together in a single stream. Again, most of the top OLAP tools can do this.

3. Create a view that automatically performs a UNION of the current and previous years' data and have the users use that view instead of the base tables.

MANAGEMENT WANTS TO DEVELOP A DATA WAREHOUSE SIMULTANEOUSLY WITH A NEW OPERATIONAL SYSTEM

A manufacturing company is in the midst of implementing a new operational system with the normal problems of any new system. Management is pushing to install a data warehouse with this new operational system's data as the source. Is there anything the data warehouse team members can do now, or should they wait until all the bugs are out before starting the work?

Sid Adelman

Trying to develop a data warehouse in parallel to the development of the source system is almost impossible. It is better to wait until the operational system is reasonably stable before working on the ETL portion of the data warehouse. However, some tasks can be accomplished in parallel. The infrastructure can be built, including installing the hardware, RDBMS, other software, and the network. People can be trained, and those people can begin working with the tools, especially the access and analysis tools. The company can build prototypes with sample data, making sure the users understand that the prototypes are throwaway samples and do not reflect real data or the reality of the business. The organization can develop project plans. Managers can write project scope agreements, create the cost justification for the project, analyze risk, and plan for risk mitigation.

Joyce Bischoff

Both systems should be built from the same underlying data model. The physical design in the operational environment will be close to third normal form, but the data warehouse model will be denormalized with multiple levels of aggregation and multidimensional structures. As long as they are based on the same data model and the requirements for both systems are completely understood, there is no reason why the projects should not proceed in parallel.

Douglas Hackney

The company can accomplish quite a bit within some important boundaries. The managers should not expect to have a fully functional warehouse the day after the new operational system goes into production. However, it is possible to fully understand the needs of the business and to design the target model prior to the completion of the operational system. The greatest challenge in this scenario is that the source system experts have zero available time for the data warehouse team. Consequently, the data warehouse team must add resources to the new OLTP team to provide source system knowledge.

Sean Ivoghli

The data warehouse team can start gathering requirements for the data warehouse and design the logical data model at any time. This mainly requires input from users. If possible, the team members should avoid getting into physical data warehouse and data acquisition design until the operational system database design has been stabilized; otherwise they will find themselves doing a lot of rework.

Chuck Kelley

The data warehouse team members might as well get ready for change, so they should start building that data warehouse. There must be a strong sales job to the business managers to get them to recognize that the data warehouse may need to be rebuilt as the business rules of the operational system changes. I would also start telling management that the data warehouse will be delivered two months after the operational system goes live. That will give time to make minor adjustments to the ETL process. The data warehouse team members must accept the fact that the operational group will "forget" to notify them of some changes that occurred at the last second. The project manager should make sure there is enough time allocated in the project plan to accommodate this.

Larissa Moss

Been there. Done that. Never again. Management must understand two important factors about data warehouses.

1. It is impossible to roll out a data warehouse at the same time as implementing an operational system. This does not mean that the data warehouse cannot be *started* while the operational system is still in development, but the data warehouse cannot be delivered at the same time as the operational system.

   Since the data warehouse is data-centric rather than process-centric, the data elements and data content of the operational source file or database must be final and stable in order to complete the design of the data warehouse database(s) and application(s). In an operational system conversion or in the development of a new operational system, this is typically not achieved until the system goes into acceptance testing or even into production. Therefore, completing the data warehouse will always lag behind by several months.

2. A data warehouse is not meant to be an operational reporting system. Therefore, there should be no requirement to have the new operational system and the new data warehouse delivered at the same time. The main reason for not using the data warehouse for operational reporting is *timeliness*. Operational reporting requirements are often time-sensitive.

   For example, a large savings and loan (S&L) association received notification from a government agency to include a new government-mandated field on a report submitted to that government agency on a monthly basis. This field had to be added to the operational system and subsequently to the data warehouse in order to be included in this operational report run from the data warehouse. Adding the field to the operational system was accomplished within a few days. Adding the same field to the data warehouse took a couple of months. There were several reasons for that, such as having to split the government code into several columns because the codes described multiple entities (dimensions). But the main reason was that regression testing for the data warehouse ETL process was much more complicated and took much longer than testing the silo operational system. The S&L was fined for not complying in a timely manner.

Bottom line: Don't use the data warehouse for operational reporting. And if it's not needed for operational reporting, there is no reason to be pressured into delivering the data warehouse at the same time as a new operational system.

Clay Rehm

It is data warehousing's most cardinal sin—do not implement a first release of a data warehouse using a new operational system as its source! Having said that, I believe the data warehouse team has the following options:

- *Build the data warehouse at the same time as the operational system.* This is the cardinal sin of data warehousing—never build a data warehouse with a new operational system under development as its source. You will spend more money this way and still not have it right. From a technology point of view, it can certainly be done; however, it will take longer to develop, and it will cost more.
- *Wait for a stable source.* The data warehouse team could wait until the operational team can provide a stable data model, business definitions, business rules, and functional definitions of the application. There are still many risks in doing this, but this may give the data warehouse team a jump start in the right direction. Management should keep in mind that until the operational system is truly in production, in use, and functional, the data model and rules can change.
- *Wait until the source system is complete.* This is the safest route. However, the business must wait for the operational system to be completed and the data warehouse designed and implemented before actually using the data warehouse.
- *Do a little with a small team.* As soon as documentation starts to appear from the operational system's team, the data warehouse team could start to model and design the data warehouse without beginning a full-blown data warehousing project. The team members should keep in mind that the operational system is not stable, so there will be many changes along the way. This is still a high-risk option, but it will allow a small data warehouse team the chance to keep the project moving.

No matter which option the project manager picks, he or she should document every decision and design option and communicate, communicate, communicate! The project manager should keep the project plan up to date and publish it to the stakeholders weekly. Updated status reports should go out weekly, with early notification of any issues and risks.

The moral of the story: Whatever option you choose, you *must* communicate decisions and issues to all stakeholders on a regular basis.

THE DATA WAREHOUSE GETS ASSIGNED THE ROLE OF A REPORTING SYSTEM

The data warehouse team members for a large bank knew early in the project that they could deliver a Web-based reporting system on time if it were done in moderation. Additional reports were to be added iteratively after the initial implementation as enhancements. This strategy was completely scrapped and the reporting requirements started to balloon as the more realistic team members were taken out of the decision-making loop. The advisory group members who made the decision to include total reporting capability failed to grasp the meaning of a data warehouse—to them it means a reporting system, period. How should the data warehouse team set the advisory group on the right path?

Sid Adelman

The data warehouse manager should bring in a high-priced consultant (executives pay more attention if they have to pay big bucks) who is willing to tell them they are about to fail, waste money, and lose important time that would have allowed them to get ahead of their competition. The consultant should support the position of the displaced team members and recommend their reinstatement to the decision-making process.

Joyce Bischoff

The advisory group needs a basic introductory data warehouse class along with an understanding of the need to empower the users to write their own queries and reports. The scope of the initial reporting system was too narrow to meet today's needs.

Chuck Kelley

What's in a name? One of the biggest issues I see in the computer industry today is that everyone wants to build a "pick your favorite name," but there is no real consensus about what that is. You can't expect the business users to think strategically until their tactical issues are solved. This is the problem at hand. The advisory group members are having problems with getting their tactical issues handled (that is, the need for a reporting system), so they look to the data warehouse to deal with it. Once these tactical issues are answered, they will be ready to think strategically. With few exceptions, every organization with which I've worked to build the first iteration of a data warehouse really moves toward an operational data store. The business units are trying to solve a tactical problem by using the term "data warehouse."

Therefore, I recommend that the data warehouse team deliver a reporting system (and call it a reporting warehouse or something different than a data warehouse) and look forward to building a data warehouse when the business users are ready.

Sean Ivoghli

I see no problems with using a data warehouse to provide operational reports as long as the reports are not required real-time and the reporting requirements do not compromise the ability of the data warehouse to provide data for analytical purposes.

Clay Rehm

The data warehouse environment must provide the data to the users who need it, when they need it. If this environment is called a data warehouse, an operational data store, or the "Name of Bank" Reporting Database, it does not matter. What does matter is that the environment is integrating data and is easy to access.

The moral of the story: Don't get hung up on a name.

META DATA NEEDS TO BE INTEGRATED ACROSS MULTIPLE PRODUCTS

An insurance company is in the pilot stage of putting together a data warehouse strategy. The software selection committee has identified a number of different products from different vendors to implement this strategy. The committee members believe meta data is critical to their success, but they are concerned about the ability to bring together meta data from multiple sources and multiple vendors. Is it possible to manage a single source of meta data across multiple vendors' products?

Joyce Bischoff

This is difficult but not impossible, provided that the different products use XML for importing and exporting data. It is also highly desirable for the various products to be based on an open, underlying, relational design.

Douglas Hackney

The software selection committee is right to be concerned. While it is possible to build an integrated meta data resource that draws the data from multiple vendors' products, it is a very complex and daunting task. Meta data is very resource intensive, especially the maintenance and sustenance of the system. The committee members should work very hard to identify the absolute most critical elements of meta data required and focus their efforts on only those to start.

Sean Ivoghli

If the vendors' products store the meta data in tables that the software can read, then the company can extract the meta data into a meta data repository the company designed and make the meta data available to users. However, I don't know of any vendors' products that allow management of meta data through another platform (such as this meta data repository).

Chuck Kelley

This situation presents a big concern, but it is possible to resolve it—although a large manual effort may be required. The meta data product will need to have a lot of extensible features. I am not a big fan of the products currently on the market. I would take the time to build a repository based on the real requirements and then see if there is a product that can come close to the design. I find it easier to build a repository from scratch and then use different mechanisms within each product to load the meta data repository.

David Marco

Building a good meta data repository is critical to any company's data warehousing effort. Without the repository the data warehouse will struggle in meeting the needs of the business users. Before the insurance company builds its centralized meta data repository, it will be vital to define the specific business and technical objectives of the meta data repository initiative. Once this is accomplished, a list of the meta data sources that will go into this repository can be defined. Once the meta data sources have been identified, the company can see if a meta data integration tool exists that could meet the company's needs.

Each of the repository tools integrates meta data through differing interfaces. However, three broad categories can be defined to classify the manner in which these interfaces integrate different sources of meta data. Each of these categories requires varying levels of integration complexity and meta model changes.

1. *Certified sources.* Certified sources of meta data are those sources that the tool can directly read, properly interpret the information, and load it into the correct attributes of the meta model. These sources are easily integrated and do not require an extension to the base meta model. In addition, because the tool is designed to accept these sources, they do not require additional programming or analysis. Common examples of certifiable meta data sources include technical meta data from data-modeling tools and transformation rules from extraction/transformation engines. Normally a repository tool is certified for several vendor tools in each of these categories.

2. *Generic sources.* Most tools allow for one or more generic meta data sources. Generic meta data sources are those in a common format— that is, CASE Data Interchange Format (CDIF), tab delimited, space delimited, comma delimited—that the tool can read. The challenge with these sources is that while the tool can easily read the sources, programming is still needed to map the source elements to the correct attributes in the meta model. As a result, it is important that the repository tool has an interface that can be easily changed to map these sources. In addition, it is somewhat common for these sources to require extensions to the meta model. The process for extending the model can range from a simple change, if all that is needed is to add an attribute to an existing table, to a complex one, if new tables are required and additional foreign keys are needed for other tables to reference them. If the repository is built on an object database, it can greatly simplify the task of administrating changes to the model. Common examples of generic sources are those technical and business meta data sources in databases and spreadsheets that are easily extracted into these formats.

3. *Nonsupported sources.* Some sources of meta data are not certified or are in a generic format. These nonsupported sources might require sophisticated analysis for design and programming. These sources contain all the challenges of generic sources with the added challenge

of a possibly complicated programming step that would be needed to transform the nonsupported source into a generic source. Nonsupported sources are common for informal business meta data sources and the meta data stored in vendor applications.

Most likely the company will not find a vendor that integrates all the meta data sources, so even if the company purchases a tool, the company will still need to do plenty of development work.

Clay Rehm

It is possible to manage a single source of meta data across multiple vendors' products through a custom solution. This can be accomplished by a team that can integrate the different business and technical meta data from multiple sources into one new meta data repository.

The new meta data repository must be designed using a meta model. A meta model is a logical data model for the meta data database. The meta model requires an enterprise focus, which will challenge most designers. The team could significantly benefit from the help of an outside consultant who has experience and success with this kind of work. The meta model must consider different types of meta data. Not only is there business and technical meta data, but the team members must also consider that any kind of documentation is meta data. Any description of anything can be considered meta data! Descriptions of business processes, rules and regulations, business rules, table names, and column lengths are all types of meta data.

Once the meta model has been completed and approved by the users, then the DBA should build the meta data database. This new database will be fed from the other meta data repositories—just like a mini data warehouse! This database should have a browser front-end for the users to view the meta data and a separate Web application that allows updates.

In Figure 13–5, the circles represent examples of the different types of meta data. This meta data must be captured, which can be done by using different mechanisms such as data modeling tools, ETL tools, homemade or purchased meta data editors, and other meta data repositories. As the data is loaded into the data warehouse, meta data is loaded into the meta data repository. The meta data repository may be a collection of databases that must be integrated, as shown in the figure. In this example, a

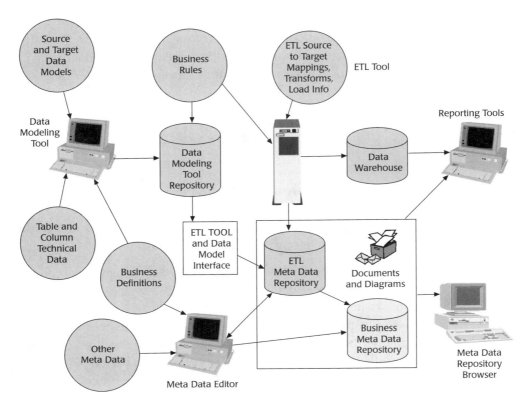

Figure 13–5: Positioning meta data

meta data repository came with the ETL tool; however, it will not contain all the meta data. In this case, the client developed another meta data database to hold additional meta data, which is linked to the ETL meta data database. To the users, it looks like the meta data is in one place.

The meta data can be displayed not only through typical business intelligence tools but also through a custom-built browser, which is more complete and can show all the meta data in the repository.

HOW CAN UPC CODE CHANGES BE RECONCILED?

A retailer is collecting data about shipments into a store and receipts of sales from a store. For example, the store may receive into inventory a 12-pack of Buzzy-Cola that might be sold as 12 single cans—and there are different UPC codes for the 12-pack versus a single can. Remember, if the analyst queries at the single can level, he or she can't do analysis on 12-pack sales! How can the data warehouse team reconcile the incoming data with the outgoing data?

Joyce Bischoff

A product master is the key to this problem. It will require a recursive data design because a product may be a part of another product.

Chuck Kelley

In the case described in the question, there would be a fact table and a product dimension (and many other dimensions that are not shown here). The fact table would have two measurement columns: SOLD_ QUANTITY and LOW_LEVEL_QUANTITY. There would be two relationships (roles) between the fact table and product dimension: ACTUAL_SOLD and LOW_LEVEL. Two foreign columns added in the fact table would hold the primary key of the product for the ACTUAL_SOLD product and the LOW_LEVEL product. In the SOLD_QUANTITY column would be "1" and in the LOW_LEVEL_QUANTITY would be "12" (based on the case described in the question). During the ETL process, there must be some process that transforms the UPC code for a 12-pack to that for 12 single cans. At this point, the users can do analysis of single cans (LOW_LEVEL_ QUANTITY) and what was actually sold (SOLD_QUANTITY) and can reconcile what was incoming and what was outgoing (LOW_LEVEL_ QUANTITY).

Clay Rehm

The single can must be tracked by some kind of identifier, if not a UPC code then something else. This may require a cross-reference table that exists in the staging process when a shipment comes in. A hierarchical dimension table and reference (lookup) tables are needed.

Level of granularity is the challenge. How can the users know that each shipment is being tracked at the lowest level of granularity unless the company maintains another table that acts as a cross-reference to the products being shipped? For example, rows in the cross-reference table for a store could contain data like that shown in Table 13–1. The ETL process will read the table, look for a match, and if it finds one, load 12

Table 13–1: Product Table

Product ID	Number of Units
COLA123	12
EGGS456	12
BAGEL443	6

rows instead of 1, with the identifier being the Product ID and then a sequential number, such as COLA123-1, COLA123-2, and so on.

This problem also requires a new application or process that keeps hierarchies intact. This is usually a problem that data warehousing can identify. Since dimension tables make the drill-up and drill-down functionality possible, these new dimensions do not have applications or processes identified to create or maintain them.

In summary: You may have to invent data storage and processes to maintain levels of granularity and hierarchies.

CHAPTER FOURTEEN

Performance

The ultimate test of management is performance

—Peter F. Drucker

OVERVIEW

Poor performance is often cited as a reason for a data warehouse failure. Performance is relevant for the response time of the queries and reports and for the time to complete the ETL process.

Many users have been spoiled with very fast and very consistent response time both with their operational systems and with their personal computers. The nature of a data warehouse is that response time is highly variable. If the users expect very fast and very consistent response time, they will ultimately be disappointed.

In many data warehouse implementations, there appears to be little governance of the data being loaded in the data warehouse, the frequency of the updates, the storage of atomic versus summarized data, or any controls on the number of years of data being stored. Without clear standards the data will proliferate at a rate that will warm the hearts of the hardware vendors.

Large databases almost always cause performance problems. The impact is on queries and on the loads, refreshes, and updates. Smaller databases take less time to load, refresh, and update. Long load, refresh, and update times may result in the data warehouse being unavailable to users when they need it. They may not see yesterday's results until 11:00 A.M., and they wanted the information when they walked in at 8:30.

Software limitations will impact performance, but these limitations can sometimes be overcome with a good design that reflects expected usage. The purpose of data marts, custom decision support applications, and dimensional designs is to support the specific needs of the user community.

The network, the operating system, the hardware, the RDBMS, and the way these systems are implemented all impact performance. The application itself and the SQL generated by the access and analysis tool will also cause response times to vary greatly. Finally, the database design will strongly influence response times and load times.

As the organization understands how the system is being used, the DBA can build summary tables and create indexes on the fields that are more commonly accessed. This understanding comes only with the ability to measure activity and comprehend what is actually being performed. Metrics are a critical success factor for good performance.

In the remainder of this chapter, we explore three performance situations and present suggested solutions for each one.

THE SOFTWARE DOES NOT PERFORM PROPERLY

An organization made a major financial, training, and implementation commitment to a software product. It now appears that the software will not perform. What should the company do?

Sid Adelman

Conversions are messy and expensive. If the software will be improved in the near future, a conversion may not be necessary. The DBA should talk to the vendor and find out if the vendor has plans to improve the performance and what the impact of these improvements would be. Also, the organization using the product may not have explored all its performance options. The DBA may also want to talk with a consulting organization that specializes in performance improvements.

Joyce Bischoff

The company should review its contract for the product for performance guarantees. Management should ask the software vendor to rescind the sale and should take legal action as needed.

Sean Ivoghli

Data warehouses involve the integration of many software products. If the lack of performance of this (or any) software threatens the success of the entire data warehouse investment, then the organization should replace the software. The cost of not doing that may be higher than the cost of replacing it. I am assuming that the organization has exhausted all alternatives in making this software perform adequately.

Chuck Kelley

The organization should have planned for this day before making an investment in the software product. It is time to meet with the head of sales for the software product to discuss the performance problems and what can be done to fix the problems. The software selection team members must be specific in their requests. This will help show the problems. If this doesn't work, then there are two choices: (1) ask the corporate attorneys to visit, or (2) eat the losses and find a new product with better terms and conditions.

David Marco

First the organization should review the contract signed with the vendor. If the contract doesn't provide any recourse, the organization has to chalk up the situation as a lesson learned and then, if applicable, purchase a new tool.

Clay Rehm

While the legal department is working with the vendor's legal department, deciding on what the outcome will be, the IT department must review other comparable tools in the marketplace. IT must be prepared to report that there is a new tool in the marketplace that can take over or be prepared to prove that an existing in-house tool can do the job for the time being. Rather than letting such a setback slow it down, the organization must find creative ways to work around the problem.

THE DATA WAREHOUSE GROWS FASTER THAN THE SOURCE DATA

The data warehouse is growing much faster than the source data that feeds it. The costs for the hardware are already over budget, and there appears to be no end in sight. Management is concerned and is asking some embarrassing questions. Should the data warehouse grow disproportionately to the source data? If not, what can the data warehouse manager do to stem the growth?

Sid Adelman

Organizations need to recognize the source of the disorderly growth of their databases and understand whether that growth is justified.

As an organization begins to understand the problem of letting the database increase in an uncontrolled manner and is willing to take appropriate steps, it should consider the following:

1. Recognize that size is important (in this case, big is bad) and that it can have a strongly negative impact on the cost, performance, availability, risk, and management of the data warehouse. This recognition needs to be communicated to everyone on the data warehouse team.
2. Develop data standards that, among other things, include standards on transformations, data replication, data stewardship, and naming.
3. Implement a cost justification methodology that can be used uniformly as funds are requested. The hard numbers can help management understand and evaluate options.
4. If possible, charge the users for the data they request. This can be very difficult because other departments may also be using the data, and distributing the costs may become complex. Charge-backs are never appreciated, but they are one of the few techniques that force users to make a business case for additional data.
5. Allow enough time to implement the data warehouse properly. Unrealistic schedules sometimes force the team members to load all the data from the source files since they do not have the time to evaluate which data is needed. Management should understand the costs and risks of an unrealistic schedule.
6. The project should be phased and the users should understand the plan and know when each grouping of data will become available to them.

7. Educate and sell the users on the importance of their participation in the process of determining data requirements. Instruct them on the costs and problems of frivolous requests for data.

8. With the users, evaluate the necessity of keeping atomic data as well as summarized data. This requirement will probably change as the data ages. Older atomic data may be archived while the summarized data will probably be retained.

9. Carefully consider the need to replicate data. Many organizations replicate for questionable reasons. ("The users want their data to be under their physical control.")

10. Understand the need for the frequency of data storage (daily, weekly, monthly).

11. Allow sharing of data rather than giving each user his or her own copy of data warehouse data. If possible, encourage sharing by lowering user costs or appealing to higher motives.

12. If data models have captured the structure of the data warehouse and if a repository has been populated with meta data about the data warehouse, the models and the meta data should be used to understand the inventory of data warehouse data and to minimize storing redundant data.

13. Give the data administration staff the authority to determine data sources and give them the responsibility for populating meta data in a repository.

14. Give the data administration staff or the data warehouse administrator the authority to control what data will be stored in the data warehouse. This would minimize the storage of redundant or unneeded data.

15. Be sure the right analysts are working on the project. They need to feel comfortable with the users and know what questions to ask. Consider a team that has analysts that come from the user departments.

16. Monitor the usage of the data. Consider archiving data that is rarely accessed and archiving data that is never accessed. (Murphy's corollary is that purged data will be requested three weeks after its deletion.)

17. Review archiving schemes to determine how much of historical data must be online and whether all atomic data must be kept online. Determine response time requirements and whether historical data may be restored from less costly but slower storage media.

18. Consider the use of data marts (departmental or subject data warehouse databases). They will not decrease the overall amount of data to be stored or the CPU to run the loads, but they can substantially improve the performance of the queries.

Joyce Bischoff

Since the data warehouse will contain detail data, summary data, and dimensional data, it may be larger than the source systems. The DBA should perform a full design review to determine whether there are opportunities to:

- Optimize the design
- Eliminate unnecessary data redundancy

The DBA should perform a data usage analysis to determine what data is used, how often, and by whom. Products on the market can assist in analyzing data usage at the table level, column level, and so on. If data is rarely used, it may be moved to offline storage, where it can be retrieved if it is needed.

Douglas Hackney

If the data warehouse is providing mission-critical capability to the organization, the relative size of the data warehouse versus the source system is immaterial. The size of the data warehouse and its aggregations, analysis data sets, and so on has no linear relationship to the size of the source system. If the questions being asked are embarrassing, it could only be that the data warehouse is not providing a solution to a critical business problem and instead was built to further a different agenda.

Sean Ivoghli

The size of a data warehouse can and frequently does grow disproportionately to the operational systems that feed it. The reason is: performance! Data warehouses store the same data repetitively in order to allow faster query performance. These duplications come in the form of aggregated fact tables and consolidated, conforming dimensions. Sometimes multiple facts that have been represented in separate fact tables are represented together in a single fact table just to prevent the joining of multiple large fact tables. Some OLAP tools require more tables and duplication than others do to perform adequately. Performance is the main driver for all of this. Performance is key to the success of a data warehouse, so storing the same data again in multiple formats (therefore duplicating its existence) is justified when done properly.

Chuck Kelley

This will depend on a couple of items. First, are the dimensions changing rapidly? If the dimensions are changing rapidly, then growth of the data warehouse will be disproportionate to the raw data and a redesign may be needed. If they are not changing, then it is quite perplexing why the data warehouse is growing disproportionately (raw data to raw data). Second, the data warehouse will grow larger depending on the indexing strategy. For the most part, every column in the dimensions should be indexed, as should the keys to the fact table(s). This is because the DBA does not know the questions that the business users will ask.

To stem growth, the DBA can create aggregate (summary) tables and then drop the indexes on the main dimensions. Then standards can dictate that the users query from the aggregates for the increased performance. If users need a lower level of granularity (that is, more granular data), they will need to understand it will take a longer time to fetch the data since there are fewer indexes.

Clay Rehm

Before anyone gets too "embarrassed," has anyone asked if the faster growth of the data warehouse is really an issue? Has anybody asked to review the original requirements? The team members could be doing what they were asked to do, and the requirements may have been forgotten. Does the design meet the original user requirements? Do the requirements ask that every change in the source systems be tracked in the data warehouse? If this is not what is happening, the data warehouse certainly has an issue to resolve.

The DBA should review the requirements and how the design supports each requirement. He or she should also review the data models, the ETL process, and the data validation process (and error logging), checking to see if:

1. The ETL process really has a problem. It may be loading duplicate records and so on.
2. The ETL process is tracking every change and keeping the history.

If the requirements stated that the data warehouse has to keep track of all changes and be able to show how the data warehouse looked at any one time, the data warehouse will grow due to all the history and overhead that is required.

Bottom line: When in doubt, review the original requirements!

LOADING THE FACT TABLE TAKES TOO LONG

The data warehouse uses a star schema for its database design. The load time for a full fact table will soon take more than 24 hours. The data in the fact table must be updated daily. What should the DBA do?

Joyce Bischoff

The DBA may consider redesigning the fact table and the processes used to load the data, keeping the following items in mind:

- If the fact table contains multiple levels of summarization, they may be split into separate tables.
- Partitioning and loading by partition may help.
- Incremental loading should be considered if the whole table is being rebuilt on a daily basis.
- Loading with a high degree of parallelism will help. Various products on the market may provide this capability.

Sean Ivoghli

I would ask the DBA the following questions:

- Are you dropping the indexes before loading?
- Are you using the bulk-loading feature of the DBMS?
- Are you loading the fact table incrementally (versus a full reload every time)?
- Is the fact table partitioned?
- Are you using the parallel loading feature of the DBMS?

If the company is using Oracle, performing updates, and using bitmapped indexes, the system will experience significant performance issues due to the decompressing and recompressing of the bitmapped indexes on updates. The DBA should drop all bitmapped indexes before the load and rebuild them afterwards.

The ETL process should be reading the primary keys of the dimensions (hopefully single column and integer) from the dimension tables and making that part of the primary key of the fact table before the records are inserted or loaded. In that case, the foreign keys of the fact table should automatically comply with the referential integrity rules, so the DBA can also turn off the referential integrity constraints before loading (and turn them back on afterwards).

Chuck Kelley

Someone once said, "With a data warehouse, the question is not whether to partition, but how to partition." This is the case regardless of whether the data warehouse uses a star schema, a snowflake schema, or a normalized data structure. Partitioning the data such that the data can be loaded in parallel without killing the disk drives is an important factor in increasing the performance of the load. The DBA needs to develop a load strategy for the database to fully realize the performance benefit due to parallelization. Databases implement partitioning differently.

Let's say the DBA has time, product, customer, and store as the dimensions. Partitioning the facts on time is generally a good way to proceed, but maybe the DBA should consider partitioning on time and store. That way he or she can break the output of the transformation process into multiple files and then load each into its partition simultaneously. This increases the number of files to load but should reduce the time to load them. Again, processor power, the number of disks, and the degree of parallelization will force the load strategy for performance.

The DBA must determine whether some features should be turned off during the ETL process. He or she will need to test the following to make sure the solution is right for the data warehouse:

- *All constraints.* The DBA will want to have the ETL process make sure the referential integrity is correct. Processing the constraint in the ETL process might be a more effective solution. However, some database optimizers will require the primary key/foreign key constraints to be turned on before star schema optimization can be used. Therefore the DBA will need to test to make sure that the time it takes to turn on the constraints will be less than the time consumed by leaving them on. Again, the DBA should check with the database vendor.

- *Disabling indexes.* The DBA should test whether indexes can or should be dropped and rebuilt within the time constraints and whether the database allows indexes to be created in parallel.
- *Partitioning data.* Even if the database product does not have partitioning by data value, the DBA can still partition the data using poor man's partitioning—namely, defining the tablespace files to be across multiple disks instead of one big disk. It is best to have several small disk drives rather than a few large ones so that the data can be partitioned. This is a common problem I see when doing configurations. The finance department wants to buy the larger disks because they are cheaper and require fewer slots, less electricity, and so on than having several smaller disks that would make up the same capacity. For example, instead of buying one 30 gigabyte disk, I would prefer to buy three 10 gigabyte disks. That way the I/Os can be spread among the three drives, not a single drive. The latency will be lower; therefore the load time will be lower. This is pure queuing theory.

David Marco

I would question how the fact table is being loaded. The fastest way to load a table is to check referential integrity during the ETL process and create a load-ready table or file and then use the database's native bulk loader, without referential integrity, to load the table or file into the data warehouse. Partitioning can be used in conjunction with this technique to greatly accelerate the load run. Also, is the fact table being completely dropped during each load or are just additions (change data capture) being brought into the fact table? Obviously, complete refreshes or updates (updates to existing rows in the fact table) take a great deal more processing time than inserts do.

Clay Rehm

Can the original requirement stating that the data in the fact table must be updated daily be changed? Can the fact table be updated every other day, for example?

The DBA must ask the sponsors or users the following questions:

- Have the requirements changed?
- Is there more data that must be loaded into the fact table because of additional source systems, or is there a change in an existing source system?

- Can the fact table be split into one or more tables, based on new or changing requirements?
- Do we have to do a full load? What data can be loaded, and what portions can be loaded?
- Is there data in the fact table that is not being used and can be archived, thus reducing the number of rows in the table?
- Is it possible to have a "current" fact table and a "history" fact table and then load only the appropriate tables at the appropriate times?
- Has the fact table been partitioned? If so, has it been partitioned based on date?

Assuming change control is in place, the DBA must get the new solution in writing with signed approvals from the sponsors or users.

The moral of the story: Before making any changes to the system, get written permission first!

Data Warehouse Glossary

This glossary is a compilation of definitions contributed by the experts. Some definitions contain terms and acronyms defined elsewhere in this glossary.

access: The act of retrieving data from the data warehouse databases.

access path: The path selected by the database management system to locate and retrieve requested data.

ad hoc query: A request for information that is normally fabricated and run a single time and cannot be anticipated in advance. It consists of an SQL statement that has been constructed by a knowledgeable user or through the use of a data access tool.

aggregation: The process by which data values are collected with the intent to manage the collection as a single unit. For example, the combination of fields for the same customer extracted from multiple sources.

analysis: The act of evaluating the data retrieved from the data warehouse.

analytics applications: Processes that produce information for management decisions, usually involving demographic analysis, trend analysis, pattern recognition, drill-down analysis, and profiling. Examples of analytics applications include customer segmentation, customer probability models, campaign measurement, up-sell opportunities, cross-channel analysis, sales distribution analysis, cross-sell opportunities, trigger inventory analysis, supply chain analysis, customer quality analysis, channel satisfaction measurement, click-stream analysis, backlog analysis, churn analysis, interaction analysis, booking analysis, billing analysis, distribution analysis, retention analysis, delivery analysis, fulfillment analysis, and promotion effectiveness.

anomaly: A deviation, irregularity, or an unexpected result. A data anomaly may occur when a data field defined for one purpose is used for another. Examples of anomalies are negative numeric fields that should be positive (for example, a negative number of dependents), abnormally high numeric values (for example, a person's weight recorded as 3,000 pounds), and pairs of values in related columns that make no sense (for example, a male patient having a hysterectomy).

application service provider (ASP): A company whose business is providing application services for its client companies. Such applications can include both tactical systems (for example, for billing) and strategic solutions (for example, for customer relationship management, which currently accounts for over half the ASP market).

architect: *See* data warehouse architect.

architecture: A framework for organizing the planning and implementation of data resources. The set of data, processes, and technologies that an enterprise has selected for the creation and operation of information systems. The blueprint that describes the environment in which the data warehouse, analysis application, or operational system is built.

ASP: *See* application service provider.

atomic data: Data at its most granular and detailed level.

attributes: In logical data modeling, the properties of an entity. Each property has one distinct value per instance of the entity. For example, if the entity is Automobile, then an attribute is Color, and an attribute value is Red. When logical models are translated into physical data models, entities become tables and attributes become columns. There is not necessarily a 1:1 correlation between the logical model objects and the physical model objects.

availability: The percentage of time during scheduled hours that the system can be used. It also can refer to the days per week and the hours per day that the system is scheduled for use. *See also* service-level agreement.

back-end: Populates the data warehouse with data from operational source systems.

base table: In relational databases, tables are defined as temporary or base. Base tables are the tables created by the CREATE TABLE command and are used for persistent storage.

batch windows: The time required to run the ETL process from beginning to end.

best of breed: The most effective, powerful, functional, and optimal choice of product in each category of tool. Organizations must decide whether they wish to choose a suite of products from the same vendor (when some of the tools in the suite may not be terrific) or choose the best product in each category (that is, the best of breed) and integrate those tools themselves.

best practices: Processes and activities that have been shown in practice to be the most effective.

beta release: A version of the vendor's software that is given to selected installations prior to the product becoming generally available. This version is often not free of defects.

BI: *See* business intelligence.

Big Bang approach: Delivering all the intended functions of the data warehouse at the same time.

bitmapped indexes: An indexing mechanism that involves building streams of bits such that each bit is related to the column value for a single row of data in a table.

business analyst: The person whose job it is to analyze the operation and data of the business to develop a business solution.

business drivers: The tasks, information, and people that promote and support the goals of the enterprise. The requirements that describe what the business wants (for example, more quality data, faster response to queries). A problem in the business that is important enough to spell the difference between success and failure for an organization.

business intelligence (BI): Normally describes the result of in-depth analysis of detailed business data. Includes database and application technologies, as well as analysis practices. Sometimes used synonymously with "decision support," though business intelligence is technically much broader, potentially encompassing knowledge management, enterprise resource planning, and data mining, among other practices.

business process engineering: The analysis and redesign of business processes and associated technology systems, with the goal to eliminate or reduce redundancy and streamline interactions.

business rules: Policies by which a business is run. The business rules contain constraints on the behavior of the business. The assertions that define data from a business point of view. (For example, the state code business rule might be the 50 United States, the District of Columbia, and the U.S. Territories.)

business sponsor: The manager or executive who acts as visionary for the data warehouse program and can articulate how the data warehouse can drive business improvements. Establishes the need, pain, or problem the data warehouse will solve, serves as a tiebreaker for issues during the project, and might actually fund some or all of the data warehouse development. *See also* sponsor.

business timestamp: A timestamp generated by a business event and not as a result of a systems operation, for example, `sales_timestamp`, `order_timestamp`, `shipment_date`, and so on. Typically, all facts in a data warehouse have at least one business timestamp, which can be traced to a transaction in the source operational system.

business user: A person who reports to the line of business and accesses the data warehouse by writing reports and queries or who uses the reports and queries generated by others. *See also* user.

caching: As related to caching reports, involves storing the results of pre-run reports in tables (instead of caching to memory as the usage of the word implies) so that when the user accesses the report for the first time, it seems to run instantaneously. This is a feature provided by the server component of many of the popular OLAP tools.

campaign analysis: Campaign analysis provides a measurement of responsiveness to campaigns by households and by individual customers. It provides the ability to measure the effectiveness of individual campaigns and different media and offers the ability to conduct cost/benefit analyses of campaigns.

Capability Maturity Model (CMM): Developed by the Software Engineering Institute (SEI); a representation of the goals, methods, and practices needed for the industrial practice of software engineering. The goal of the model is to have processes that are repeatable, defined, managed, and optimized.

CASE Data Interchange Format (CDIF): A family of standards and interfaces with an architecture for exchanging meta data and other information among modeling tools and meta data repositories.

CASE tools: Computer Aided Software Engineering tools that support logical and physical data modeling.

CDIF: *See* CASE Data Interchange Format.

CEO: Chief executive officer.

CFO: Chief financial officer.

champion: The (high-level) person in the organization who supports and promotes the data warehouse, its use, and those who developed and maintain it. A person with sufficient clout in the organization who believes in and sells the idea of the data warehouse and helps solve problems between groups.

channels: The method/means by which a product or service is marketed, ordered, and delivered.

charge back: The process of assessing and assigning the costs of a system to the departments that use it.

check totals: A loose term used to describe the total sum of the values in an additive column of data across all rows of data that are within scope. This total is usually calculated before and after moving data across platforms or processing data in order to ensure no data was lost.

CIF: *See* corporate information factory.

CIO: Chief information officer.

CKO: Chief knowledge officer.

class: A collection of objects that share common properties, definitions, and behaviors.

click stream: A series of page visits and associated clicks carried out by a Web site visitor when navigating through the site. Analysis of clickstream data can help a company understand which products, Web site content, or screens were of most interest to a given customer.

CMM: *See* Capability Maturity Model.

conformed dimension: A dimension whose use and semantics are agreed upon across the enterprise. *See also* dimension.

consultant: Someone who provides expertise and can be an advisor or a deliverer of tasks. Consultants are hired for their expertise when the company has none. Consultants often help define the data warehouse strategy and assess the organization's ability to implement the data warehouse.

contractor: A person who provides the delivery of tasks. The contractor might be responsible for building the ETL process or for overseeing the DBA functions. Contractors are hired when the company has a shortage of skilled workers. The company tells them what needs to be done, and the contractors perform the work.

control totals: The addition of values of specific fields to verify that the ETL job streams have run properly. Cross-footing of numbers to verify that a process (for example, ETL) has run successfully.

COO: Chief operating officer.

corporate information factory (CIF): The framework that surrounds the data warehouse. Typically contains an ODS, a data warehouse, data marts, DSS applications, exploration warehouses, data-mining warehouses, alternate storage, and so forth.

cost/benefit analysis: The process by which the value of a project is estimated based on the expected costs compared to the tangible benefits, usually expressed as increased revenue or reduced cost.

critical success factor: An element that contributes to the success of a project, without which the project will fail.

customer relationship management (CRM): Infrastructure that enables delineation of and increase in customer value and the correct means by which to increase customer value and motivate valuable customers to remain loyal—indeed, to buy again. A collection of integrated applications that facilitate the seamless coordination between the back-office systems, the front-office systems, and the Web. The DSS expansion of CRM analytics refers to customer-centric analytics applications.

cross-organizational: Includes multiple departments within an organization. A nonredundant and horizontally cross-functional view of the business.

cross-selling: Selling an additional category of products as a result of the customer's original purchase.

CTO: Chief technology officer.

customer segmentation: Separating customers by factors such as age, gender, educational background, and whether or not they like Wayne Newton.

DASD: *See* direct access storage device.

data administrator (DA): The role responsible for the enterprise's data resources and for the administration, control, and coordination of all data-related analysis activities. The DA has the responsibility for planning and defining the conceptual framework for the overall data environment. The functions of the DA typically include requirements definition, logical data modeling, data definitions, logical to physical mapping, maintenance of inventory of the current system, data analysis, and the meta data repository.

data analysis: The systematic study of data so that its meaning, structure, relationships, origins, and so on are understood.

data architecture: The framework for organizing the planning and implementation of data resources. The set of data, processes, and technologies that an enterprise has selected for the creation and operation of information systems.

data definition language (DDL): The SQL syntax used to define the way the database is physically defined.

data loading: The process of populating a data warehouse. It may be accomplished by utilities, user-written programs, or specialized software from independent vendors.

data mapping: The process of identifying a source data element for each data element in the target environment.

data mart: An implementation of an analytics application serving a single department, subject area, or limited part of the organization. Usually refers to a physical platform on which summarized data is stored for decision support. Data marts are commonly used for specific analysis purposes by a single organization or user group.

data mining: The discovery mode of data analysis, or analyzing detail data to unearth unsuspected or unknown relationships, patterns, and associations that might be of value to the organization. Advanced analysis used to determine certain patterns within data. Most often associated with predictive analysis. A process of analyzing large amounts of data to identify patterns, trends, activities, and content of data content relationships.

data owners: People who have the responsibility for determining the required quality of the data, for establishing security and privacy for the data, and for determining the availability and performance requirements for the data. Data originators who have the authority, accountability, and responsibility to create and enforce organizational rules and policies for business data.

data quality: The degree of excellence of data. High-quality data is stored according to data types, is consistent, not redundant, timely, complete, and well understood. Such data also follows business rules, corresponds to established domains, and satisfies the needs of the business. The user is satisfied with the validity of the data and the information derived from that data, and there are no duplicate records. For example, data quality ensures that a customer's name is spelled correctly and the address is correct.

data staging: The storage of data prior to it being loaded into a data warehouse or data mart. *See also* staging area.

data stewardship: The responsibility for the quality of the business data; an information expert about a particular subject area.

data warehouse: A collection of integrated, subject-oriented databases designed to support the DSS function, where each unit of data is relevant to some moment in time. The data warehouse contains atomic data and lightly summarized data.

data warehouse architect: A person who defines how to build the environment for the data warehouse, analytics application, or operational system.

data warehouse manager: The person who has overall responsibility for all the organization's data warehouse initiatives, for data warehouse standards, and for data warehouse tools. The project managers may report to the data warehouse manager or they may report to individual sponsors.

database administrator (DBA): The person responsible for the physical aspect of the data warehouse. This includes physical design, performance, and maintenance activities including backup and recovery.

database design schema: *See* physical data model.

database management system (DBMS): Software that controls and supports the storing and access of data. This includes loads, updates, deletions, and access. A DBMS supports the backup and recovery of the data as well as the support of securing the data. *See also* relational database management system (RDBMS).

DDL: *See* data definition language.

deadline: The point in time by which a project must be completed.

decision support system (DSS): An implementation that provides tactical and strategic capabilities to management and knowledge workers through reports and the ability to launch ad hoc queries.

deliverable: The tangible output from a task or a project; for example, a logical model, a project agreement, a database design, or an application.

delta: A change, for example, the difference from one period to the next.

demo: Short for demonstration, as in a vendor demonstration of software to impress the users.

denormalization: Data or data design elements that do not conform to the rules of data normalization. Denormalized data structures are often used in databases to provide rapid access for specific user needs. Denormalization usually results in some degree of data redundancy in a data record. A process of combining like data into a single entity (table or file). This combining will create duplicate data.

departmental systems: A data mart implementation that serves the needs of only a single department, such as human resources or finance. *See also* enterprise systems.

derivations: The transformation of data in the ETL process in which the data is created through the use of an algorithm based on data from multiple sources.

derived data: A new data element created from or composed of other data elements.

design review: A peer review of project deliverables, such as design specifications, program code, or test specifications. The objective of the review is to find weaknesses, errors, and problems. Different groups are given access to the design to provide input on how it might be changed to (a) work best with the tools selected or (b) be complete in its solution to the problem.

dimension: Defines either the organization of the measures (facts) or how an organization measures a fact.

dimension data: An entity used to describe, qualify, or otherwise add meaning to "facts" in a star schema fact table. Dimensions are the "by" items in analysis of facts "by" product, market, time, period, and so on. Data that describes the measurements (facts) that business users wish to analyze.

dimensional hierarchy: The different levels of data within a dimension that data can be rolled up or down to for analysis. This can be represented in a data model by a series of related tables with parent–child relationships (snowflaked schemas) or by multiple columns within a dimension table (standard star schemas) called hierarchy columns. For example, the dimensional hierarchy of a sales organization could include the following levels: salesperson, branch, territory, region, and company.

direct access storage device (DASD): Rotating magnetic disk storage.

domain: A set of data values that represent the full range of allowable values that may be used for a given data attribute. (Synonym: valid values.) Defines validity criteria for a particular column or field. For example, Gender could be a domain defined as having the data type of Character of 1 byte containing "F" for Female, "M" for Male, and "N" for Not Sure.

dotted-line (reporting, responsibility): Indirect responsibility.

DSS: *See* decision support system.

EAI: Enterprise application integration.

EIS: *See* executive information system.

end-user: *See* user, business user.

enterprise data model: A logical data model that incorporates all the important components of an enterprise data architecture. Components include entities, attributes, relationships (roles), rules, and definitions stated in business terms. A schematic defining the data and their relationships that is applied to the whole organization. Diagram of a single, nonredundant view of business data, showing how data is used by the business activities of an organization.

enterprise data warehouse: A collection of data that can be defined and shared across the whole enterprise along the lines of common dimensions to be used for analysis.

enterprise resource modeling (ER modeling): Illustrates entities and their relationships with each other. ER modeling represents the requirements of the business; it does not represent a technical architecture.

enterprise resource planning (ERP): Tying together and automating of diverse components of a company's operations, including ordering, fulfillment, staffing, and accounting. This integration is usually done using ERP software tools.

enterprise systems: Systems that support and are used by the entire enterprise. *See also* departmental systems.

entity: A person, place, thing, concept, or event about which an organization collects data.

ETL: *See* extract/transform/load.

executive information system (EIS): A system that lets upper management view the organization's performance at a highly summarized level, usually in a graphical representation.

extract/transform/load (ETL): The process of extracting data from operational data sources or external data sources, transforming the data (which includes cleansing, aggregation, summarization, and integration, as well as basic transformation, for example, "1" becomes "Male" and "2" becomes "Female"), and loading the data into some form of the data warehouse (ODS, enterprise data warehouse, data mart). ETL can also refer to the vendor software that performs these processes.

fact table: The central table in a star join schema, characterized by a composite key, each of whose elements is a foreign key drawn from a dimension table. Facts are information about the business, typically numeric and additive. A table that contains the measures that the business users wish to analyze to find new trends or to understand the success or failure of the organization.

FAQs: *See* frequently asked questions.

federated database system (FDS): A collection of independently managed, heterogeneous database systems that allow partial and controlled sharing of data without affecting existing applications. An FDS presents an enterprise view of data.

file transfer program (FTP): A program that transfers data from one computer to another.

foreign keys: Columns on one table that are inherited from the primary key of another table by means of a dependent or independent relationship.

frequently asked questions (FAQs): Questions that are repeated, usually asked by the users of the help desk or of the project support team. Software vendors also have FAQs, which are usually asked by technical people who use the vendors' software. To minimize support requirements and to assure a consistent response, FAQs are normally captured, validated, and made available through a Web site.

front-end: The access and analysis piece of the data warehouse architecture.

FTP: *See* file transfer program.

gap analysis: The analysis of the difference between what is needed and what is available. The difference between where you are and where you want to be.

Global 2000: The 2000 largest companies worldwide.

goal: An objective to be achieved within a specific period of time.

granularity: The level of the measures within a fact table represented by the lowest level of the dimensions.

guideline: A guideline is a recommendation, like "You should if your situation warrants," while a standard is "Thou shall, regardless of the situation."

hard-dollar benefits: Tangible benefits that can be measured. Hard-dollar benefits can result from an increase in revenue or a reduction in cost.

historical data: Data from previous time periods, in contrast to current data. Historical data is used for trend analysis and for comparisons to previous periods.

information center: An old approach to delivering information to management. It involved a dedicated staff that would respond to management requests for information, usually in the form of reports.

information technology (IT): The department that builds and maintains computer systems.

infrastructure: The architectural elements, organizational support, corporate standards, methodology, data, processes, physical hardware and network, and so on that make up the data warehouse environment.

instance: The objects that belong to a class and contain only their particular values.

integration: The activity of combining data from multiple data sources to present a single collection of data to the warehouse.

I/Os: Inputs and outputs.

IPO: Initial public offering (of stock).

islands of automation: Systems that were developed without consideration for their ability to interface with each other. As a result, data stored in these systems is often redundant and inconsistent. *See also* silo, stovepipe.

IT: *See* information technology.

iteration: The division of a project in which functionality is provided to the users in a series of phases.

iterative development: The process of implementing a total system in phases or increments. This provides users with usable capabilities and value without having to wait until the entire system is delivered.

joining: Within the context of SQL, refers to the comparison of similarly valued keys across multiple tables for the purpose of selecting rows of data from multiple tables. This is done by means of an SQL `SELECT` statement in which the comparison of the keys is performed in the `WHERE` clause.

justification: The process by which each project is evaluated to determine whether there is financial viability in its implementation. The justification process also allows management to prioritize projects. *See also* cost/benefit analysis, return on investment.

knowledge transfer: The act of transferring knowledge from one individual to another by means of mentoring, training, documentation, and other collaboration.

legacy system: Any existing production or operational system. Legacy systems often provide the source data for the data warehouse. *See also* operational system.

libraries of queries and reports: Sets of programs that have been created, fully tested, quality assured, documented, and made available to the user community. The programs in these libraries are variously called canned, predefined, parameterized, or skeleton queries and reports. They are launched by the user, who enters only a variable such as a date, region number, range of activity, or some other set or sets of values the program needs to generate a query or report.

lines of business: Divisions of a company responsible for the production and creation of the organization's products and/or services. The IT, human resources, and accounting departments are not lines of business.

logical data model: An abstract formal representation of the categories of data and their relationships in the form of a diagram, such as an entity-relationship diagram. A logical data model is process independent, which means it is fully normalized and therefore does *not* represent a process-dependent (for example, access-path) database schema.

logical database design: *See* physical data model.

market penetration: The percentage of the market owned by a company as represented by share of revenue.

massively parallel processing (MPP): A parallel hardware organization that deemphasizes the sharing of memory resources.

matrix management: A reporting structure in which the manager does not hold the performance and payroll card of the subordinate. This is synonymous with dotted-line responsibility.

mentor: A person who provides guidance and recommendations to a more junior person for courses of action and behavior.

meta data: Data about data. Usually refers to agreed-on definitions and business rules stored in a centralized repository so business users—even those across departments and systems—use common terminology for key business terms. Can include information about data's currency, ownership, source system, derivation (for example, profit = revenues − costs), or usage rules. Prevents data misinterpretation and poor decision making due to sketchy understanding of the true meaning and use of corporate data.

methodology: Proven processes followed when planning, defining, analyzing, designing, building, testing, and implementing a system.

metrics: Any type of measurement. Metrics could include business results, quantification of system usage, average response time, benefits achieved, and so on. The measures that an organization believes is vital for its success.

milestone: A tangible event used to measure the status of the project. Markers during the execution of a project that shows its movement in the right direction.

mission: A high-level set of goals of the organization, for example, to be the low-cost producer or the company with the highest level of customer satisfaction.

MPP: *See* massively parallel processing.

multidimensional database: The aggregation of data along the lines of the dimensions of the business, for example, sales by region by product by time.

near-line storage: Data storage that is not online and not immediately accessible.

networking: (1) Connecting with people of like interests for the purposes of uncovering opportunities, identifying land mines, and learning best practices. (2) The ability to tie more than one component together through protocols (for example, TCP/IP).

object: An instance that is a member of a class.

objective: A desired outcome of the delivery of the project. An objective can be measured.

object-oriented: Describes a self-contained module of data and its associated code.

OCM: *See* organizational change management.

ODS: *See* operational data store.

OLAP: *See* online analytical processing.

OLTP: *See* online transaction processing.

online analytical processing (OLAP): "Drilling down" on various data dimensions to gain a more detailed view of the data. For instance, a user might begin by looking at North American sales and then drill down on regional sales, then sales by state, and then sales by major metropolitan area. Enables a user to view different perspectives of the same data to facilitate decision making.

online transaction processing (OLTP): The transaction processing that supports the daily business operations.

OO: *See* object-oriented.

operational data: Data that supports the productions systems that run the business. This includes but is not limited to OLTP systems.

operational data store (ODS): A data store that contains only current data. It can be used for analytical and reporting purposes by the access and analysis tools to understand current data, not historical data.

operational system: The system that creates, updates, and accesses production systems. The operational system does not access or update decision support systems. *See also* legacy system.

organizational change management: Management of major change in which performance of job functions requires most people throughout the organization to learn new behaviors and skills. It can encompass an entire workforce and will focus on innovation and skill development. To some degree, the downside effects of change are inevitable. Whenever groups of people are forced to adjust to shifting conditions, discomfort will occur. The key is to proactively recognize the effects of change, plan for the change, and develop skill sets and tools to support the change and inevitable discomfort associated with it. Without this proactive approach, the risk of poor project implementation increases significantly and reduces the opportunity to achieve expected compliance.

outsourcing: Assigning to a vendor outside of the organization the responsibility for all or a portion of the activity and tasks involved in developing and/or running and maintaining a system.

ownership: One of the more controversial and disputed ideas in data warehousing. Owners have the responsibility for determining the required quality of the data, for establishing security and privacy for the data, and for determining the availability and performance requirements for the data. Data originators have the authority, accountability, and responsibility to create and enforce organizational rules and policies for business data.

pain: An unfulfilled business need that jeopardizes the success of the organization.

parallelism: The ability to run the same process simultaneously (in parallel) within more than one processor.

partitioning: The ability to divide a table into pieces (partitions). The division can be horizontal by data value (for example, by date) or vertical by columns (for example, by the most-used columns in one partition, the least-used columns in another partition).

periodicity: The frequency of load/update/refresh of the data warehouse, for example, daily, weekly, monthly.

PERT chart: A graphical representation showing the critical path for a project applied to a calendar.

phasing: The method of delivering the data warehouse in separate groupings of functionality to particular groups of users rather than delivering everything at once to all the intended users.

physical data model: A formal representation of data and its relationships in the form of a diagram, depicting the physical placement of data in a database. A physical data model is process dependent, which means it is denormalized to provide maximum performance efficiency. It is commonly referred to as *logical database design* or *database design schema*.

pilot: The initial implementation of a data warehouse. A pilot always provides a subset of the intended functions and includes a subset of the total set of users. A partially built system to show the capabilities of a full implemented system. A pilot may become a live system. The terms *pilot*, *proof-of-concept*, and *prototype* are sometimes used synonymously.

platform: The hardware, operating system, and database management or file system on which the data warehouse runs.

political agenda: The plans of an individual to enhance his or her position in the organization.

power user: A knowledge worker who is capable of writing complex queries and reports with little help.

primary key: The column(s) on a relational table that uniquely define a row of data on that table.

project agreement: A document that outlines the scope of a project, including the deliverables, functions, tools to be used, service-level agreements, responsibilities, and schedule. The project agreement sometimes includes the anticipated milestones.

project management office: The office or department responsible for establishing, maintaining, and enforcing project management processes, procedures, and standards. It provides services, support, and certification for project managers. Sometimes called *project office*.

project manager: The person who has overall responsibility for a project's successful implementation. The project manager defines, plans, schedules, and controls the project. The project plan must include tasks, deliverables, and resources (the people who will perform the tasks). The project manager monitors and coordinates the activities of the team and reviews the deliverables. If contractors and consultants are used, the project manager assigns the tasks, monitors activities and deliverables, and assures that knowledge transfer is indeed taking place.

proof-of-concept: A software trial that allows a prospect to try out the product before buying it. Delivers a realistic slice of functionality and is often used as the foundation for the first application. A system built quickly to show the capabilities of an idea. A proof-of-concept should not become a live system but usually does. The terms *pilot*, *proof-of-concept*, and *prototype* are sometimes used synonymously.

prototype: A less formal experimental and experiential development process of a proposed application for the purpose of demonstrating some or all of its functional capabilities. A prototype does not have the same rigorous testing, documentation, and implementation requirements as a software release or an application does and should therefore never be implemented as is. The terms *pilot*, *proof-of-concept*, and *prototype* are sometimes used synonymously.

QA: *See* quality assurance.

quality: The absence of any defect. A system of quality has the following characteristics: (a) maintainability (making it easy to add new functions); (b) conformance to specifications and the original design (fulfilling user requirements); (c) a long mean time to failure (few bugs or abnormal terminations); (d) performance that is adequate or as expected; (e) well-tested functionality, user interface, and performance; (f) good documentation; (g) ease of use; and (h) use of standard interfaces.

quality assurance (QA): The department, role, or process responsible for validating that which is proposed to ensure a correct outcome. The planned and systematic activities that provide confidence that a product or service will fulfill requirements for quality.

rapid application development (RAD): A process in which the time is set (timeboxed) and a small set of deliverables is implemented in a reasonably short period of time.

RDBMS: *See* relational database management system.

real time: The current moment in time. Real time refers to what is happening to any piece of data right now.

real-time data: Data that is captured and made available as it is happening. Real-time data reflects the latest status of the organization's operational transaction data. For analysis, some people want to see current rather than historical data.

recursive: A relationship between two instances of the same entity, as in recursive data design.

referential integrity: The concept of enforced relationships between tables based on the definition of a primary key and foreign key.

relational database management system (RDBMS): Software that controls and supports the storing and access of data. This includes loads, updates, deletions, and access. A RDBMS supports the backup and recovery of the data as well as the support of securing the data. An RDBMS provides relations or connections between tables by column values and access by column value. A major capability of an RDBMS is that it can process a set of data with a single statement. Examples of an RDBMS are DB2, Oracle, SQL Server, and Sybase.

release concept: A new approach to development that produces a fully tested, fully documented, high-quality, but only partially functioning application until the final release, which completes the application. The release concept severs the notion that a project deliverable must equal a complete application. Instead it tightens and expands on the concept of a pilot by producing a partially functioning application, which is refined and enhanced several more times through several more releases before it becomes a fully functioning application. This concept is the embodiment of iterative development and is fully compatible with XP (extreme programming) and the new agile and adaptive methodologies.

request for proposals (RFP): A formal request to vendors to submit proposals to provide a product or service.

resources: People and budget needed to perform the data warehouse tasks.

return on investment (ROI): Usually represented as a percentage of tangible monetary value in relation to the cost of the system.

RFP: *See* request for proposals.

ROI. *See* return on investment.

rolled up: Aggregated to a higher level.

scalable: Provides the ability to increase the number of users, the size of the databases, and the complexity of the queries and reports without having to replace the existing platform or architecture.

scope: An itemized accounting and definition of the agreed-upon project deliverable in terms of functionality as well as data. In data warehousing, the data scope is more critical than the functional scope for correctly estimating the development effort.

scope creep: The addition of new requirements, source data, or users to the initial agreement of what the project will deliver.

semantic layer: A layer between the end-user tool and the database. This allows the end-user tool to present the data most effectively for the end-user's understanding and then allows the end-user to generate the proper query to the database.

service-level agreement (SLA): The definition of a level of service provided by the IT department for a particular system. Service-level agreements can be established for availability (for example, 24 hours per day, 7 days per week, and 98 percent during scheduled hours), for performance (for example, response time for 95 percent of queries in 1 minute or less), for timeliness of the data (for example, weekly data available by 6 A.M. Monday morning), or for other reasons. A contract with a service provider—be it an internal IT organization, an ASP, or an outsourcer—specifying discrete reliability and availability requirements for a given system. Might also include such requirements as support of certain technology standards or data volumes. The outsourcer's failure to adhere to the terms laid out in the SLA could result in financial penalties.

shelfware: Software that is not being used. (It's "sitting on the shelf.")

sign-off: The process of agreeing in writing to the scope of a project or the acceptability of a deliverable.

silo: A system that cannot easily integrate with any other system. Results in multiple versions of the same data, violating the idea of a single version of the truth. *See also* islands of automation.

siloize: To create a silo.

single version of the truth: A primary goal of the data warehouse wherein the data to be accessed resides in only one database so that there will be no conflicting data and no inconsistent reports.

SLA: *See* service-level agreement.

SMP: *See* symmetrical multiprocessing.

snowflake structure: A star schema with normalized dimensions.

SOP: *See* standard operating procedure.

source data: The data from the operational or legacy systems that feed the ETL process.

source system: An operational system or ODS used as the source or input to the ETL process.

sponsor: The person in the organization, usually from the business side, who supports the project. This person should be someone with power, money, and commitment to the project. *See also* business sponsor.

staging area: Where the ETL programs run and where the source data is prepared for the data warehouse. *See also* data staging.

stakeholder: A person who has a vested interest in the success of the project or is involved in the implementation of the project.

standard: A standard is "Thou shall," while a guideline is a recommendation, more like "You should if your situation warrants." There are data warehouse standards for, among other things, meta data, terminology, data stewardship, and privacy.

standard operating procedure (SOP): A procedure usually followed in the course of business.

star schema: A modeling paradigm that has single object in the middle (fact table) connected to a number of objects (dimensions tables) around it radially.

stovepipe: A system that cannot easily integrate with any other system. Results in multiple versions of the same data, violating the idea of a single version of the truth. *See also* islands of automation.

strategy: An approach taken that will affect the overall direction of the organization and will establish the organization's future environment.

subject areas: The primary categories of data that run the enterprise. The two basic subject areas in data warehousing are (a) the data subject area, which comprises fundamental entities that make up the major components of the business, for example, customer, product, employee; and (b) the function subject area, which comprises a business function or business activity, for example, sales, order processing, inventory.

suite of products: A collection of software products from the same vendor, either developed or bundled by that vendor. The idea is to provide a complete set of tools from modeling through access and analysis. Vendors offer a range of functional software modules that interact with each other. Suites should eliminate integration complexity.

supply chain: The management of the components, manufacture, and distribution of a manufactured commodity. The supply chain management includes warehousing and tracking inventory.

SWAT team: A small team of skilled and experienced practitioners who can pull a failing project out of the ditch. This team does not tolerate political interference as it makes decisions and takes actions to bring the project to fruition.

symmetrical multiprocessing (SMP): A parallel hardware organization that emphasizes the sharing of memory resources.

system timestamp: A timestamp that is generated by a systems operation, for example, `record_create_date`, `last_update_date`, and so on.

systems integration: The art and science of integrating processes, functions, people, and data so the end result is a seamless and tight-knit system.

tactical: An approach taken to achieve a specific objective or to solve a specific problem.

target: The database into which data will be loaded from a source database or file. The data store accessed by the users.

terabyte: 1,000 gigabytes.

third normal form: A database in which each attribute in the relationship is a fact about a key, the whole key and nothing but the key. Usually refers to a fully normalized structure.

tie and foot: The process of validating the number of rows, summarizations, and monetary totals of the source data with the data loaded into the data warehouse.

time dimension: A table of descriptive attributes about the date/timestamp, for example, day of week, month, quarter, season, year, century, holiday, and so on.

time variance: A characteristic of a data warehouse that defines the moment in time that the data or variant of the data is valid. If Order 123 has a value of $1,500 on December 1 and $1,700 on December 10, December 1 and December 10 show us the difference of the two values on the dates shown.

timeliness: The act of getting the data to the users at the most opportune time, a function of the users' requirements for currency, consistent with user expectations. Data is valuable and useful to analysts only if it represents organizational activities that are reasonably current. Timeliness is usually measured by how soon the data is available after some distinctive end of a period, such as two days after the close of the month.

topology: The manner in which the components of a subject are arranged or interrelated.

total cost of ownership: The cost to the organization for the initial implementation and maintenance of the system.

transformation: The manipulation of data to bring it into conformance with the business rules, domain rules, integrity rules, and other data within the warehouse environment.

triage: The process by which projects or activities are prioritized to determine which should be attempted first, second, and so on and which projects or activities should never be done at all. This process applies similarly to the cleansing process. Triage considers the value of cleansing, the complexity, the cost, and the order in which the cleansing should be accomplished.

trickle feed: The process by which data updates the target database a little at a time, in contrast to massive updates that take place after the close of a period such as the day, month, or quarter. The process of feeding data from one system to another in either real-time or small time intervals.

universal product code (UPC): A unique bar code embossed on every product, used for inventory control.

user: A knowledge worker, business analyst, statistician, or business executive who will access the data in the data warehouse to perform some type of business analysis. *See also* business user.

value added: The notion of additional benefit being provided by some activity or service.

very large database (VLDB): An inexact term since the perception of what constitutes a VLDB continues to grow. A 1 terabyte database would normally be considered a VLDB.

virtual enterprise data warehouse: An enterprise data warehouse constructed of multiple data marts and a request broker computer application. The data warehouse does not physically exist except throughout the formation of the integrated data marts.

vision: The direction of the data warehouse—what it is intended to accomplish.

visionary: The person in the organization who articulates the data warehouse direction and intended purpose.

visualization: The presentation of results in a format other than just numbers with a display that may include graphs and charts making copious use of colors and figures.

VLDB: *See* very large database.

work breakdown structure (WBS): A detailed list of tasks to be performed on the project.

workload: The quantity of processing to include the machine cycles and the disk I/Os.

Colloquialism Glossary

These definitions are given primarily in the context of a data warehouse and the impossible situations and their solutions presented in this book. Some definitions in this glossary use terms defined in Appendix A, Data Warehouse Glossary.

A-level people: The best people possible who can work on the project.

A plus: The best evaluation possible.

B grade: An evaluation that is not the best.

bad apples: Members of the team who are incompetent, are lazy, have a bad attitude, or all of the above.

bad-mouth: To make a disparaging reference.

bake-off: A contest in which more than one set of software is exercised, usually at the customer's site, and the superior product is recognized as the winner, which most often leads to the purchase of the winning product.

balloon: To grow or expand beyond acceptable limits.

bandage: A solution that does not solve the problem but only delays an inevitable catastrophe.

bang their heads against the wall: To perform an action that is unlikely to succeed and is also painful.

bare-bones methodology: A set of minimal methods used in implementing the data warehouse.

be on board: To accept what is being proposed.

be on the bench: To have no current assignment.

bean counter: A derogatory term used to describe a bureaucratic or an accounting-type person who cares only for hard-dollar results and is very wary of anything that costs money. A nitpicker, dedicated to detail down to the last bean, but one who fails to see the big picture.

beat the bushes: To diligently search for something.

best bet: The approach that is most likely to succeed.

best of breed: The most effective, powerful, functional, and optimal choice of product in each category of tool.

Big Bang approach: Delivering all the intended functions of the data warehouse at the same time.

Big Brother: (1) An organization or boss that is overcontrolling. (2) A governmental agency that has the authority to observe the actions of a person or an organization.

big bucks: Outrageous fees charged by overpriced consultants.

big dog: The person in the organization who wields the most power and influence and is the person the data warehouse must satisfy.

bite the bullet: To address the most difficult issue and take action even though the solution may be unpleasant. Biting the bullet requires overcoming hesitation and procrastination.

black eye: An unfavorable reputation for an activity gone bad.

blackballed vendor: A vendor that offended a client organization and is therefore no longer allowed to market to that organization.

bleeding-edge technology: Technology (mostly likely software) that has not been thoroughly tested in real applications. Bleeding sometimes refers to the money fruitlessly wasted as organizations test and find problems in vendor software.

Blinky the three-eyed fish: An attempt at humor by one of the experts describing a mutated fish found in a pond surrounding a nuclear facility.

blown deadline: A deadline that has been missed.

blue-sky requirements: In an RFP, requirements for product capabilities that are impractical but may possibly be available sometime in the distant future.

blurb: (1) A publicized notice. (2) A piece of text.

bodies are buried: Information about seamy events in the organization.

boilerplate: Standard verbiage that can be used multiple times for the same purpose. Material in an RFP response that is generic and not written specifically for the organization sending out the RFP. Vendors may respond to RFPs with boilerplate so they do not have to write the same material multiple times.

bottom line: The most important and conclusive issue or point being made.

brainstorming: Collaborating to think of possible solutions without excluding ideas that could be considered outrageous, for example, bringing in a tool that is still in beta.

bread and butter: The most important components without which the company could not function.

bugs (software): Errors in the code that would cause serious problems or would cause the system to fail.

burning bridges: (1) Eliminating all but one option. (2) Deliberately performing an action that would preclude you from ever working with the injured party again. (Julius Caesar burned a bridge that eliminated the chances that his troops could retreat.)

bury the hatchet: To make peace, settle differences.

buy-in: Acceptance, most importantly by management.

buzz: Enthusiastic talk and interest about a subject.

call in the cavalry: To request more powerful people to come to the rescue, most probably to assist a data warehouse team that is terribly behind schedule. In the American Old West the cavalry was called in to save the day and to extricate those in trouble.

canned: Already built, established, predefined, or prewritten, for example, a canned report.

cards are stacked: A reference to a poker game that a person whose cards were prearranged (stacked) against him or her has no chance of winning.

career-limiting move: An activity that would foreclose promotions, such as taking an unpopular position or challenging a powerful manager.

cashing in: Taking advantage financially.

chalk up: To attribute.

cookie-cutter approach: A very standard way of approaching a problem. The approach would not vary from situation to situation.

cooking the books: Making changes to the reported results or profits of a division or company to make the results look more favorable.

cooks in the kitchen: *See* too many cooks in the kitchen.

cool: Interesting, desirable. Often describes a deliverable that has exciting features, particularly those that would be of interest to some of the more junior members of the organization.

corporate ladder: An organization's hierarchy. As you move up the corporate ladder, you achieve more responsibility and authority, a higher salary, a nicer office, and a more attractive assistant.

cover (provide cover): To protect from harm.

cronies: People you know well who will support you regardless of your stupidity.

crunch time: The point in the project when you have to make things happen and you have to deliver.

devil's advocate: A person who takes a position contrary to one embraced by the majority, usually to generate discussion and disagreement.

dinosaurs: Systems that are old and should be extinct.

Dirty Dozen: Refers to the ability of a dysfunctional team of misfits to deliver a successful project. Based on the 1967 movie *Dirty Dozen*, about 12 misfits and criminals who carry out a dangerous assignment in World War II.

dirty laundry: Unfavorable or embarrassing characteristics of the organization that you would not want known outside your immediate group.

do your own thing: To make your own independent decisions and take your own independent actions.

dog and pony show: A presentation that contains exciting elements but is often short of real content.

done deal: An activity that has been finalized and cannot be changed.

don't air your dirty laundry: An admonition against talking badly about an organization to outsiders.

down the road: Something to be done at a future date.

dregs (staff): Personnel that no one wants—people who are unskilled, have bad attitudes, have questionable hygiene habits, and are, on the whole, distasteful to work with.

drop-dead date (and time): A serious and nonnegotiable deadline. The time and date by which the project must be successfully completed. (In ancient times, the project manager was put to death if the project did not complete on time.)

dust off: To resurrect or reinstate and begin to make use of, as in to dust off a plan that had been set aside.

Easter Bunny: An imaginary rabbit that (get this) lays and distributes eggs to children at Easter time. A fantastic and implausible scenario. The likelihood of having a successful data warehouse implementation without a project plan is just a little short of actually encountering such an animal under your petunias.

eat the costs: To absorb the costs. In an organization where all the costs are charged back, there are times when the organization implementing the system is unable to fully charge back all the expenses incurred; in this case, the IT department would have to absorb the costs.

end of your rope: You have no other options and no solutions to your problems. The phrase comes from mountaineering—when you are at the "end of your rope" you have nowhere to go but down and very fast at that.

ETL jockey: A person who is responsible for and specializes in the ETL process.

fast-forward: To advance in time, for example, it is now three months later.

fat: Extra allowance or padding of an estimate.

fiefdoms: Areas of power in which managers can exert total authority.

field of dreams: The misguided notion that if IT builds a data warehouse, the users will show up, run queries, and be ecstatic about the results. A reference to a 1989 movie, *Field of Dreams*, in which a man builds a baseball diamond without first having the players or spectators.

finger pointing: Blaming another person or department other than oneself.

fire fighting: Dealing only with immediately critical issues or creating solutions that are not based on any strategic plan.

firewall: An impenetrable security barrier to restrict access.

flak jacket, wearing a: A metaphor for taking action to protect yourself from harm to your career.

flu: A metaphor for a wrong way of thinking.

fluff: Something of little value or importance.

free lunch: As in "There's no such thing as a free lunch," indicating that even though something has been represented to be free, you will somehow ultimately have to pay for it. In the American Old West, saloon keepers offered a free lunch to attract customers, knowing the price of the drinks would more than offset the cost of the free lunch.

frontal assault: A nonsubtle approach to winning over other members in the organization. A frontal assault lacks subtlety and finesse.

fuzzy: Not specific, intangible.

get over it: To disassociate from emotional involvement.

get the ear: To get the attention of someone (for example, the CIO)

gig: An engagement or contract to perform work, such as a consulting contract to train the end-users on an access and analysis tool.

give them the boot: To dismiss them from the organization or from the team.

gloss over: To pretend a problem is not important.

go behind your back: To take action without your knowledge that will cause you to be disadvantaged. This is usually done in secret.

go down with a sinking ship: To stay with a project that is doomed to fail.

"go/no go" decision: A decision to either continue with the project or to abort it.

goodies: A generic term for something desirable such as money, bonuses, an all-expense-paid trip to Kauai, or a T-shirt emblazoned with "I built the financial data mart and all I got was this crummy T-shirt."

graveyard shift: The nighttime part of the workday, usually from midnight to 8:00 A.M.

green eyeshade: Headgear to shade the eyes from the glare of incandescent bulbs. Green eyeshades are the preferred apparel of financial types eager to kill any project that cannot be guaranteed to be economically justified.

gut feel: An estimate based on experience and intuition.

head count: The number of people allocated to work on a project.

heart-to-heart: A conversation that is both serious and honest.

heat seeker: A person who constantly searches for and exercises the newest and usually risky technologies, only some of which may have value to the project.

hired gun: A consultant from outside the organization, usually one with required skills and an unusually high billing rate.

homework: Research required before beginning an activity.

hogs (CPU and RAM): A reference to piggish appetites. A process, software, or design that makes overly generous use of the resources of the machine, often requiring more hardware than had been anticipated.

hot spot: The application that can make the greatest contribution to the organization.

hung up: Inappropriately and overly concerned about an issue. When a person is hung up, he or she is often paralyzed and unable to carry out designated activities.

industrial strength: Anything (for example, software, designs, or processes) that will hold up to heavy and sometimes abusive usage and still deliver high availability and good performance.

jump start: To facilitate getting a task or a project started.

kick the tires: To research in a cursory, superficial manner. This relates to evaluating data warehouse tools without performing the proper due diligence.

kickback: An activity that is underhanded and usually illegal—paying a party that has rendered a service or made a decision in your favor.

lead hat: The person leading the project.

lemming philosophy: The mind-set that would cause members of the organization to self-destruct by following other members in dysfunctional and destructive behavior. The reference is to small rodents that, in their migration, will sometimes follow each other off a cliff. Data warehouse lemmings continue to follow practices that are well known and destined to fail.

life-threatening: Capable of causing a project or business to fail.

lip service: To appear to accept something (as reflected in words) but to actually not accept it (as reflected in actions).

lock-in: An activity that makes an outcome unalterable.

look over the shoulder: To review, observe, and validate the work of someone else.

macho: Robust, manly.

marching to the beat of a different drummer: Changing direction or following a new leader.

milk: To take financial advantage of someone, perhaps unethically.

mind-set (organizational): The common perception or culture within the organization. An organization's culture is often difficult to change.

Mongolian horde: A very large group of people, often consultants descending on a client all at once.

most valuable player: The person on the data warehouse team with the most skills and experience; the person who would be missed most if he or she left the team.

neat: Exciting and intriguing, for example, the features of a deliverable.

new-fangled: Something new but often untried or untested.

nip in the bud: To stop an activity before it gets started.

not on board: Usually refers to a person who does not believe in or is not in agreement with a proposed plan. The plan is in place, everyone else is in agreement, and the project has sailed, except for the person who is not on board.

no-win: A situation in which there is no possibility of success.

off the shelf: Something that is standard, that does not have to be customized.

off-Broadway: The deliverable is shown to a group who is willing to make constructive comments about problems in the deliverable without damaging the reputation of the project or the team.

ol': Old (and often familiar).

on board: Refers to a person who has accepted an agreed-upon position.

one size fits all: Originally from the label on pantyhose that indicated the panty hose would fit any size person equally well. In the world of software, the "one size" of the products doesn't work for anyone.

on the bench: To have no current assignment.

on the line: To be at risk. A person's reputation or career is at risk if the project fails.

only game in town: The only option; no other place to go. There is no alternative.

opening night: The first time management sees the major deliverable.

out: A way to gracefully exit, as in "allow you an out."

outside the box: A nontraditional manner, as in "thinking outside the box."

pecking order: An indication of the importance of the people involved in the project.

pitch: A sales presentation, often to management by internal personnel.

Pollyanna: An annoying optimist who sees only good even in terrible circumstances.

poor man's alternative: A minimal effort to do something. Not a robust undertaking, but better than nothing. For example, a minimum effort to improve the quality of the data warehouse.

power play: An action that takes advantage of political clout and position, often to the detriment of others in the organization.

powers that be: The important decision makers in the organization.

prima donna: A temperamental person who has an unrealistically high opinion of him- or herself and wants to be treated very specially.

Project Management 101: The basics or fundamentals of knowing the concepts and application of project management.

pronto: Right away, without delay.

provide cover: To protect from harm.

pull: Strong influence, as in "The senior executive has some pull in the organization."

pull it off: To extricate a difficult situation from impending failure, as in "if the team pulls it off."

purse strings: Refers to the person who controls the allocation of funds and is capable of not making money available to the project, that is, "closing the purse strings."

put on hold: To prevent further activity taking place on the project; to delay until a later time.

quick hitters: Personnel able to accomplish tasks in an expedient manner.

query from hell: A query that does bad things to your CPU, memory, and database. A query that runs forever and rarely gives you what you were expecting.

radar: Knowledge within an organization that something is occurring.

ragtag team: A team with little coherence, with a minimal set of skills and experience, and very little experience working together.

raise the red flag: To alert the organization about a problem with the project.

reality check: A review to determine whether what is being proposed or implemented is feasible (or realistic) and whether it will ultimately be successful.

red tape: Bureaucratic and officious requirements that slow down or even kill a project.

ride herd: To closely manage. The expression comes from cowboys encircling their herds to keep them moving.

road show: A "traveling" demonstration of applications given to multiple departments or people in the organization.

rock star: A team member who has extraordinary skills.

rolling out tools: A phased approach to installing and training new users on the tools.

rule of thumb: An accepted standard based on experience, not scientifically supported. In old English law, a man was allowed to beat his unfaithful wife with a stick no thicker than his thumb.

sacrificed on the altar: A project cancelled or dismembered, or a person blamed for a project error.

sanity check: A review to determine whether what is being proposed is realistic and is likely to be successful, as in "We need to have a sanity check to determine whether the project has any chance for success."

seat of the pants: An estimate or action based on instinct and experience, not based on factual evidence or precise rules.

send the vendor packing: To dismiss the vendor.

sexy: Attractive, visually appealing (and even exciting) to management.

shelfware: Software that is not being used and is sitting on the shelf (usually unwrapped). Shelfware is found in organizations that are good at buying software but bad at making use of it.

shoot: To target or aim at an objective.

shortcut: An action that shortens the time to accomplish an activity.

show stopper: A situation or major occurrence that would significantly impede progress or cause the project to fail.

Siberia: An undesirable locale. For example, when a team member is "sent to Siberia," he or she might be assigned to an undesirable project.

silver bullet: A very effective (almost miraculous) method for dealing with a problem but one that rarely exists in the real world. The Lone Ranger used silver bullets that never, ever missed their marks.

singing from the same hymnal: Refers to everyone on the team having the same objectives, terminology, and plans.

sinking ship: A project that is doomed to fail.

sit-down: A serious meeting in which difficult issues are addressed.

skunkworks: (1) A rogue and unofficial project being developed "under the radar," apart from the sanctioned data warehouse project that might be under way. Skunkworks projects can jeopardize the reputation and funding of the authorized projects by raising questions about their value, timeliness, or planned deliverable. (2) A group within a company tasked with evaluating new products, cobbling tools together to see if they work, and testing new procedures to determine whether they can be of use to the organization.

slam-dunk: A spectacular success.

spaghetti web: A system that has many inputs, interfaces, and transformations that are highly interwoven, difficult to understand, and very difficult to maintain.

spin: To provide a slant on the measurements that can make the results more favorable to the person or group doing the spinning.

spoon feed: The necessity to communicate at a detailed level. The requirement to support almost every minor detail.

start from scratch: To begin without using anything that has already been developed.

steer the ship: To be in charge. Effectively managing, as with a project.

sticking it out: Staying to the end of the project. Being persistent, not giving up.

sugarcoat: To make something appear better than it really is. To hide the flaws and problems associated with the system. As team members are being recruited, the characteristics of the project may be sugarcoated to make the project appear to be more attractive.

SWAT team: A small and very effective team that can fix a project that's in trouble. Refers to a Special Weapons and Tactics team used in the military.

swing shift: The evening portion of the workday, usually from 4:00 P.M. to midnight.

tab: Cost, expense.

tactical fire-fighting solutions: Solutions that deal only with immediately critical issues or that are not based on any strategic plan.

take it on the road: To demonstrate the system to different groups of users, probably in different locations.

take the heat off: To remove pressure.

team player: A person who looks after the success of the team and the project rather than focusing on his or her own success.

tell it like it is: To be honest and straightforward.

thick-skinned: Not upset by criticism, as in "a thick-skinned person."

three strikes: Originally from baseball. After making three mistakes or failing three times, you do not get another chance.

too many cooks in the kitchen: Too many people making decisions about a project that ultimately will cause the soup to taste terrible and the data warehouse deliverables to also be unpalatable.

tool jockey: A team member skilled in a specific product.

toot your own horn: To boast. To represent how well you have done rather than waiting for someone else to sing your praises.

touchy-feely: Someone who goes out of his or her way to be empathetic and understanding of another person. Managers who are people oriented rather than technically oriented.

track record: The record of success of individuals or teams. Derived from the performances of racehorses.

warts: Deficiencies or problems in the software.

wearing a flak jacket: A metaphor for taking action to protect yourself from harm to your career.

weenie: A person in IT who is emotionally and unnaturally involved with the technology.

well-oiled team: A team that works well together and has the resources to work productively.

what makes a person tick: What motivates a person.

whole cloth: Refers to a deadline mandated "out of whole cloth," that is, created without the benefit of information about what is involved (tasks, skills, deliverables, and so on) in the project.

whole enchilada: The entire project, deliverable, concept, or meal.

win points: To get credit for accomplishing something.

win/win: A situation in which both parties benefit from a decision, negotiation, or solution.

work out the kinks: To uncover problems and fix them.

Bibliography

PUBLICATIONS

Adelman, Sid. 2001a. "Data Strategy Introduction." *DMDirect*, November.

———. 2001b. "Standards for Business Intelligence." *Cutter IT Journal* XIV(11).

———. 2000. "Top Ten Tips for Data Warehouse Success." *The Data Administration Newsletter*.

———. 1998. "Calculating Intangible Benefits." *Data Warehouse Report*, September.

———. 1997. "Organizational and Cultural Issues of the Data Warehouse." *Journal of Data Warehousing*, Winter.

———. 1996. "The Data Warehouse Database Explosion." *DM Review*, December.

———. 1995a. "People-Oriented Issues: Exploring the Data Warehouse's Organizational and Cultural Issues." *Database Programming & Design*, June.

———. 1995b. "Readiness Test for the Data Warehouse." *InfoDB*, February.

Adelman, Sid, and Larissa Moss. 2001. "Data Warehouse Risks." *Journal of Data Warehousing*, Winter.

———. 2000a. "Data Warehouse Goals and Objectives." *DMDirect*, July.

———. 2000b. *Data Warehouse Project Management*. Boston, MA: Addison-Wesley.

———. 1999. "Indicators of Success: Measures of Data Warehouse Success and Failure." *DMDirect*, July.

Adelman, Sid, and Joe Oats. 1999. "How Lack of Project Management Can Sink a Data Warehouse Project." *TDAN Newsletter*, June.

Barquin, Ramon, and Herb Edelstein. 1997a. *Building, Using, and Managing the Data Warehouse.* Upper Saddle River, NJ: Prentice Hall.

———. 1997b. *Planning and Designing the Data Warehouse.* Upper Saddle River, NJ: Prentice Hall.

Berry, Michael J. A., and Gordon Linhoff. 1999. *Mastering Data Mining: The Art and Science of Customer Relationship Management.* New York: Wiley.

———. 1997. *Mastering Data Mining Techniques for Marketing, Sales and Customer Support.* New York: Wiley.

Bischoff, Joyce, and Ted Alexander. 1997. *Data Warehouse: Practical Advice from the Experts.* Upper Saddle River, NJ: Prentice Hall.

Brackett, Michael H. 2000. *Data Resource Quality.* Boston, MA: Addison-Wesley.

———. 1996. *Data Warehouse Challenge: Taming Data Chaos.* New York: Wiley.

Brooks, Frederick P. 1995. *The Mythical Man-Month.* Reading, MA: Addison-Wesley.

Cabena, Peter, Pablo Hadjinian, Rolf Stadler, Jaap Verhees, and Allesandro Zanasi. 1997. *Discovering Data Mining from Concept to Implementation.* Upper Saddle River, NJ: Prentice Hall.

Devlin, Barry, and Lynne Doran Cote. 1996. *Data Warehouse: From Architecture to Implementation.* Reading, MA: Addison-Wesley.

Dyché, Jill. 2002a. "Choosing Your CRM Tool." *Computerworld*, February.

———. 2002b. "The CRM Backlash." *CIO Magazine*, February.

———. 2002c. "Making Hay: Building the IT Infrastructure When Times Are Tough." *Teradata Magazine*, March.

———. 2002d. "Resurrecting CRM." *Intelligent Enterprise*, January.

———. 2001a. *The CRM Handbook: A Business Guide to Customer Relationship Management.* Boston, MA: Addison-Wesley.

———. 2001b. "Have a Data Warehouse? What to Do Next." *Journal of Data Warehousing*, Spring.

———. 2000a. "The Data Warehouse RFP." *DM Review*, February.

———. 2000b. "Data Warehousing, Metadata, and Middleware." *EAI Journal*, September.

————. 2000c. *E-Data: Turning Data into Information with Data Warehousing.* Boston, MA: Addison-Wesley.

————. 1998a. "Give Consultants a Break!" *Information Week*, December.

————. 1998b. "Scoping Your Data Mart Implementation." *DBMS*, August.

Dyché, Jill, and Evan Levy. 1999. "Beating the Data Mart Blues." *Teradata Magazine*, Spring.

Edelstein, Herb. 1997. *Data Mining: Products and Markets.* Potomac, MD: Two Crows Corp.

English, Larry P. 1999. *Improving Data Warehouse and Business Information Quality.* New York: Wiley.

Hackney, Douglas. 2002. "The Challenges and Opportunities for BI Professionals in the Information War." Accessed in January 2002 at *http://www.egltd.com/production/columns/01-02-We-can-17.htm.*

————. 2001a. "Processes Are the Most Often Neglected Element of Your BI System, Yet You Cannot Live without Them." Accessed in January 2001 at *http://www.egltd.com/production/columns/01-01-power-of-process-06.htm.*

————. 2001b. "The Team-Person-Days Realities of Product Bake-offs." Accessed in August 2001 at *http://www.egltd.com/production/columns/08-01-Bakeoff-06.htm.*

————. 2001c. "Tips for Manager/Executive Team Communication." Accessed in September 2001 at *http://www.egltd.com/production/columns/09-01-troops-09.htm.*

————. 2000a. "Frequently Asked Questions Regarding a Federated BI System." Accessed in April 2000 at *http://www.egltd.com/production/columns/4-00%20Federated%20FAQ%2005.htm.*

————. 2000b. "The Secret to Requirements Gathering and Political Success for Your BI System." Accessed in October 2000 at *http://www.egltd.com/production/columns/10-00-vein-of-pain.htm.*

————. 2000c. "Seven Steps to Achieving a Federated Business Intelligence System." Accessed in August 2000 at *http://www.egltd.com/production/columns/6-00%20How%20to%20Federate%2002.htm.*

————. 2000d. "What Happens When You Only Ask IT the Questions." Accessed in February 2000 at *http://www.egltd.com/production/columns/2_00_The_Price_of_Hubris.html.*

————. 1999a. "Every Company's Most Valuable Asset, and How It Will Be Recognized and Valued." Accessed in October 1999 at *http://www.egltd.com/production/columns/10_99_1_Hidden_Assets.html.*

————. 1999b. "Key Lessons to Maximize System Success and Customer Satisfaction." Accessed in June 1999 at *http://www.egltd.com/production/columns/6-99_Gift_of_the_Amish_02.htm.*

————. 1999c. "The Parallels between Data Warehousing and Parenthood." Accessed in February 1999 at *http://www.egltd.com/production/columns/2-99-04_Parenthood.htm.*

————. 1997. *Understanding and Implementing Successful Data Marts.* Reading, MA: Addison-Wesley.

Hoberman, Steve. 2002. *Data Modeler's Workbench: Tools and Techniques for Analysis and Design.* New York: Wiley.

Imhoff, Claudia, Lisa Loftis, and Jonathan G. Geiger. 2001. *Building the Customer-Centric Enterprise.* New York: Wiley.

Inmon, W. H. 1996. *Building the Data Warehouse,* 2nd Ed. New York: Wiley.

Inmon, W. H., Claudia Imhoff, and Greg Battas. 2001. *Building the Operational Data Store.* New York: Wiley.

Inmon, W. H., Claudia Imhoff, and Ryan Sousa. 1997. *Corporate Information Factory.* New York: Wiley.

Inmon, W. H., and Chuck Kelley. 1994a. *RDB/VMS: Developing the Data Warehouse.* New York: Wiley.

————. 1994b. "The 12 Rules of Data Warehouse for a Client/Server World." *Data Management Review,* May.

Inmon, W. H., J. D. Welch, and Katherine L. Glassey. 1997. *Managing the Data Warehouse.* New York: Wiley.

Inmon, W. H., John A. Zachman, and Jonathan G. Geiger. 1997. *Data Store, Data Warehousing and the Zachman Framework.* New York: McGraw-Hill.

Kelley, Chuck. 1995. "Enterprise Data." *Data Management Review,* April.

Kelley, Sean. 1996. *Data Warehousing: The Route to Mass Customization.* New York: Wiley.

Kimball, Ralph. 1998. *The Data Warehouse Lifecycle Toolkit: Expert Methods for Designing, Developing and Deploying the Data Warehouse.* New York: Wiley.

———. 1996. *The Data Warehouse Toolkit.* New York: Wiley.

Marco, David. 2002a. "IT Portfolio Management." *DM Review*, April.

———. 2002b. "Meta Data Repositories: Where We've Been and Where We're Going." *DM Review*, February.

———. 2002c. "Revisiting the Top 10 Mistakes to Avoid When Building a Meta Data Repository, Part 1." *DM Review*, May.

———. 2002d. "Revisiting the Top 10 Mistakes to Avoid When Building a Meta Data Repository, Part 2." *DM Review*, June.

———. 2001a. "Data Warehousing Meta Data Standards: The OMG and Where the Industry Should Head." *Application Development Trends*, March.

———. 2001b. "Evaluating Meta Data Tools." *Application Development Trends*, October.

———. 2001c. "A Meta Data Repository Is the Key to Knowledge Management." *DM Review*, December.

———. 2001d. "Meta Data Repository ROI." *Application Development Trends*, September.

———. 2001e. "Which Should Come First, the Meta Data Repository or the Data Warehouse?" *DM Review*, September.

———. 2000a. *Building and Managing the Meta Data Repository.* New York: Wiley.

———. 2000b. "The e-Dilemma, www.EWSolutions.com/Newsletter.asp." *Real-World Decision Support*, July.

———. 2000c. "XML Bringing Order to Chaos." *Database Trends*, June.

———. 2000d. "XML Uses in Data Warehousing: Getting Data Out." *DM Review*, July.

Marmel, Elaine. 2002. *Microsoft Project 2000 Bible.* New York: Wiley.

Moss, Larissa. 2002. "Business Intelligence Roadmap." *DM Review*, February.

———. 2001a. "BI Methodologies: Agile with Rigor?" *Cutter IT Journal*, December.

———. 2001b. "Data Warehouse Key Issues." *eBusiness Executive Report, Taiwan*, January.

————. 2001c. "Organizational and Cultural Barriers to Business Intelligence." *Cutter Consortium Executive Report* 1(7).

————. 1999. "Practical Guidelines for Data Acquisition/Data Cleansing." *The Navigator*, Spring.

————. 1998a. "Data Cleansing: A Dichotomy of Data Warehousing?" *DM Review* 8(2).

————. 1998b. "Planning for the Evolution of a Data Warehouse." *The Navigator*, Fall.

Moss, Larissa, and Sid Adelman. 1999a. "Data Warehouse Goals and Objectives, Part 1." *DM Review* 9(8).

————. 1999b. "Data Warehouse Goals and Objectives, Part 2." *DM Review* 9(9).

————. 1999c. "Data Warehouse Goals and Objectives, Part 3." *DM Review* 9(10).

Moss, Larissa T. and Shaku Atre. 2003. *Business Intelligence Roadmap.* Boston, MA: Addison-Wesley.

Swift, Ronald S. 2001. *Accelerating Customer Relationships.* Upper Saddle River, NJ: Prentice Hall.

Whitten, Jeffery, Lonnie Bentley, and Kevin Dittman. 2000. *Systems Analysis and Design Methods.* New York: McGraw-Hill.

WEB SITES

Architecture, Colin White, and Mike Fergeson:
http://www.databaseassociates.com

Data administration:
- Enterprise Warehouse Solutions: *http://www.EWSolutions.com/newsletter.asp*
- *The Data Administration Newsletter*: *http://www.tdan.com*

Data mining, Herb Edelstein: *http://www.twocrows.com*

Data quality, Larry English: *http://www.infoimpact.com*

Data warehouse consultants: *http://www.bialliance.com*

Data warehouse general information:
- The Data Warehousing Community: *http://www.datawarehouse.com*

- The Data Warehousing Information Center:
  http://www.dwinfocenter.org

The Data Warehouse Institute: *http://www.dw-institute.com*

Data warehouse journals:
- *DM Review: http://www.dmreview.com*
- *Intelligent Enterprise: http://www.intelligententerprise.com*

Database and Data Warehouse Information Exchange:
http://www.searchdatabase.com

Database issues and solutions: *http://www.Dbazine.com*

DCI's CRM community: *http://www.crmcommunity.com*

Jill Dyché, Baseline Consulting Group: *http://www.baseline-consulting.com*

Enterprise Information Architecture: *http://www.methodfocus.com*

ETL tool comparison: *http://www.ewsolutions.com/research_paper.asp*

Douglas Hackney, Enterprise Group, Ltd.: *http://www.egltd.com*

Bill Inmon: *http://www.billinmon.com*

Sean Ivoghli, The Data Warehouse Consulting Group: *http://www.dwcg.com*

Chuck Kelley: *http://www.excellenceindata.com*

Ralph Kimball: *http://www.rkimball.com*

Meta data—David Marco, Enterprise Warehousing Solutions:
http://www.ewsolutions.com

Meta Data Tool Comparison Study:
http://www.ewsolutions.com/research_paper.asp

Pieter Mimno, tool comparisons: *http://www.mimno.com*

Larissa Moss: *http://www.methodfocus.com*

Multidimensional research, Nigel Pendse and Richard Creeth:
http://www.olapreport.com

Negotiations, Joe Auer: *http://www.dobetterdeals.com*

Organization, roles and salaries, David Foote: *http://www.footepartners.com*

Project Management Institute: *http://www.PMI.org*

Security:
- International Information Systems Security Certification Consortium:
  http://www.isc2.org
- IS Audit and Control Association: *http://www.isaca.org*

- MIS Training Institute: *http://www.misti.com*
- National Research Council—*Cybersecurity Today and Tomorrow: Pay Now or Pay Later: http://www.nap.edu/html/cybersecurity*
- Systems Administration, Networking Security Institute: *http://www.sans.org*

Tools/products:

- DSstar: *http://www.dsstar.com*
- itoolbox.com: *http://www.itoolbox.com*

Experts' Bios

Sid Adelman

Sid Adelman is a principal in Sid Adelman & Associates, an organization that specializes in planning and implementing data warehouses and in establishing effective data architectures and strategies. He jointly developed a methodology, MapXpert for Data Warehouse, that provides a master plan for implementing data warehouses. He is a regular speaker at The Data Warehouse Institute and IBM's DB2 and Data Warehouse Conference. Mr. Adelman chairs the "Ask the Experts" column at *http://www.dmreview.com*. He is a frequent contributor to journals that focus on data warehousing. He coauthored *Data Warehouse Project Management* [2000b] with Larissa Moss.

Mr. Adelman is a founding member of the BI Alliance, whose members include Herb Edelstein, Larry English, David Foote, Douglas Hackney, David Marco, Pieter Mimno, Neil Raden, and Colin White. Mr. Adelman can be reached at *sidadelman@aol.com*.

Joyce Bischoff

Joyce Bischoff, president of Bischoff Consulting, Inc., is an internationally recognized consultant, writer, and lecturer specializing in all aspects of data warehousing, database design, and design methodologies. She has been involved in planning, designing, implementing, and performing design reviews of data warehouses in more than 50 companies in the credit card, chemical, pharmaceutical, insurance, financial, oil refining, publishing, and hospital industries. She is the lead author of the book *Data Warehouse: Practical Advice from the Experts* [1997], which brings together opinions from 20 contributing authors, and a member of the expert panel for the monthly column "Ask the Experts" at *http://www.dmreview.com*. She is the author of numerous articles and frequently presents at data warehousing conferences all over the world. She may be reached at *JoyceBischoff@cs.com*.

Jill Dyché

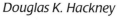

Jill Dyché is a partner and cofounder of Baseline Consulting Group, a consulting firm that specializes in designing, building, and analyzing customer databases. As vice president in charge of Baseline's management consulting practice, Ms. Dyché leads teams through front- and back-end reviews of strategic technology initiatives, including data warehouse, database marketing, and CRM implementations.

Ms. Dyché is the author of *The CRM Handbook* [2001], a CRM best-seller. She speaks regularly at marketing and technology conferences and has advised key technology vendors on their CRM strategies. Her work has been featured in *CIO Magazine*, *Computerworld*, *Information Week*, *Intelligent Enterprise*, the *Wall Street Journal*, and *The Chicago Tribune*, among others. Her first book, *eData* [2000c], has been published in four languages. Ms. Dyché can be reached at *JillDyche@Baseline-Consulting.com* or through the Baseline Web site, *http://www.baseline-consulting.com*.

Douglas K. Hackney

Douglas Hackney is the president of Enterprise Group Ltd., a consulting company specializing in business intelligence (BI). Mr. Hackney has over 20 years of experience in business management and in designing and implementing BI solutions for Global 2000 organizations. A recognized BI industry leader who regularly serves as a voice of the industry and as a chair of industry conferences, he is particularly noted for his pragmatic and vendor-independent perspective.

Mr. Hackney is a frequent and highly rated speaker at industry conferences, at private and public events, at industry user conferences, and at industry, educational, and product seminars and conferences around the globe. A frequent lecturer at leading MBA programs across the United States, he is a founding board member of the International Data Warehouse Association and often serves as a judge for industry awards. Mr. Hackney is the founder of the BI Alliance, a marketing and resource-sharing consortium of the BI market's thought and implementation leaders.

Mr. Hackney is the author of *Understanding and Implementing Successful Data Marts* [1997]. He is a contributing editor who writes a monthly column for *DM Review,* and he contributes to and is quoted often in other industry publications such as *eWeek, Computerworld, Enterprise Systems Journal*, and *Forbes.* His Web site is *http://www.egltd.com* and he can be reached at *dhackney@egltd.com.*

Sean Ivoghli

Sean Ivoghli is the founder and president of Digital Symmetry, Inc., formerly the Data Warehouse Consulting Group, a consulting firm that specializes in providing end-to-end data warehousing, business intelligence, and data/application integration solutions. He has over 12 years of experience in full life-cycle data warehouse and information systems development, and he provides expert consulting services in data warehouse design, development, project management, and information management strategies. Mr. Ivoghli is the coauthor of *Compass*, a comprehensive data warehousing methodology that offers multiple tracks for developing scalable, flexible, and high-performance data warehousing and data mart solutions in a cost-effective manner. He can be reached at *sivoghli@digitalsymmetryinc.com* and at *sivoghli@dwcg.com.*

Chuck Kelley

Chuck Kelley is an internationally known expert in database technology. He has over 25 years of experience in designing and implementing operational/production systems and data warehouses. Mr. Kelley has worked in some facet of the implementation process of over 45 data warehouses. Mr. Kelley teaches seminars on SQL, Database Internals, Implementing the Data Warehouse, Designing and Implementing the Star Schema from Your Operational System, and other database and data warehousing topics. He has been a speaker at Database World, Client/Server World, UniForum, COMDEX, Rdb Conference, DECUS Symposia, and many data warehouse conferences. He coauthored a book with W. H. Inmon [1994] on data warehouses and is a member of the panel on the "Ask the Experts" column at *http://www.dmreview.com*. Mr. Kelley has been published in many trade magazines on database technology, data warehousing, and enterprise data strategies. He can be reached at *chuck.kelley@excellenceindata.com* or at his Web site at *http://www.excellenceindata.com*.

David Marco

David Marco is an internationally recognized expert in the fields of data warehousing, e-business, XML, and business intelligence, and he is the world's foremost authority on meta data. He authored the book *Building and Managing the Meta Data Repository* [2000b]. Mr. Marco also serves as the editor of *Real-World Decision Support*, an electronic newsletter focusing on business intelligence and e-business topics (*http://www.EWSolutions.com/newsletter.asp*). Mr. Marco has published over 80 articles and is a columnist for *Application Development Trends*, *Database Trends*, and *DM Review* magazines. Mr. Marco has been selected as a judge for the 1998–2002 *DM Review* World-Class Solutions, 2002 TDWI Pioneering Solutions, and 1999–2002 Microsoft Industry Solutions awards. In addition, Mr. Marco was a finalist for the 2000 DAMA Individual IT Achievement award.

Mr. Marco has presented over 70 keynote addresses and courses at all the major data warehousing and meta data repository conferences throughout the world. He also cosponsors with Pennsylvania State University a certified series of courses on data warehousing and business intelligence, and he teaches data warehousing at the University of Chicago. Mr. Marco is the founder and President of the Chicago-headquartered Enterprise Warehousing Solutions, Inc. (EWS), a strategic partner and systems integrator dedicated to providing clients with best-in-class business intelligence solutions using data warehousing and meta data repository technologies. EWS provides strategic consulting services and full life-cycle implementation services for Global 2000 corporations and government institutions and has been awarded a government GSA Schedule. In addition, EWS presents the Marco Master's Series, which is the industry's first and only certified meta data training course. Visit *http://www.EWSolutions.com* for more information about EWS and the Marco Master's Series. Mr. Marco may be reached at *DMarco@EWSolutions.com.*

Larissa T. Moss

Larissa Moss is founder and president of Method Focus, Inc., a company that specializes in improving the quality of business information systems. She has over 20 years of experience with information management. She frequently speaks at data warehouse, business intelligence, customer relationship management, and information quality conferences around the world on the topics of information asset management, data quality, enterprise information architecture, project management, and organizational realignment. She lectures worldwide on data warehouse development, data modeling, and project management, as well as data audit and control.

Her articles are frequently published in *The Navigator, Analytic Edge, TDWI Journal of Data Warehousing, Cutter IT Journal,* and *DM Review.* She coauthored *Data Warehouse Project Management* with Sid Adelman [2000b] and the forthcoming *Business Intelligence Roadmap: The Complete Lifecycle* with Shaku Atre. Ms. Moss is a member of the IBM Gold Group, a senior consultant at the Cutter Consortium, a contributing member of ExperNet (a consulting service provided by Giga Information Group), and a member of the panel on the "Ask the Experts" column at *http://www.dmreview.com.* She is also a member of the Data Administration Management Association (DAMA) and a frequent speaker at various national DAMA chapters. She can be reached at *methodfocus@earthlink.net.*

Clay Rehm

Clay Rehm, CCP, PMP, is president of Rehm Technology (*http://www.rehmtech.com*), a consulting firm specializing in data integration solutions. He provides hands-on expertise in project leadership and management, assessments, methodologies, data modeling, database design, meta data and systems analysis, design, and development. He has worked in multiple platforms, and his experience spans operational and data warehouse environments.

He is a technical book editor and author, instructor, and speaker. He serves on the panel of the *DM Review* "Ask the Experts" Web site (*http://www.dmreview.com*) and on the Carroll College Business Advisory Council.

With a passion for data architecture, he is well versed in DB2, SQL Server, and Access. He is Access 2000 Microsoft Office User Specialist (MOUS) Certified, a Certified Computing Professional (CCP), and a certified Project Management Professional (PMP). He holds a bachelor's of science degree in computer science from Carroll College and is currently working on his master's degree in software engineering.

He is a member of the Data Management Association (DAMA), the Professional Society of SQL Server (PASS), and the Project Management Institute (PMI). He can be reached at *clay.rehm@rehmtech.com*.

Index